TURNING THE TIDE

TURNING THE TIDE

The Battles of Coral Sea and Midway

BRITANNIA NAVAL HISTORIES OF WORLD WAR II

This edition first published in the United Kingdom in 2013 by
University of Plymouth Press, Portland Square, Plymouth,
Devon, PL4 8AA, United Kingdom.

Paperback   ISBN 978-1-84102-333-5
Hardback   ISBN 978-1-84102-334-2

© University of Plymouth Press 2013

The rights of this work have been asserted in accordance with the Crown Copyright, Designs and Patents Act 1988.

A CIP catalogue record of this book is available from the British Library.

Publisher: Paul Honeywill
Commissioning Editor: Charlotte Carey
Editor: Miranda Spicer
Series Editors: G. H. Bennett, J. E. Harrold, R. Porter and M. J. Pearce
Publishing Assistant: Maxine Aylett

All rights reserved. No part of this publication may be reproduced, stored in a retrieval system or transmitted in any form or by any means whether electronic, mechanical, photocopying, recording, or otherwise, without the prior written permission of UPP. Any person who carries out any unauthorised act in relation to this publication may be liable to criminal prosecution and civil claims for damages.

Historical content courtesy of Britannia Museum, Britannia Royal Naval College, Dartmouth, TQ6 0HJ.

Cover image © Edward Stables 2013

Typeset by University of Plymouth Press in Janson 10/14pt.
Printed and bound by Short Run Press, Exeter, United Kingdom.

The historical documents reproduced here appear as unedited text, apart from minor changes made to date formats and corrections to typing errors found in the original. Throughout *Turning the Tide*, Pearl Harbor carries US spelling.

MIX
Paper from responsible sources
FSC
www.fsc.org   FSC® C014540

Britannia Royal Naval College

A majestic landmark, which towers above the harbour town of Dartmouth in Devon, Britannia Royal Naval College was designed by royal architect Sir Aston Webb to project an image of British sea power. A fine example of Edwardian architecture, the College has prepared future generations of officers for the challenges of service and leadership since 1905.

The Britannia Museum opened in 1999 to safeguard the College's rich collection of historic artefacts, art and archives and promote greater public understanding of Britain's naval and maritime heritage, as a key element in the development of British history and culture. It also aims to instil a sense of identity and ethos in the Officer Cadets who pass through the same walls as their forbears, from great admirals to national heroes, to royalty.

www.royalnavy.mod.uk/The-Fleet/Shore-Establishments/BRNC-Dartmouth

Contents

Foreword 8
Introduction 12

PART I
Battle summary No. 45
The Battle of Coral Sea 28

PART II
Battle Summary No. 46
The Battle of Midway 102

Biographies 231

Britannia Naval Histories of World War II Series 233

Diplomacy and Military History 239

Foreword

Captain John Rodgaard

During the early months of 1942, America and its allies were reeling from the Axis onslaught. This was the first full year that America was at war. Victory seemed difficult to contemplate. However, by mid-year, the Allies had fought the Axis powers to a standstill during a series of battles on land and at sea. By the end of the year, it could be said that victory's door had been prised open. Churchill said as much on 10 November 1942 when referencing the Allied successes in North Africa:

> "Now this is not the end. It is not even the beginning of the end. But it is, perhaps, the end of the beginning."

The battles of the Coral Sea and Midway were two of America's contributions to the end of the beginning.

The Battle of the Coral Sea was the first major battle between the Imperial Japanese Navy and the United States Navy. The battle was noteworthy on several levels. It was the first of six battles between aircraft carrier forces of both navies. As such, the Coral Sea marked the first time that combat damage and losses occurred against opposing fleets at sea, solely from aircraft action. It was the first naval battle in which surface forces never sighted one another or directly fired upon one another. The Battle of the Coral Sea confirmed to both navies the primacy of the aircraft carrier as an offensive weapon. Seventy years later, the aircraft carrier remains the centrepiece of the United States Navy and something for other navies to emulate, especially China's.

The role that naval operational intelligence played leading up to the battle and during its aftermath was another first. Although the United States Navy's cryptologic capability had not completely 'broken' the Japanese naval code, the intelligence personnel at Pearl Harbor and Melbourne were able to piece together the enemy's plans. The intelligence derived by their efforts gave the United States and Australia the chance to thwart the great Japanese offensive that had begun five months earlier. It laid the groundwork for the Allies' strategic victory in the Battle of the Coral Sea. Furthermore, naval operational intelligence established a level of credibility that would have enormous consequences a month later at the Battle of Midway.

In May 1942, Commander Joseph Rochefort, USN and his cryptologic team decrypted enough of the Japanese code to provide sufficient detail of Admiral Yamamoto's attack plan against Midway Island. Based upon the intelligence, Admiral Nimitz deliberately calculated that the odds had evened out. Against the Japanese carrier juggernaut known as Kido Butai, Nimitz deliberately set a trap, which resulted in the Battle of Midway.

The loss to the Imperial Japanese Navy of four aircraft carriers, with their highly trained crews, and approximately one quarter of its naval aviators, was a heavy blow to its overall war effort. The cumulative attrition of Japanese naval combat power from both battles allowed the Allies to go on the offensive for the rest of the Pacific War with the amphibious landings on Guadalcanal in August, followed by a series of fierce naval battles off the same location between August and November. Coral Sea and Midway blunted Japanese offensives at the strategic level. Even after Midway, the Imperial Japanese Navy's combat power was still much greater than the US Navy's, especially in the number of aircraft carriers and aircrews that were available. Guadalcanal became the first offensive operation for the US and the successive carrier and surface ship battles ground the IJN down to such an extent that it was unable to go back on the offensive.

The knowledge of intelligence code breaking we have today gives a different perspective when reading the combat summaries that follow. At the time they were written, the fact that the Allies had succeeded in breaking the Japanese code (JN-25) was still a closely guarded secret. The same can be said about the Allies breaking the German Enigma codes. When you, the reader, encounter statements such as "American intelligence indicated" or "The concentration of Japanese ships ... was reported by Allied intelligence", I suggest these are allusions to code breaking.

Another notable 'first' was the role that radar played in both battles. Air search radars provided the Americans with a distinct advantage. These early radar sets could detect incoming flights of Japanese aircraft and thus provide tactical warning for surface gunnery and airborne intercept. Although the Grumman F4F Wildcat was inferior to the famed Japanese Zero fighter, it would have been far less effective if the information derived by radar to vector the Wildcats toward the incoming raids had not been available.

To lose both battles would have had tremendous strategic consequences. The threat to Australia was considerable, and although the Japanese had no intention of invading Australia at that time, losing the Battle of the Coral Sea would have compromised Australia's sea lines of communication to the Americas. The conquest of the Dutch East Indies (Indonesia) by the Japanese had already threatened Australia's western sea lanes across the Indian Ocean. A Japanese victory would have opened the door to Port Moresby and all of New Guinea. As the Australian ambassador to the United States, the Honourable

Kim Beazley, said during the 70th anniversary ceremony in Washington DC:

> "The survival of Australia and its participation in the war solely depended on the outcome of this battle… This was the battle which turned the tide… Australia had to look in different directions partly to our own resources and self reliance but also for new allies, and we looked to the United States."

The foundation on which the current nature of the American and Australian alliance rests is a result of the Battle of the Coral Sea and the bloody campaigns which Americans and Australians fought across the Pacific. Furthermore, the operational intelligence that affected the outcome remains a key component of the alliance today.

Losing the Battle of Midway would have certainly extended the war in the Pacific and might have reversed America's strategic priorities. The Roosevelt Administration had agreed with Britain on a 'Europe first' strategy. An American defeat would have brought about tremendous pressure to change course; the implications of which would have been enormous for the conduct of the war. One wonders what the world would have looked like today if the United States Navy had lost the Battle of Midway.

Seventy years have now passed and these two battles have become an intrinsic part of how the United States Navy sees itself. Of the two, the Battle of Midway has become the United States Navy's Battle of Trafalgar and it is commemorated each year as such. Ironically, the Battle of the Coral Sea has failed to rise to that level of commemoration. Ah, but ask an Australian.

Written seven years after the war, these previously classified battle summaries of the Battles of the Coral Sea and Midway represent the historical foundation, which subsequent historians have built upon through the 20th century and into the 21st. They are, by themselves, a testament to the high degree of cooperation and interaction that existed between the Royal and United States Navies, as well as that of the Canadian, Australian and New Zealand Royal Navies. This level of cooperation and integration continues to the present.

It is a tribute to the Britannia Royal Naval College that these summaries now see the light of day. I believe it is the responsibility of each generation to re-examine the history that has been given to them and to make it relevant for their own times. It is my hope that the overall series Britannia has brought forward will serve as a touchstone and inspire future historians.

Introduction

Philip D Grove

An understanding of the battles of the Coral Sea and Midway in the early summer of 1942 is crucial in appreciating their significance in naval history, and World War II in particular. The following Naval Staff History, including Battle Summaries Numbers 45 and 46, is an excellent aid to this.

The battles represent two momentous naval events. Firstly, they are the turning point in the course of the Pacific War. These are America's first naval victories against the Imperial Japanese Navy (IJN) and begin the long road to victory, following months of US and Allied defeats at the hands of the seemingly unstoppable Japanese 'juggernaut'. Secondly, the battles become the recognition point by the United States Navy (USN) that the aircraft carrier had become the primary weapons platform at sea, replacing the battleship that had dominated naval warfare for centuries. It is now 70 years since the battles and the carrier remains the USN's capital asset. For the first time during the actions in the Coral Sea and off Midway, naval fleets engaged each other beyond the visual sight of the ships involved. Ships no longer carried the large calibre guns, which had been the arbiter of battle for hundreds of years, and now the aircraft were the instruments of destruction carried onboard the ships. Battle Summaries Numbers 45 and 46 follow the course of both these pivotal and ground-breaking battles, which heralded the twin age of US dominance in the Pacific and the pre-eminence of the aircraft carrier in the US Navy.

Prior to the outbreak of the Pacific War, the US and Japan had experienced a decade of ever-worsening relations. Allies in World War I, they had become implacable foes by the 1940s, due to a multitude of factors. That said, in the aftermath of World War I, the victorious powers had, by the early 1920s, moved to a series of understandings to avoid very real tensions among themselves. International agreements at Washington in 1922, and throughout the decade, were reached on arms limitations and naval disarmament, with other treaties dealing with naval power, bases, the future of China specifically and Asian security in general.[1] However, by the 1930s, a wave of militarism and nationalism had effectively swept away the pliable democratic Japan of the 1920s. Japan's nationalists began a search for autarky and this rapidly resulted in her annexing Manchuria and other Chinese provinces before full-scale war between the two erupted in the summer of 1937.

Four years later, the war in China was not going well, but the Imperial Army and Navy had demonstrated considerable capabilities by seizing China's coastline, operating deep into the mainland and by absorbing French Indochina following France's defeat at the hands of Nazi Germany. This last act in 1940 and 1941 was the final straw for President Roosevelt's administration. It resulted in a series of trade embargoes imposed on Japan by the US, the British Empire and the Dutch East Indies. The embargoes would ultimately have crippled Japan's war machine. To the militarist dominated Japanese government only two options were available: relinquish its gains in the face of western pressure and lose face at home and abroad, or seize the resources the embargo denied them from the rich western-controlled territories of South East Asia. The latter option would bring them into direct conflict with the US, Great Britain, Australia and the Dutch East Indies and see World War II become a global struggle.

Prior to World War I, the US and Japanese Navies had been markedly inferior to the Royal Navy. However, during World War I, both the younger navies strove to expand their size and capabilities, but both with a suspicious eye firmly on each other's actions. Following the arms limitations treaties of the 1920s, Japan's expansion plans had been drastically curtailed but she still possessed the largest naval force in the Pacific. The overall larger, but now limited, US Navy was split between the Pacific and Atlantic Oceans, passing an obvious advantage to the Japanese Empire. Japan's naval hierarchy built on this beneficial state by exploiting the new naval technologies that had been developed during World War I; namely carrier air power and the submarine. By the outbreak of World War II, the IJN possessed the most modern submarine arm in the world, including its oxygen-powered Long Lance torpedoes and, more importantly, the largest and most capable carrier force in the world. This latter development would become a force multiplier, acting both as a widely spread power projection asset to be deployed anywhere in the Pacific, neutralising enemy air and sea forces, and then as a mobile floating reserve, a sort of fire brigade, to be sent to shore up any defences in the newly acquired Empire, should the western Allies be foolish enough to try to counter Japanese actions.

Yet the IJN in 1941 was portrayed by many as outdated, poorly equipped and trained, and also badly led. Japanese pilots were painted in the west as having genetic eye conditions, which was patently untrue, but which supposedly precluded them from flying at night. They were believed only capable of fighting other Asian countries, such as China. Their abilities had been deliberately downplayed in Washington, even though reports from American advisors, such as General Chennault, had shown the true situation. Thus, when the IJN launched the largest geographical offensive in history (in December 1941) across the Pacific, on a 6,000-mile front, employing 10 aircraft carriers and some 1,400 aircraft, it seemed unbelievable. They also seemed unstoppable.

By 1941, the IJN had more operational carriers than either the US or Britain, with more experienced and trained skilled aviators, and were flying aircraft that outclassed their western naval and land-based counterparts in the Pacific and Asian theatres. All of this came as a shock to the Allied forces in the Western Pacific, as the Japanese quickly gained air and sea supremacy, which led to the conquering of the islands of South East Asia and directly threatened India, Australia and the US mainland itself. Spearheading the IJN's onslaught was not its sizeable battlefleet, which stayed mostly in Japanese waters until the Midway operation, but its carrier forces and the elite air and ground crews onboard. The Mitsubishi A6M Zero fighters, Aichi D3A dive bombers and Nakajima B5N torpedo and level bombers, supported by land-based naval and army machines, swept all before them creating more than just an image of invincibility.

The IJN carriers were being operated in a doctrinal way, far ahead of anything else at the time, as a result of evolving dynamic and fluid Japanese naval thinking during the 1930s. The IJN had already realised the benefit of operating carriers in pairs and then in multiple pairs, allowing a greater concentration of offensive capability than afforded by one ship, and this was clearly demonstrated in the first six months of the Pacific War. The quality of the aircraft was the result of having control of the design and procurement of these flying machines; the right people in the right places at the right time, and of the aircrews' experience of air warfare against the Chinese – and to a lesser degree the Russians prior to the war. The training regime of the Japanese aviators was extremely demanding and, at the outbreak of the war, the longest of any naval air service in the world. The result was a hugely powerful, yet flexible, sea-based asset that could achieve knockout blows, so sufficiently strong that the western Allies would be forced to accept the new Asian order. Japan now controlled their former colonies and territories in South East Asia and the Western Pacific.

The onslaught began with near-simultaneous attacks against the US Pacific fleet at Pearl Harbor in Oahu in the Hawaiian Islands and attacks across multiple targets in South East Asia including neutral Thailand and British Malaya. Air and sea forces were targeted and subdued, allowing the numerically fewer Japanese land forces to overwhelm far greater Western ground forces. The temporary loss of the US battlefleet at Pearl Harbor at the hands of six IJN carriers was followed by loss after loss for the Allies, as Hong Kong, Wake, Guam, Singapore and countless other islands succumbed to Japanese forces. Western sea, land and air units were neutralised, outmanoeuvred and dislocated by well-planned and timed attacks. Allied seapower and airpower in theatre had effectively ceased to exist by the end of February, allowing the IJN to threaten ever more targets beyond its initial line of advance far more quickly than even it had anticipated. By the end of May, the Japanese defensive perimeter enclosed the territories of Malaya, Singapore, the Gilbert, Marianas, Marshall and Solomon Island chains, the Dutch East Indies, the Philippines, the majority of New Guinea and Burma.

In April, a major IJN raid involving five carriers was mounted into the Indian Ocean in an attempt to destroy a hastily formed and somewhat motley Royal Navy fleet, to push Britain further from the theatre.[2] Although the British refused to give battle, the raid did achieve the desired intention of securing the Japanese western advances and protecting the key rubber and oil supplies of Malaya and the Dutch East Indies. Dissension in the Japanese naval hierarchy over a Western naval policy and continued advance into the Indian Ocean – versus an Eastern one with total neutralisation of the USN in the Pacific – was decided on in the late spring, as a result of a number of developments. These led directly to the Battles of the Coral Sea and Midway.

Not everything had been seized in South East Asia. Australian troops had clung to the Owen Stanley mountain range in New Guinea, denying Japan the southern half of the island and an easy route from southern New Guinea into Northern Australia. Moreover, Australia was quickly becoming the forward operating base for the US and needed to be neutralised. Worse yet, the USN had begun mounting carrier raids against Japanese-held islands, demonstrating a capability and resolve that should have been destroyed at Pearl Harbor. The US Pacific carriers had not been at Pearl on 7 December and so were missed by Admiral Chuichi Nagumo's carrier striking force. Ironically, some had been delivering aircraft to the US Pacific island garrisons in an attempt to forestall Japanese intentions and increase their chances of defence.

The USN realised that all it had left, following the attack, were carriers. It learnt quickly how to employ them against the newly acquired Japanese Pacific islands. Of greater significance to the IJN and its Commander-in-Chief of the Combined Fleet – Admiral Isoroku Yamamoto, the overall architect of the Pearl Harbor attack – was a US raid on the Japanese home islands. The famous Halsey/Doolittle Raid on 18 April 1942, launched from the flight deck of the carrier USS *Hornet* and escorted by the USS *Enterprise*, achieved little tangible military significance, but it proved to be a catalyst for Yamamoto. He needed to avenge the attack and destroy, once and for all, the USN's Pacific carriers and its naval capability for the remainder of 1942. The result was his Midway operation scheduled for June.

In the meantime, the IJN needed to remove the growing Australian/US enclave in New Guinea and pressurise Australia itself. This would be achieved by an operation in May 1942 that led to the Battle of the Coral Sea and the world's first carrier-to-carrier fleet engagement. Both battles were intrinsically intertwined: had the outcome of the first been any different, the engagement at Midway would also have seen a differing result and the whole course of the Pacific Campaign and World War II would not have been fought as history has written.

The Battle of the Coral Sea

The intention was clear to the IJN high command. The aim was to seize the port in the south of Papua New Guinea, Port Moresby. This would stop the flow of allied equipment to the frontline on the Owen Stanley Range and, more importantly, act as a pincer movement catching the Australian/US forces between two simultaneous Japanese thrusts; one from the south and one from the north. The resulting victory would allow unfettered operations against northern and eastern Australia, enabling the IJN to increasingly close down US shipping and the growing forces that were heading there. That would then allow Japan's new Imperial southern flank to stabilise and become protected. Simultaneous with the seizure of Port Moresby, a series of other islands and ports including Tulagi in the Solomon Island chain would also be taken, strengthening Japan's island defensive screen and further isolating Australia.

Were any allied forces to intervene during the seizure, these would be dealt with and destroyed by superior escorting forces, further aiding the Japanese situation in the Pacific. If attempted intervention came after the successful seizures, the Japanese would deal with the Allied forces by the same escorting units, joined by the enlarged and strengthened land-based air forces as a result of taking the other targets during the operation. Either way, success would bring immense benefits to securing Japan's earlier expansion.

The IJN plans did not go as intended. Certain similarities are shared by the Coral Sea plan (Operation Mo) and the Battle of Midway. Japanese planning was overly complicated, with a large use of split forces deployed on underestimations of the actions and capabilities of the Allies, combined with overestimations of its own forces. Scant attention was paid to securing Japanese information traffic, while even less attention was paid to finding out what the Allies were doing.

As the plan stood, there were six task forces to be deployed for Operation Mo. Firstly the Tulagi invasion force, which was designed to establish a seaplane base. Once Tulagi was seized from Australian forces it would enable IJN reconnaissance assets to cover the eastern half of the Coral Sea. This force, comprising a large transport, two destroyers and minesweepers, was to move from Rabaul in New Britain, north-east of New Guinea and occupy the island on 3 May. The second force was designed to allow reconnaissance in the western half of the Coral Sea by seizing the island of Misima to the east of New Guinea. Two light cruisers, gunboats and a seaplane carrier provided the assets.

The third force was the Port Moresby invasion force with five transports, minesweepers and six destroyers, the aim of which was to land troops there, seizing the facilities on 7 May. This was covered by the fourth force, which included the light carrier *Shoho* and four heavy cruisers and was designed to provide air support to the invasion. The fifth force in theatre was the carrier task force commanded by Vice Admiral Takeo Takagi, comprising the large fleet carriers *Shokaku* and *Zuikaku*, both veterans of the Pearl Harbor raid. Overall, there were some 70 IJN ships involved, all coming under the direction of the Fourth Fleet, commanded by Vice Admiral Shigeyoshi Inouye.

Finally, the land based air garrison at Rabaul made up the sixth force and was designed to support the sea-going assets in the Coral Sea. Its 150 or so aircraft easily had the range to reach Port Moresby and Tulagi. The Japanese anticipated US intervention and were confident that *Shoho* attacking from the west, together with *Shokaku* and *Zuikaku* attacking from the east supported by Rabaul-based aircraft, would intercept any USN units that attempted to disrupt the Port Moresby invasion and destroy them. But Admiral Chester Nimitz, the USN Pacific Fleet Commander, was aware of Japanese plans through naval intelligence services led by Commander Joseph Rochefort at his Hypo centre in Hawaii. Americans had been breaking Japanese codes since World War I and were particularly able at deciphering naval transmissions, if not completely, to the extent that they could position Japanese forces fairly accurately and in the correct time frame. Nimitz's problem was moving assets into the Coral Sea in time and in sufficient strength to stop the IJN.

Of the five carriers in theory at his disposal, *Saratoga* was under repairs from a torpedo attack, while *Hornet* and *Enterprise* were returning from the Halsey/Doolittle raid. *Lexington*, under Rear Admiral Aubrey Fitch, was in Pearl Harbor receiving new guns, while the only carrier in the South Pacific was *Yorktown* as part of Rear Admiral Jack Fletcher's Task Force 17 (TF 17). Two heavy cruisers, one American and one Australian, plus an Australian light cruiser under the command of Rear Admiral John Crace, were also available.[3] Thus *Yorktown* and *Lexington* (TF 11) task forces together with Crace's Task Force 44 (becoming TF 17.3 for the Battle) would have to suffice as the main response to the IJN thrust and were duly dispatched to the Coral Sea, where they had combined by 6 May. Some 23 warships in total, supported by potentially 500 allied land-based aircraft, relatively few of which had the range to take part in the battle, were all that Nimitz could muster against a far more numerous enemy. Although they were dispatched faster than the IJN expected and they were larger than anticipated, Takagi was confident that three carriers and a land-based air garrison would be sufficient to destroy any US response. Unfortunately, for both the Japanese and the Americans, none of the operations went according to any of their plans.

The battle itself, which is covered in the following Battle Summaries in great detail, resulted in the Japanese calling off the offensive against Port Moresby. Both sides were hampered by surprise, poor reconnaissance, bad weather and vastly exaggerated claims by their bomber pilots. But the USN had held the IJN's Coral Sea advance. Admiral Inouye had decided that they could not push through to the southern coastline of Papua New Guinea without sustaining even heavier losses. He felt that Takagi had insufficient aircraft to protect the invasion force because by 6 May, the light carrier *Shoho* had been sunk by US naval aircraft, to the famous radio transmission of "Scratch one flattop".[4] The fleet carrier *Shokaku* was badly damaged and the air group of Zuikaku mauled. Takagi was subsequently sent back by the Combined Fleet Commander Yamamoto to finish the USN force but failed to find Fletcher's force as he had withdrawn by 10 May. The USN, in its turn, saw the large *Lexington* sunk and her consort *Yorktown* badly damaged, and large losses in air group strength with 66 aircraft failing to return.

It was arguably a Japanese tactical victory, but strategically and more significantly an American one. However, in the aftermath, Nimitz realised they had won their first sea battle against the IJN. Prior to this engagement, no Japanese ship larger than a destroyer had been sunk. The USN now knew that even with what were regarded as inferior aircraft and less experienced aircrew, Japanese carrier forces could be held and defeated. It was going to be a lesson that would be repeated a month later off the atoll of Midway where the core of the IJN striking force would meet its end. The Japanese did not truly appreciate this setback. Their losses at Coral Sea were not regarded as prohibitive for the IJN and the subsequent Midway mission (Operation MI). The sinking of the small *Shoho* was considered a minor inconvenience, the temporary loss of *Shokaku* and *Zuikaku* through damage and inability to restock the airwings more so. The forces selected for Midway were regarded as strong enough to deal with the USN in any eventuality, but this depended on the Americans once again behaving as they were expected to.

The Battle of Midway

The Battle of Midway was fought in the Central Pacific around the strategically vital American islands from 4–7 June 1942. It is now regarded as the pivotal turning point of the Pacific War. The US forces on and around the Midway islands faced a vastly superior force of IJN assets, numbering some 200 ships, including eight aircraft carriers, but spread across the Central Pacific. By sheer numbers, Yamamoto should have been victorious. The USN could spare only three carriers to face the might of the Japanese Combined Fleet. However, what should have been a rout for the IJN ultimately saw the heart of its First Carrier Air Fleet, and all four of its carriers, sunk for the loss of only one US carrier.

Admiral Yamamoto's response to the Halsey/Doolittle Raid of April 1942 had been to seek immediate destruction of the remnants of the USN. Never again would it be able to bomb Japan and threaten the Emperor. Some commentators now believe that this drive blinkered Yamamoto and greatly influenced his decisions and actions. Consequently, Operation MI, the plan for Midway, became fundamentally flawed and laid the foundations for the IJN's defeat. With this, other factors combined to create a situation whereby Japan would lose its best asset to forestall defeat at the hands of the US later in the war. With the loss of four of its finest and largest carriers, taken with Japan's industrial weaknesses and thorough, yet rigid, aircrew training system, the IJN was never able to field a force of sufficient skill or power as it did in the early summer of 1942. By contrast the USN, in 1943, would start to deploy growing numbers of larger *Essex* class carriers together with more highly trained and equipped aviators.

The failure to sink the USN Pacific carriers at Pearl Harbor had already seen Yamamoto begin planning for the decisive engagement that would see Nimitz's carriers finally dispatched. The April raid against Japan and the battle of the Coral Sea in May simply confirmed this desire. But the plan that was constructed to deal the decisive blow was extremely rigid in nature, yet again, overly complicated with a myriad of split and diversionary forces to be involved. The plan took on a larger role with the Aleutian Islands chain, part of Alaska in the northern Pacific, in what most saw as a pointless diversion, splitting IJN assets and now creating Operation AL as well.[5]

Operations AL and MI would see the dispatch of IJN task forces. Separate invasion forces sailed for the Aleutian Islands of Attu and Kiska under the overall command of Vice Admiral Moshiro Hosogaya. A carrier striking force with *Junyo* and *Ryujo* and cruisers under the command of Rear Admiral Kakuji Kakuta – whose mission was to attack Dutch Harbor, to the west of the invasion points – were to neutralise America's main defensive base in the Aleutians. There was also a support force including four battleships under Vice Admiral Shiro Takasu's command, should the US attempt to interfere with the IJN surface ships.

The Midway forces were larger and even more widely spread. The Midway occupation and invasion forces, together with elements of the Second Fleet, both commanded by Vice Admiral Nobutake Kondo, sailed from Japan and Guam with battleships, cruisers and the carrier *Zuiho*. This was supported by Rear Admiral Takeo Kurita's support force with heavy cruisers from Guam and a separate minesweeping force from Saipan. These would be shielded from surprise US attack by a large submarine screen, which was to be placed between Midway and Hawaii, as well as more submarines performing other support missions in the Central Pacific. Overall, three submarine squadrons deployed in total. The island itself was to be neutralised by Admiral Nagumo's First Carrier Striking Force. This comprised four carriers, *Akagi*, *Kaga*, *Hiryu* and *Soryu*, with the Combined Fleet Commander, Yamamoto, hundreds of miles behind him, commanding three of the IJN's battleships, the carrier *Hosho* and the seaplane carrier *Chiyoda*. Both groups sailed from Japan. Long range reconnaissance flying boats would also have a role to play, providing updates of USN carrier movements throughout the Pacific.

Yamamoto's plan had failed to implement a key principle of war, that of concentration of effort. Of his eight carriers, he had one, Nagumo had four, two were with the Aleutian force and the eighth was with the Midway support force. Worse was that previous air losses over the last six months of operations had not been fully replaced and many that had, were replaced with inexperienced aircrew. Had the IJN carriers been merged together, their attack, defensive and reconnaissance capabilities would have been vastly improved. Moreover, had the fleet been concentrated, the defensive firepower of the ships' guns would also have been improved and early warning of potential US air raiders made possible, as the only radars in the IJN fleet were in Yamamoto's battleship force. The course of the battle, which the following Battle Summaries cover in great detail, would have been radically altered. As it was, this large, if very disparate, group of ships sailed as a result of a rigidly formulated plan to Midway, lacking flexibility and forewarning of US intentions and capabilities. It was a plan which, when run in exercise prior to the battle, had seen the IJN lose. It was only due to Yamamoto's force of personality and his desire to avenge the April bombings that he ensured it was adopted.[6]

The USN suffered none of these problems. Nimitz's main concern was marshalling sufficient assets to stop the Japanese. Through Commander Rochefort's codebreaking team, Nimitz once again knew the intentions of Yamamoto, the size of the force and the nature of the Aleutian diversion.[7] In comparison, he was only able to muster three carriers in response, *Hornet* and *Enterprise*, comprising Task Force 16 under the command of Raymond Spruance, and the badly damaged *Yorktown*, still TF 17, which many Japanese had thought lost at the Coral Sea. *Yorktown* remained under the command of Admiral Fletcher. These three were also packed with aircraft, unlike their Japanese counterparts. Moreover, Nimitz was able to send as many personnel and Navy, Marine and Army aircraft to Midway as possible, creating a fixed fourth carrier. This would be pivotal, as at the crucial point of contact at Midway, both sides would effectively be equal in carrier numbers and the IJN would actually be outnumbered in terms of aircraft. In addition, Midway and the task force carriers all possessed radar to provide early warning of Japanese attack. Ultimately, whoever found the enemy carriers first, and hit first and hardest, would win. It would be Fletcher.

To the surprise of the IJN, the USN would be there to strike at Nagumo's carriers first, as it was able to sail before the Japanese submarine cordon was in place and also to disrupt the long-range Japanese reconnaissance flights, blinding the Japanese due to the forewarning of Rochefort's team. Thus, on the morning of 4 June, the US Task Forces were off to the north east of Midway while Fletcher's aircraft and those on Midway searched for Nagumo's carriers that were to the north west. The following Battle Summaries take the reader through the immensely confusing and constantly active scenario of 4 and 5 June, which saw the exchanges between Midway and the IJN carriers and then the opposing carrier fleets themselves that ultimately culminated in the disabling and sinking of Nagumo's four carriers and Fletcher's *Yorktown*. The latter finally sank on 7 June, following two successful Japanese carrier attacks and an IJN submarine attack.

The result of the battle was damning for the Japanese. Again they failed to maintain their effort, as after Nagumo transferred his flag to a cruiser from the stricken *Akagi*, Yamamoto passed command to Kondo who was told to finally, perhaps far too late, merge the IJN forces. However, shortly afterwards, Yamamoto changed his mind and called for a withdrawal of all forces from the theatre. Midway and the Central Pacific had been held. The IJN, knowingly or not, was mortally wounded.

There are similarities and themes in both battles that should be mentioned. Both see the IJN mounting overly complicated, rigid plans, with divided forces and diversions as a norm. It failed, in both operations and also in later ones, to concentrate its overwhelming firepower. The IJN failed to deploy all its carrier assets and failed to operate with full air groups. The Japanese planners attempted to gauge US intentions and predict with certainty the actions of the USN, but they lacked the intelligence to support their contentions. Imperial naval codes were transmitted sloppily and open to breaking, yet they did not pose the same challenge as US codes. They have been accused of suffering from 'victory disease' and overconfidence. More likely, they were suffering from losses and, critically, exhaustion from six months of near constant activity against the Allies, with little hope of relief, due to the inflexible and slow-moving Japanese training regime.

Nimitz and the USN displayed similar characteristics in both battles. Superior security and excellent code-breaking abilities gave the US an immediate advantage. This could have been nullified, however, had

Yamamoto concentrated his forces, which he did not. Nimitz and Fletcher ensured in both battles that all available carriers with full air groups were employed. US command and control was far more flexible than the IJN. Its planning was simpler and robust; it ensured it maintained the aim in both engagements – and this all helped to create the conditions for victory.

On the other hand, both engagements can be painted in the light of luck, uncertainty, poor reconnaissance, bad weather and employment of air assets. In the Coral Sea and Midway battles, Yamamoto came within a hair's breadth of victory and Nimitz and the US Government were aware of this. Yamamoto was portrayed as America's number one enemy and following pyrrhic Japanese tactical victories in the Eastern Solomons and Santa Cruz battles during the later Guadalcanal campaign, he was assassinated by US aircraft in the spring of 1943. This was only one legacy of Coral Sea and Midway. The other was the loss of the four IJN carriers, a number of aircrew and, crucially, the well-drilled deck crews. These two battles, followed by the attritional engagements off Guadalcanal, saw the pride of the Japanese striking force destroyed. It had dominated East Asia, the Pacific and the Eastern Indian Ocean. New ships would be built, new variants of existing aircraft manufactured and new air and ground crew trained. But none of them ever lived up to the Japanese force that had launched Japan into war in the first six months of the struggle in the Pacific. The Japanese had been stopped and the course of the remainder of the war assured as a result of the Coral Sea and Midway battles.

The Battle Summaries, the Coral Sea and Midway Literature

Battle Summaries 45 and 46 take the reader through both battles in the greatest of detail. Beginning with thorough discussions of the strategic situation prior to the engagements, they then follow the actions of the combatants and highlight the lessons of the engagements. Appendices are included, detailing operational orders, forces employed and losses, together with relevant maps and glossaries. Published for the benefit of the Royal Navy in 1952, they are a result of combining mostly US sources, written during and after the war, up to 1951. The individual sources are all still available and a number of writers including Samuel E. Morison (author of the monumental series concerning USN operations in World War II – see Further Reading, page 26) employ them heavily. However, these Battle Summaries are somewhat different, as they cross-refer and blend the official publications more than published works of the same era. Most narratives of battle, published post war, had a tendency to rely on a handful of sources and would often recount a story peppered with inaccuracies and myths. Others, particularly Japanese-sourced accounts, were written deliberately for the US market and perpetuated the myths further. Most notable of these fictions was the outnumbering of the USN, when at the crucial carrier-to-carrier battles, the Americans actually outnumbered the IJN. Instead, a sort of successful 'Alamo scenario' is often portrayed by some writers. The Battle Summaries also employ the Naval Analysis Division of the United States Strategic Bombing Survey (USSBS) 1947 publication, *The Japanese Story of the Battle of Midway*, and therefore draw on the most official Japanese publication possible.[8] This work was the result of interviews with IJN personnel at the time of Midway.

Since 1952, much has been published – the amount of literature concerning both battles, especially Midway, is immense and more continues to be written. Some crucial information had not come properly to light, such as the role of code breaking, and the Summaries make clear that the information was sourced from what was available, up to May 1951. However, controversy continues 70 years after the events. Various decisions, mostly by the IJN, are continually raked over and even some concrete facts and events are debated. Were the Japanese carrier decks full of aircraft or not? Why were IJN reconnaissance procedures so poor? Was Nagumo far too slow in reacting? We are not able to answer all these questions, but the following Battle Summaries assist in understanding the battles, and their place as the turning point in the Pacific War – and might bring us closer to finding some answers.

1. The Washington Naval Conference was called by the US to forestall a global naval arms race and attempt to diffuse tensions over China. The most famous result was the Five Power Treaty which saw reductions and limitations imposed on the navies of Great Britain, America, Japan, France and Italy, using the ratio of 5:5:3:1.75:1.75, applicable to their battleships, battlecruisers and aircraft carriers.
2. A fleet strong on paper, but not in reality, was sent following the loss of HMS *Prince of Wales* and HMS *Repulse* on 10 December to IJN land-based air attack. Admiral Somerville, the British Fleet commander of the new force, fully understood he was outmatched, especially once the carrier HMS *Hermes* and two heavy cruisers were sunk by IJN air attack.
3. Crace was Australian born.
4. Lt.-Cdr. Robert E Dixon, USS *Lexington*'s second Douglas Dauntless dive bomber leader, was responsible for the transmission, "Scratch one flattop! Dixon to carrier. Scratch one flattop!"
5. The Aleutians were far from a diversion. Yamamoto knew that fighting on US soil off the Alaskan mainland would be as important as Midway.
6. Yamamoto had offered his resignation in an attempt to ensure the plan remained intact.
7. Rochefort's hand-picked team in Hawaii were decrypting some 140 Japanese messages a day throughout May.
8. Available via the US Naval Historical Center.

Further Reading

Agawa, H., *The Reluctant Admiral: Yamamoto and the Imperial Navy* (Tokyo: Kodansha International, 1979)

Buell, T.B., *The Quiet Warrior: A Biography of Admiral Raymond A. Spruance* (MD: Naval Institute Press, 2009)

Carlson, E., *Joe Rochefort's War: The Odyssey of the Codebreaker who Outwitted Yamamoto at Midway* (MD: Naval Institute Press, 2011)

Chesnau, R., *Aircraft Carriers of the World* (London: Arms & Armour, 1992)

Francillon, R.J., *Japanese Aircraft of the Pacific War* (London: Putnam, 1987)

Grove, P., *Battles in Focus* (London: Brassey's, 2004)

Hoyt, E.P., *Blue Skies and Blood: The Battle of the Coral Sea* (NY: Jove Books, 1975)

Lundstrom, J.B., *Black Shoe Carrier Admiral Frank Jack Fletcher, at Coral Sea, Midway and Guadalcanal* (MD: Naval Institute Press, 2006)

Morison, S.E., *Coral Sea, Midway and Submarine Operations May 1942–August 1942: History of US Naval Operations in World War Two Volume Four* (NY: Little Brown and Co, 1954)

Morison, S.E., *The Rising Sun in the Pacific: History of US Naval Operations in World War Two Volume Three* (NY: Little Brown and Co, 1951)

Parshall, J., & Tully, A., *Shattered Sword: The Untold Story of the Battle of Midway* (VA: Potomac Books Inc., 2005)

Peattie, M., *Sunburst: The Rise of Japanese Naval Air Power, 1909–1941* (MD: Naval Institute Press, 2001)

Perras, G.P., *Stepping Stones to Nowhere: The Aleutian Islands, Alaska, and American Military Strategy, 1867–1945* (British Columbia: UBC Press, 2003)

Symonds, C.L., *The Battle of Midway* (NY: OUP, 2012)

Part I

C.B. 3305 (1) BR 1736 (47)

RESTRICTED – Attention is called to the penalties attaching to any infraction of the Official Secrets Acts

NAVAL STAFF HISTORY
SECOND WORLD WAR

BATTLE SUMMARY No. 45

BATTLE OF CORAL SEA
4 – 8 MAY, 1942

This book is invariably to be kept locked up when not in use and is not to be taken outside the ship or establishment for which it is issued without the express permission of the Commanding Officer.

This book is the property of H.M. Government.
It is intended for the use of Officers generally, and may in certain cases be communicated to persons in H.M. Service below the rank of Commissioned Officer who may require to be acquainted with its contents in the course of their duties. The Officers exercising this power will be held responsible that this information is imparted with due caution and reserve.

T.S.D. 30/51
Training and Staff Duties Division (Historical Section),
Naval Staff, Admiralty, S.W.1

CONTENTS

Overview 32

Chapter I
Strategic Situation in April 1942
Decision by Japan to Expand the Defensive Perimeter 33
Japanese Naval Forces 34
Japanese Air Forces 37
Allied Forces 37

Chapter II
The Action at Tulagi
Allied Forces Concentrate 42
Japanese Occupy Tulagi 43
First Air Strike at Tulagi 46
Second Air Strike at Tulagi 47
Third Air Strike Launched at Tulagi 48
Results of the Operation 48

Chapter III
The Action off Misima and Japanese Air Attacks
Allied Forces Reorganised 50
Japanese Movements 51
Support Group Detached 52
Enemy Occupation Force Sighted off Misima 52
Sinking of the *Shoho* 54
Japanese Attempts to Locate U.S. Carriers 55
Attack on the *Neosho* and *Sims* 58
Attacks on the Support Group 61

Chapter IV
Air Battles
Japanese Carriers Sighted 64
The *Yorktown*'s Group Attacks 65

Attack By the *Lexington*'s Group 67
Preparations to Meet Japanese Air Attack 68
Combat Air Patrol Goes Out 70
The Attack Opens 72
Attack on the *Yorktown* 73
Attack on the *Lexington* 78
Sinking of the *Lexington* 79
Japanese Plan Abandoned 81
Lessons of the Battle 82

Annex 83

Appendices
Appendix A 88
Appendix B 94
Appendix C 96

Endnotes 99

U.S. Navy and Army Aircraft

Navy

Types.
- F2A   *Buffalo*. Single engine fighter, manufactured by Brewster.
- F4F   *Wildcat* (Br. *Martlet*). Single engine fighter, manufactured by Grumman.
- SBD   *Dauntless*. Single engine scout bomber manufactured by Douglas.
- SB2U *Vindicator* (Br. *Chesapeake*). Single engine scout bomber, manufactured by Vought-Sikorsky.
- PBY   *Catalina*. Twin-engine patrol bomber (flying boat) manufactured by Consolidated-Vultee.
- TBF   *Avenger*. Single engine Navy torpedo bomber, manufactured by Grumman.

General terms.
- VF   Fighter.   VSB Scout bomber.
- VPB Patrol bomber.   VTB Torpedo bomber.

Army

- B.17   Heavy bomber, 'Flying Fortress', originally manufactured by Boeing.
- B.26   Medium bomber, 'Marauder', originally manufactured by Martin.

Note:-

Times in this Battle Summary are Zone – 11½ *i.e.*, 11½ hours fast on G.M.T. up to 1700/7 when clocks were altered to Z –11.

Bearings and courses are true, unless otherwise stated.

Overview

The Battle of the Coral Sea was the outcome of a Japanese expedition to capture Port Moresby, in south-east New Guinea. It consisted of the following six separate though related air actions:–

Attack on 4 May 1942 by the *Yorktown*'s air groups on enemy shipping engaged in occupying Tulagi, in Florida Island (Solomon Is.).

Attempts on 7 May by both U.S. and Japanese to locate the other's task forces, resulting in:–

> Attack by Task Force 17 aircraft on Moresby occupation force off Misima Island, Louisiade Archipelago, and sinking of Japanese light carrier *Shoho*.
>
> Attempted Japanese carrier-borne attack on Task Force 17 at night.
>
> Sinking of U.S. oiler *Neosho* and destroyer *Sims* in the Coral Sea by carrier-borne air attack.
>
> Attack by land-based Japanese aircraft on the reinforced Australian squadron proceeding to attack the enemy expedition off Jomard Passage, Louisiade Archipelago.

Simultaneous attacks on 8 May by Task Force 17 air groups on the Japanese carriers *Zuikaku* and *Shokaku* resulting in the latter being put out of action, and on the U.S. carriers *Yorktown* and *Lexington* by air groups of the two Japanese carriers, causing the loss of the *Lexington*.

Strategic Situation in April 1942[1]

Decision by Japan to Expand the Defensive Perimeter

The advance of the Japanese to the south and east after the attack on Pearl Harbor on 7 December 1941 was so rapid that in the space of four months they practically completed Phase I of the Basic Plan for the Greater East Asia War, namely the occupation of the Philippines, Guam, Hong Kong, Burma, and the rich British and Dutch lands in the south, possession of which was to render Japan self-sufficient.

By the middle of April 1942 a point had been reached at which Phase II, the consolidation and strengthening of a defensive perimeter for the 'Southern Resources Area' and the Japanese mainland should have been put into effect. As originally conceived this perimeter consisted of the Kuriles, Wake Island, the Marshall Islands, Bismarcks, Timor, Java, Sumatra, Malaya and Burma.

The unexpected ease with which the first part of the war plan had been carried out caused the Japanese to underestimate the present strength of the United States in the Pacific, just as, when deciding upon war, they had overestimated their own war making capacity and underestimated the huge Allied potential. Many of their leaders were persuaded that advantage should be taken of the present situation, to embark on further expansion. Their argument received reinforcement on 18 April 1942 when U.S. Army bombers, flown from the aircraft carrier *Hornet*, raided Tokyo. Though no more than a token raid, it was used as an argument to point out the need for additional bases to the east; and it was eventually decided that the defensive perimeter should be moved outward to include the western Aleutians, Midway, Samoa, Fiji, New Caledonia, and Port Moresby in south-eastern New Guinea.

The decision proved an irretrievable mistake. The strategic sphere was already too large. Neither military strength, shipping, nor the Japanese national economy, were of a calibre capable of supporting further expansion;

and the attempt used up resources which should have been employed in consolidating the already huge gains.

Vital areas were perforce left insufficiently organised for defence whilst operations were set in train for the capture of Port Moresby, Midway and the Aleutians. The strategy that inspired these operations might be defensive, but it entailed a tactical offensive and resulted in a situation the opposite of that which it was intended to bring about: instead of strengthening the Japanese position, the attempt at expansion actually weakened it. Losses were incurred which could not be made good and consequently hampered future operations; and the eventual return to the original plan found the Japanese with insufficient strength remaining to carry it through successfully.

The first operation in the expansionist plan was the capture of Port Moresby to form a southern outpost in the Japanese defensive system. The Japanese were already established on the north-eastern shores of New Guinea. Establishment on the Gulf of Papua would deprive the Allies of a potential base within air range of the main Japanese base at Rabaul (New Britain) and would place the Japanese in a position to dominate the entire island of New Guinea, and if they desired, to threaten northern Australia, though even in their present mood of inflated morale, they apparently did not contemplate this latter eventuality.

Whilst en route to Port Moresby the expedition was to seize Tulagi in Florida Island, South Solomons, and establish a seaplane base. Tulagi, which was lightly held by Australian forces, was a strategically important point from which the main line of communications from the U.S.A. to Australia and New Zealand could be attacked. It had one of the best harbours in the South Solomons.

Japanese Naval Forces (Appendix B)

The great conquests already made by the Japanese found them with their naval, military and air strength unimpaired, and that of the Allies severely reduced. In the air and on the ground the Japanese losses were insignificant; shipping sunk to date amounted to less than 300,000 tons; and losses of major naval vessels were no more than five destroyers sunk.

On the other hand, the attempt of the Allies to withstand the Japanese advance in Malaya and the Netherlands East Indies had resulted in the piecemeal destruction of the Dutch and British naval forces in the south-west Pacific and the withdrawal of the United States Asiatic Fleet to Australian and South Pacific bases, whilst even in the more distant waters of the Indian Ocean the British Eastern Fleet had been compelled to withdraw from the Ceylon area, thus enabling the Japanese to proceed with their war plan in the Pacific unhampered by a vulnerable western flank.

A feature of the Japanese operations, which was to set the pattern for the Pacific, was the spearhead employment of carrier-based aircraft with battleship and cruiser support. Japanese carrier-based aircraft had caused the most important Allied losses of warships to date, and had also sunk thousands of tons of auxiliaries and merchant ships and destroyed hundreds of Allied aircraft, as well as docks, hangars and base facilities, all with complete immunity to the carrier striking force; in fact, it had seldom been sighted. The Battle of the Coral Sea was the first occasion on which it was effectively attacked.

The Japanese Carrier Striking Force which wrought this havoc was made up from the First Air Fleet (six fleet carriers, four light carriers), with a battle squadron (two battleships), a cruiser squadron (two cruisers), and screen. Behind it stood the main body of the Second Fleet, two battleships, four heavy cruisers and destroyers, which supported the lighter forces – cruisers, light carriers, seaplane carriers, destroyers and ancillary vessels – engaged in carrying out the operations in the Philippines, Malaya and the Netherlands East Indies. This powerful striking force of fast battleships, aircraft carriers, and several cruisers and destroyers returned to Japanese home waters from operating across a third of the globe, from Hawaii to Ceylon, on 18 April, the day of the U.S. air raid on Tokyo, and a squadron was formed without delay, for the attack on Port Moresby, known as the MO Operation.

The forces for the Moresby expedition were under the command of Vice-Admiral S. Inouye, who flew his flag on board the light cruiser *Kashima* at Rabaul (New Britain). Only one of the three squadrons of the carrier striking force was available to operate in general support of the expedition, so heavy had been the drain of war on the air groups. This was Carrier Squadron 5, consisting of the *Zuikaku*, flagship of Rear-Admiral K. Hara, and the *Shokaku*. Their aircraft complement comprised fighters, bombers, and torpedo aircraft to the number of 63 and 72 respectively. The remainder of the 6th Squadron, as the supporting force was termed, consisted of the 5th Cruiser Squadron (the 8-inch cruisers *Myoko*, *Haguro*, and *Ashigara*) under Vice-Admiral T. Takagi, two destroyer divisions (six destroyers in all), a minelayer, the seaplane carrier *Kiyokawa Maru*, and an oiler. Had the expedition gone according to plan, the force would subsequently have carried out an attack on Townsville, in Queensland, where the Japanese had information that there were American and Australian ships and that aircraft were being delivered. The presence and near composition of this force in the area was known to the Americans.

The Occupation Force for Port Moresby and Tulagi consisted of two cruiser squadrons, the 6th with four 8-inch cruisers, and the 18th consisting of two light cruisers, the *Shoho* (one of the two light carriers of the 4th Carrier Squadron) carrying 12 fighters and 9–12 torpedo aircraft, and a destroyer; the 6th Destroyer Flotilla (light cruiser *Yubari* and six destroyers); an auxiliary seaplane tender and a minelayer. Five transports carried the troops.[2] The task of the *Shoho* and her supporting cruisers was purely defensive, to guard the transports in the Occupation Force against submarine and air attack.

The organisation also included six submarines of the 8th Flotilla. The Battle of the Coral Sea developed whilst these six submarines were off the east coast of Australia. They concentrated south of the Solomon Islands to attack the Allied task force, but although there appeared to be close co-ordination between the Japanese air reconnaissance and the submarines, the latter obtained no results.

The Occupation Force and its escort sailed from Rabaul on 30 April, part of the escort being provided from Truk.

At Truk the Japanese had a naval base which, since the Caroline Islands were under their mandate, they had been enabled to develop in peace time, directly contrary though this was to the provisions of the Washington Conference, 1922. Their main base for operations in the Solomons, Bismarcks, and New Guinea was Simpson Harbour (Rabaul) in New Britain, though there were numerous anchorages in the area which could be used by naval ships, *e.g.* Gasmata (New Britain); Kavieng (New Ireland); Salamoa and Lae (New Guinea); Watom, Ulu and Dyaul Islands (Northern Bismarcks). Manus Island in the Admiralty Islands was occupied by the Japanese on 4 April 1942, but the Allies had no information whether they were using the great Sea Eagle Harbour. For the most part, however, naval units remained at sea at this date.

Japanese Air Forces

In addition to their carrier-based aircraft, the Japanese had in the Bismarcks a naval air flotilla, the 25th, shore-based at Rabaul, and estimated by the Allies to number 12 fighters, 20 bombers, 17 patrol aircraft, and four small seaplanes, total 53. American intelligence indicated that air reinforcements to Rabaul from the Marianas and Marshall Islands were being hastened. The airfield at Kavieng, in the adjacent island of New Ireland, was known to be used by enemy bombers. The only airfield known to be used by the enemy in New Guinea was Lae, at the head of Huon Gulf, where it was estimated that 15 heavy bombers, 30 fighters and four patrol aircraft were based. Patrol seaplanes used Salamoa on Huon Gulf, and were also based at Shortland Island, south of Bougainville in the Solomons, long range aircraft of this type being employed by the Japanese for reconnaissance, thus relieving the carriers of this task. There were no other land-based naval air forces nearer than Kendari in the Celebes, where the 23rd Air Flotilla was established in February 1942; and no Army air forces nearer than the Philippines (Fifth Air Army) and Malaya-Burma (Third Air Army).

Allied Forces

The concentration of Japanese ships near Truk and Palau (West Caroline Is.) at the end of April was reported by Allied intelligence in sufficient time for the Americans to assemble a strong force to oppose the expected move through the Solomons. Admiral C. W. Nimitz, Commander-in-Chief, U.S. Pacific Fleet, had operating under him in the central and south Pacific areas three American task forces, two of them, Nos. 17 and 11, containing each one fleet carrier and the third, No. 16, two carriers. Task Force 17 (Rear-Admiral F. J. Fletcher) consisted of the carrier *Yorktown* (flag), the three 8-inch cruisers *Astoria*, *Portland* and *Chester*, and six destroyers. The ships had been at sea continuously since leaving Pearl Harbor on 14 February, operating against Wake, Marcus and Lae-Salamoa, and were returning to the Coral Sea after a week spent in maintenance and replenishment at Tongatabu in the Tonga Islands. Task Force 11, consisting of the carrier *Lexington*, the 8-inch cruisers *Minneapolis* and *New Orleans*, and seven destroyers, under Rear-Admiral A. W. Fitch, had proceeded to Pearl Harbor after the raid on Lae-Salamoa on 10 March, and sailed from there on 16 April for Christmas Island. The third carrier force, Task Force 16, which included the two carriers *Enterprise* and *Hornet*, did not return to

Pearl Harbor until 25 April after the air raid on Tokyo. The Australian Squadron, including the 8-inch cruiser *Australia*, which had taken part in the Lae-Salamoa operation, and the light cruiser *Hobart*, under the British Rear-Admiral J. G. Crace, was at Sydney, Australia.

The aircraft complement of the U.S. carriers was some ten less than that of the Japanese, the difference being accounted for by the greater number of fighters, 27 against an average of 17, borne aboard the Japanese carriers. Both the Japanese fighters and torpedo aircraft were superior in performance to the American types.[3] The U.S. torpedo aircraft were obsolescent and their low performance reduced the effectiveness of their attacks. The Commander-in-Chief U.S. Pacific Fleet was not satisfied with the effectiveness of the U.S. bombs and torpedoes; the speed of the latter was so low that the Japanese stated they could turn and run from them.

There were at this date the following Allied advanced bases in the area, outside Australia:–

(a) Tongatabu in the Friendly Is., a limited monarchy under British protection, was in process of development as an intermediate operating base. The anchorage could accommodate 12 deep draft and 36 medium and light draft vessels, but pending the installation of minefields it was insecure. The shore defences were not strong, but were being increased. There was an airfield.

(b) Numea in New Caledonia (French) had an excellent anchorage for ships of any draught, but until the defences were completed it was not considered a secure anchorage for carriers.

(c) Efate in the New Hebrides, an Anglo-French condominium, was being organised as a defended base. There was known to be a landing field, but the report on its condition and suitability was still awaited.

(d) Suva and Nandi in Fiji, and Tutuila, a U.S. protectorate south-east of Samoa, were considered suitable for ships of any draught and their entrances were mined and their defences well organised. They were considered secure anchorages for other than carriers.

The Allied task forces operated in strategical co-ordination with aircraft of the South-west Pacific Area based in Australia, at Port Moresby, and at Tulagi, Florida Island (Solomon Is.), until evacuation of the latter by the Australian forces on 1 May, two days before the Japanese began to move into the island. At Numea in New Caledonia there were fleet patrol aircraft and army pursuit squadrons.

These shore-based air forces obtained information of the enemy which was of much value, and their almost daily attacks on shipping were of cumulative assistance, but they did not co-operate tactically, for this problem had not at that date been solved. Numbers of aircraft were inadequate and the Australian bases were remote. Difficulties of communication were being overcome, but there was still much to be done in providing for the readiness and training of shore-based aircraft to co-ordinate their operations tactically with fleet units, to relieve carrier-based aircraft of long range reconnaissance as did the Japanese, and to be ready to attack, with full groups, any targets located.

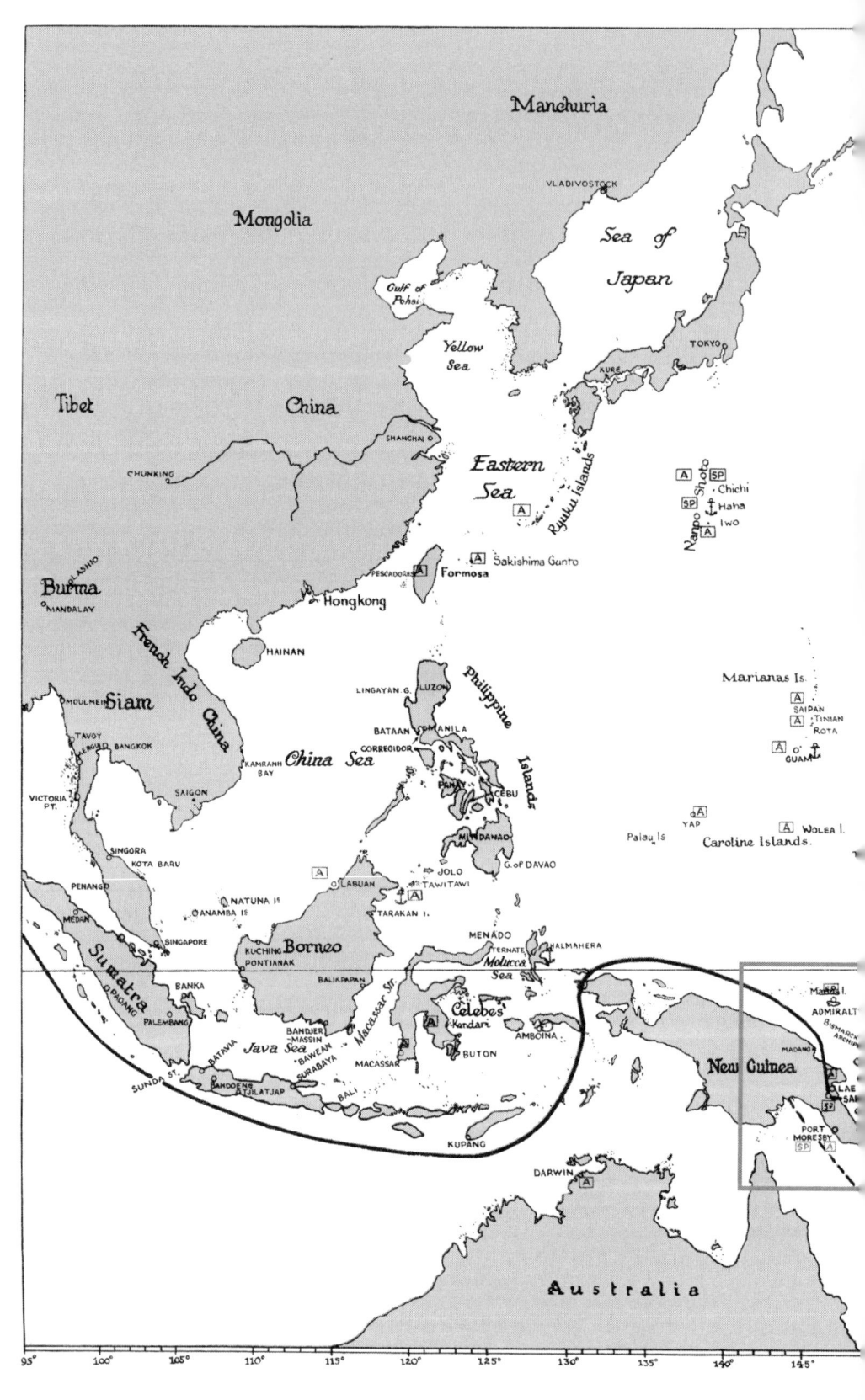

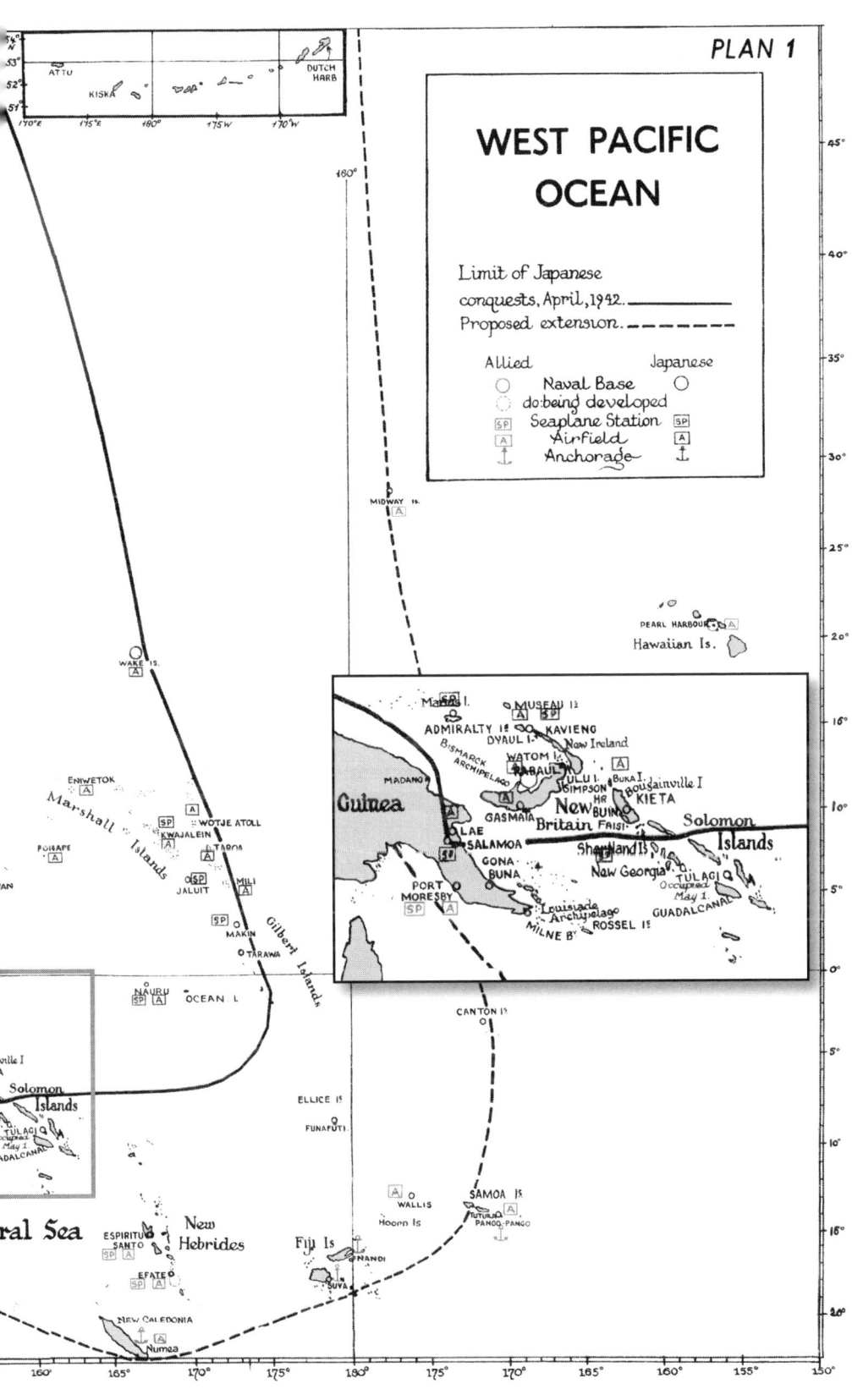

The Action at Tulagi

Allied Forces Concentrate (Plan 2, Appendix C)
U.S. intelligence reports indicated that a Japanese airborne attack on Port Moresby might occur in the first week in May, and concentration of the available Allied forces in the Coral Sea, Task Forces 17, 11, 16 and the Australian Squadron, to oppose it was accordingly ordered. Task Force 11 had left Pearl Harbor on 16 April for Christmas Island; it was now diverted to the Coral Sea, where the Australian Squadron was also to join up. Task Force 16 at Pearl Harbor was unable, in the event, to arrive before battle was joined.

Task Forces 17 and 11 made rendezvous as arranged at 0545 on 1 May in latitude 16° 16' S., longitude 162° 20' E., some 300 miles west of the New Hebrides. Two of the three oilers used for servicing the fleet, the *Neosho* and *Tippecanoe*, were in the area; Rear-Admiral Fletcher directed Rear-Admiral Fitch to meet the *Tippecanoe* with her escort the *Chicago* and *Perkins* in latitude 16° 00' S., longitude 161° 43' E., and fuel, steering to rejoin Task Force 17 next morning, the intention being to retain the *Neosho* as a reserve and to send the *Tippecanoe* back empty to Efate (New Hebrides). Task Force 17 completed fuelling from the *Neosho* on 2 May, but Rear-Admiral Fitch reported that he did not expect to finish until noon on 4 May. With enemy action now reported imminent, Commander Task Force 17 could not contemplate remaining so far to the south-eastward; he set course to the north-westward, directing Rear-Admiral Fitch to fuel his destroyers, if practicable, at night, on the same course and rejoin Task Force 17 at daylight on 4 May in latitude 15° 00' S., longitude 157° 00' E., the position in which Rear-Admiral Crace had been directed to rendezvous with the *Australia* and *Hobart* from Australia.

At 1515 on 2 May, shortly before the two task forces separated, one of the *Yorktown*'s reconnaissance aircraft sighted a submarine on the surface in latitude 16° 04' S., longitude 162° 18' E., 32 miles to the northward, but in spite of being closely depth charged by three aircraft sent out to attack it, the enemy escaped. The Americans thought that they had been sighted and that wireless signals intercepted subsequently pointed to the probability of their position having been reported, but actually this was not so.

Rear-Admiral Fletcher continued to the north-westward during the night 2/3 May, and topped up his destroyers from the *Neosho* next day; it was his consistent practice to top up his light craft from tankers, cruisers or carriers whenever they could take some 70 tons. He intended to fuel the remainder of his ships after effecting concentration next day with Task Forces 11 and 44. The latter consisted of the Australian Squadron reinforced by the cruiser *Chicago* and two U.S. destroyers. Before this could take place, however, news came in which completely altered the situation.

Japanese Occupy Tulagi

On 30 April the Japanese occupation force with its escort of six cruisers, the light carrier *Shoho*, and a screen of destroyers and submarines, sailed from Rabaul to the southward. Part of the expedition was sighted by aircraft of South-west Pacific Forces at 1700 on 2 May, off the southern end of Santa Isabel Island, possibly heading for Tulagi in Florida Island. This strategically important point in the South Solomons, from which the main line of communications from the U.S.A. to Australia and New Zealand could be attacked, had been evacuated by the Australians on 1 May. Two transports were reported unloading troops into barges in the harbour, though no indication was given of the time at which the occupation commenced.

The intelligence reached Commander Task Force 17 at 1900 on 3 May and Rear-Admiral Fletcher at once headed for Tulagi (2000) and worked up to 27 knots to reach a position for an air strike at daylight. With his flagship, the *Yorktown*, were the heavy cruisers *Astoria*, *Chester*, *Portland* and *Chicago* and the destroyers *Hammann*, *Anderson*, *Perkins*, *Walke*, *Morris*, and *Sims*. To wait for the *Lexington* and Task Force 11 might have jeopardised the success of the operation; he detached the *Neosho*, with the destroyer *Russell* as escort, with orders to proceed to the rendezvous in latitude 15° 00' S., 157° 00' E., arranged for 4 May, and inform all ships that a new rendezvous would be made in latitude 15° 00' S., longitude 160° 00' E., at daylight on 5 May.

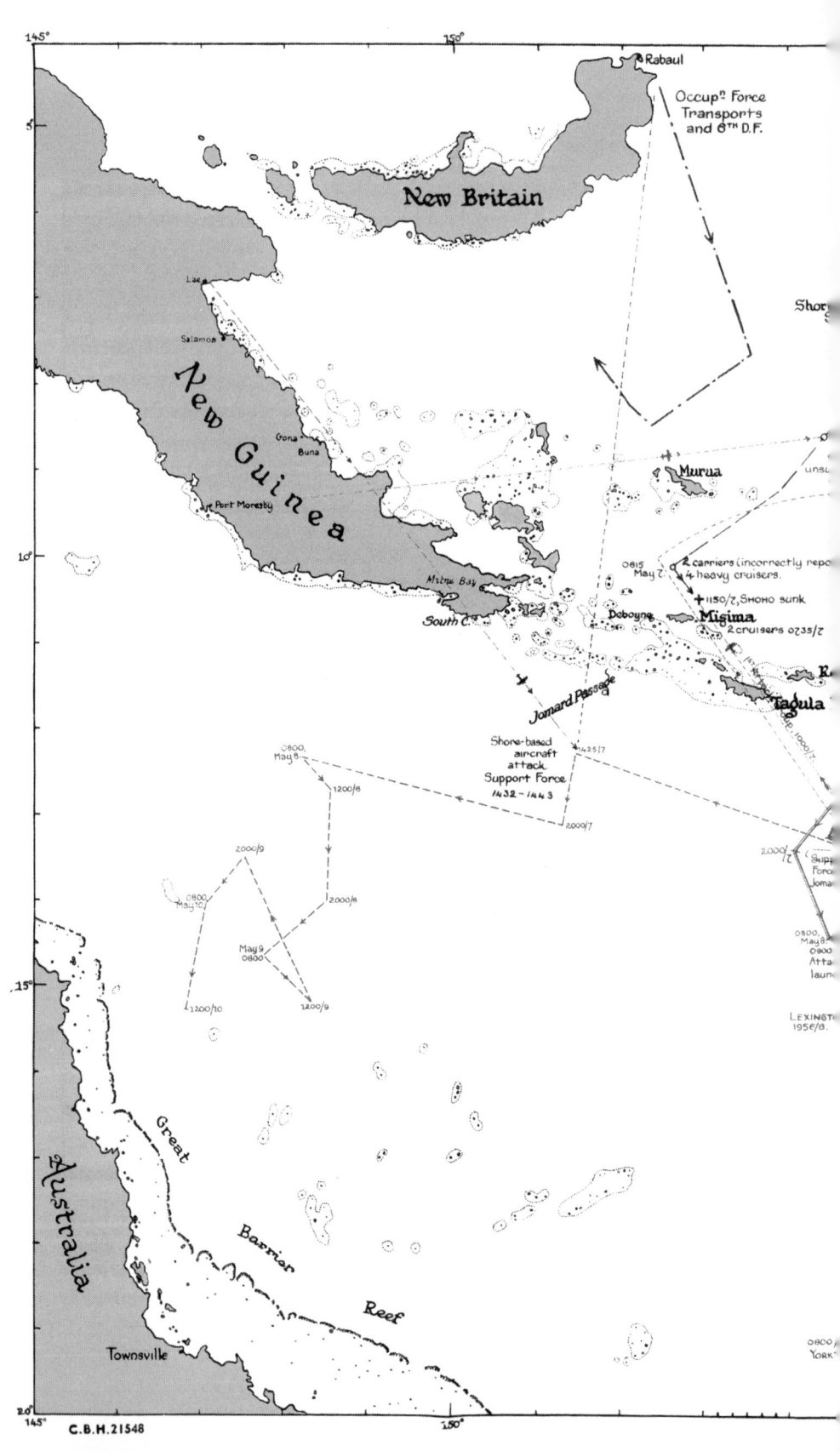

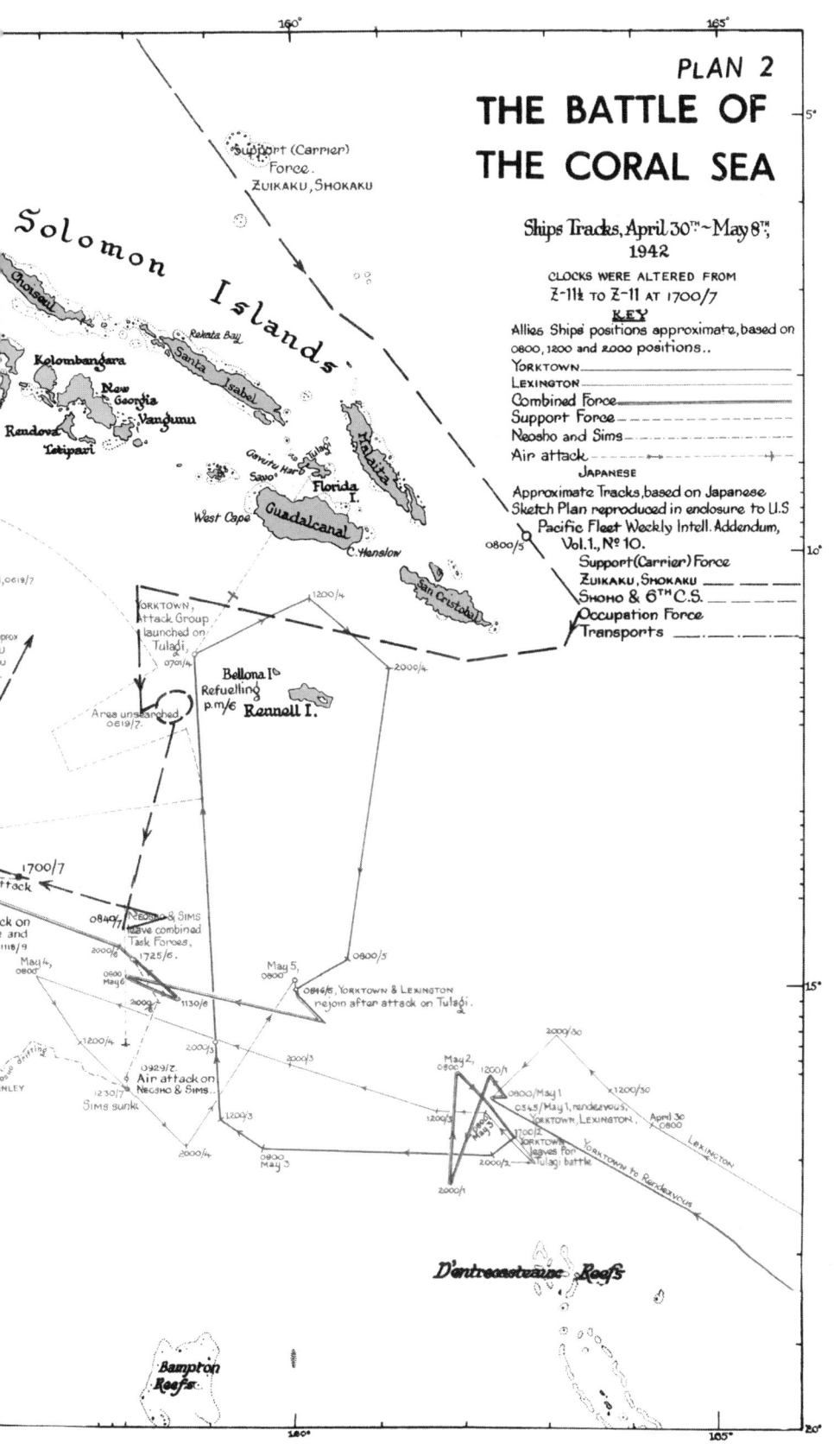

First Air Strike at Tulagi

By 0631 on 4 May Task Force 17 had reached a suitable position for launching strikes, in latitude 11° 18' S., longitude 158° 49' E., about 100 miles south-west of Guadalcanal Island. A wide zone of bad flying weather covered Guadalcanal and extended southward for a distance of 70 miles. Visibility was limited by showers from cumulo-nimbus and strato-cumulus clouds in the morning, which gave way to scattered squalls in the afternoon. In the launching area, the wind gusts varied in force from 17 to 35 knots. At Tulagi harbour, however, conditions were somewhat better, with broken to scattered cumulus at 3,000 feet and winds between 10 and 15 knots from the south-east.

Launching now began of a combat air patrol of six fighters and an attack group made up of 12 torpedo aircraft under Lieut.-Commander J. Taylor, 13 reconnaissance aircraft led by Lieut.-Commander W. O. Burch, and 15 bombers under Lieut. W. C. Short. Torpedoes were set to 10 feet, and both the reconnaissance aircraft and the bombers were armed with 1,000-pound bombs. Similar armament was used in all attacks that day. A combat air patrol of six fighters was kept overhead throughout 4 May, and the cruisers maintained inner air patrol. Task Force 17 remained south of Guadalcanal Island, the general course steered during the action being easterly.

Torpedo, reconnaissance and bomber aircraft respectively proceeded independently, with instructions to co-ordinate their attacks. Coordination was not, however, achieved. They found Tulagi off guard. In the inner harbour and adjacent Gavutu Harbour they reported there were two large transports or cargo ships of 800 to 10,000 tons, one 5,000-ton cargo ship, four gunboats, two destroyers, a light cruiser (the *Okinoshima*, an old ship used as a minelayer), the seaplane carrier *Kiyokawa Maru*, as well as a number of small patrol boats and launches, and five seaplanes moored off Makambo Island where the Japanese had established a seaplane base for the operation against Port Moresby. There was no sign of the carrier *Shoho* or the powerful cruiser escort of the transports, whilst the carriers *Zuikaku* and *Shokaku* with the Moresby Task Force, covering the operation, were still far away to the northward of Tulagi.

The scouts arrived first and commenced their attacks at 0815, taking as their target the *Okinoshima* and two destroyers which were moored together. Altitude of bomb release was 2,500 feet, angle of dive 70 degrees. Heavy but ineffective A.A. fire was encountered from the ships in harbour and from the shore. Four bomb hits were claimed. At 0931 the first of the scouts returned to the *Yorktown* and commenced landing. Rearming began at once.

The torpedo aircraft attacked five minutes after the scouts, seven of the 12 attacking the same target, though one aircraft failed to release its torpedo. Three hits were reported. Three aircraft attacked a large cargo ship but made no hits. The remaining two each reported making a hit on another cargo ship. All torpedo releases were made individually from a reported altitude of about 50 feet, at ranges of 400–500 yards.

The 15 bombers attacked in three divisions of five aircraft each, commencing at 0830. Only one certain hit was reported on the seaplane carrier. All dives were made downwind from about 10,000–11,000 feet, dive angle 70 degrees, altitude of release 2,500 feet.

Second Air Strike at Tulagi

By 1036 all aircraft were back on board the *Yorktown* and the serviceable machines had been rearmed and refuelled and a second group was despatched to attack. This group comprised 14 bombers, 13 reconnaissance and 11 torpedo aircraft, the squadrons proceeding independently as before. The bombers attacked first. About five miles east-north-east of Savo Island they sighted what were taken for three gunboats but were probably landing barges, making the best of their way from Tulagi, for every ship that could steam was now getting out of harbour. The 14 bombers attacked (1115) in three sections of 5, 5, and 4, each section taking one landing barge, two of which they blew to pieces with direct hits. The third escaped for the moment by manoeuvring, but was shortly afterwards reduced to a sinking condition by strafing and was later seen beached.

The reconnaissance aircraft covered the area to the west and northwest of Florida Island, sighting the seaplane carrier and a destroyer steering north-westward between Tulagi and Savo Island, and a cargo ship standing out of Tulagi Harbour. The first of these was attacked (1210), two hits being claimed. The torpedo aircraft were divided tactically into two divisions, both of which attacked the same target (1245). Six of them made their releases from ranges of 2,000 to 3,000 yards, target angle from about 10 degrees on the starboard bow to broad on the port bow, the remainder attacking five minutes later, from 1,000 to 1,500 yards range, target angle being abaft the beam. The seaplane carrier increased speed from 10 to 25 knots on being attacked, and manoeuvred under full helm. None of the 11 torpedoes hit, the length of range at which they were released enabling the seaplane carrier to avoid them.

Third Air Strike Launched at Tulagi

Before sending off the third air strike to Tulagi the *Yorktown* at 1310 launched four fighters to destroy enemy seaplanes which had attacked bombers and reconnaissance aircraft engaged in the second strike. Three of the *Kiyokawa Maru*'s fighters were encountered and shot down, and a destroyer heading away from Tulagi was strafed. Two of the American fighters became lost and were forced to land on the south coast of Guadalcanal Island, whence the destroyer *Hammann* with difficulty rescued the pilots that night. All attempts to set fire to the two aircraft failed and the Americans had to be content with destroying papers and secret equipment.

The third and last group of aircraft, 12 reconnaissance and nine bombers, was launched at 1400. Apart from launches, there was only one cargo ship in Tulagi harbour. This was attacked by dive-bombing at 1500; it put up light A.A. fire and got under way; one bomb hit was reported by the reconnaissance aircraft, which also reported sinking several launches and the beached landing barge after the earlier attack. The nine bombers at 1515 attacked in two divisions, one from the westward and the other from the southward, the seaplane carrier that had been the target of previous attacks, which they located by following up an oil streak left by a destroyer in its company. Both ships increased speed on sighting the aircraft, and the seaplane carrier manoeuvred to avoid bombs. No hits were made.

By 1632 the last aircraft had landed aboard the *Yorktown*.

Results of the Operation

Ammunition expenditure in the attack at Tulagi was high compared with results achieved; more particularly, since there was practically no air opposition and very little anti-aircraft fire. In the light of subsequent knowledge, the results were even smaller than was believed at the time.

Damage to the Enemy

	Estimated		Actual
Sunk:	2 destroyers, 1 cargo ship, 4 gunboats, several small launches.	*Sunk*:	1 destroyer (*Kikuzuki*), 4 landing barges.

Damaged:	1 seaplane carrier, 1 cargo ship.	*Damaged*:	1 minelayer (*Okinoshima*) (repaired at Shortland). 1 destroyer *(Yuzuki*. Personnel casualties only, from strafing).

Total expenditure was 22 torpedoes; 76 1,000-lb. bombs; 82,665 rounds of machine gun ammunition. Five Japanese single float seaplanes operating from the *Kiyokawa Maru* were shot down. The Americans lost three aircraft; in addition to the two fighters lost on Guadalcanal, one torpedo aircraft was forced to land in the sea and was lost, the crew being recovered later.

Admiral C. W. Nimitz, C.-in-C., U.S. Pacific Fleet, cited the performance as an example of the manner in which proficiency drops off in wartime and of the necessity for target practices at every opportunity. The first strike, in which the reconnaissance aircraft commenced their dives at 19,000 feet and the bombers from 10,000–11,000 feet, was adversely affected by fogging of sights and windshields, to such an extent that the sights could not be used, a condition which did not occur in dives commenced at lower altitudes.

The Action off Misima and Japanese Air Attacks
(Plan 2)

Allied Forces Reorganised

After landing-on the *Yorktown*'s aircraft Rear-Admiral Fletcher ran to the southward during the night 4/5 May for the rendezvous previously arranged with Task Force 11 and the Australian Squadron in 15° S., 160° E. The destroyer *Perkins* was left behind to search for the crew of the lost torpedo aircraft, and the *Hammann* recovered the pilots from the two fighters forced to land on Guadalcanal: both destroyers rejoined on the morning of 5 May.

Rear-Admiral Fitch (Task Force 11) was making for the rendezvous from the southward on an almost opposite course. Rear-Admiral Crace was bringing the Australian Squadron from Sydney.

At 0755 on 5 May the *Yorktown* launched four fighters to investigate radar contact on an aircraft bearing 252 degrees, distance 30 miles; they found an enemy four-engined flying boat which they shot down at 0820 in position 15 miles from the *Lexington* and 27 from the *Yorktown*. One of the latter's reconnaissance aircraft had reported an enemy submarine at 0738, bearing 285 degrees, distance 150 miles, course 105 degrees, and it was thought the aircraft was directing the submarine on to one of the U.S. task forces. Three torpedo aircraft searched for the submarine without success.

Task Forces 17, 11 and 44 (the Australian Squadron plus the *Chicago* and two destroyers) made rendezvous at 0846/5. Task Force 17 fuelled from the *Neosho* on that and the following day and combined with Task Forces 11 and 22 as Task Force 17, and at 0700/6 the operation orders issued by Rear-Admiral Fletcher at sea on 1 May were put into effect (see Appendix A). The role of the combined task force was to 'destroy enemy ships, shipping and aircraft at favourable opportunities in order to assist in checking further advance by enemy in the New Guinea–Solomon area'. Task Force 17 was organised in five groups. An attack group of five cruisers and seven destroyers under Rear-Admiral T. C. Kinkaid, had the dual role of operating against the Japanese forces reported advancing southward in the New Guinea–

Solomons area and defending the carriers against air and submarine attack whilst in company. A support group under Rear-Admiral Crace, consisting of Task Force 44, had also a dual role of defending the carriers against air, surface and submarine attack and supporting or operating tactically with the attack group. Rear-Admiral Fitch in the *Lexington* commanded the Air Group; two destroyers were assigned to the Fuelling Group; and Rear-Admiral Fletcher had also under his orders a search group consisting of the seaplane tender *Tangier* with 12 patrol aircraft which operated from Numea in New Caledonia.

Japanese Movements

The orders specified that the force was to operate generally in the Coral Sea about 700 miles south of Rabaul (*i.e.*, outside the range of Japanese shore-based reconnaissance aircraft) until word was received of an enemy advance, the anticipated date of which was given by the Commander-in-Chief, Pacific Fleet, as 7 or 8 May. On 5 May reports began to come in from the C.-in-C., Pacific Fleet and the Commander South-west Pacific Area of the sighting of numerous enemy ships in the New Guinea–New Britain–Solomon Islands area. It was fairly definitely established that three aircraft carriers were amongst them, but although almost every type of ship was reported, including (incorrectly) a battleship, the forces were scattered and there seemed to be no common direction of movement.

Actually, the Japanese occupation force was engaged on 4 and 5 May in effecting its final rendezvous in the Shortland Islands, in the north-west part of the Solomons, in preparation for the advance on Port Moresby. On the morning of 6 May it was sighted and attacked by a division of some five U.S. long-range bombers (B.17s), about 150 miles south-west of Buin, but no hits or damage occurred. The course of the enemy indicated that the invasion fleet would pass through the Jomard Passage, in the Louisiade Archipelago, the south-eastward prolongation of New Guinea, with Port Moresby as its probable objective, and establish a base in the Deboyne Islands in the Louisiades.

By the morning of 6 May, however, the Japanese came to the conclusion that the Allied air reconnaissance had been sufficiently thorough to discover their intentions. When, therefore, on this same morning one of their reconnaissance aircraft sighted the Allied task force, the Occupation Force transports were ordered to retire towards Rabaul and orders went out for the escorting naval units to concentrate with the support force for attack on the Allied force. The order to retire seems to have been rescinded during the afternoon, and the transports steered once more for the Jomard Passage.

Support Group Detached

During the forenoon of 6 May the wind and sea had made it necessary to fuel Task Force 17 on a south-easterly course; at 1130, however, course was altered to the north-westward in order to reach a position for a strike on the invasion fleet at daylight on 7 May. Fuelling was discontinued and the *Neosho* was detached to the southward with the destroyer *Sims* as escort, at 1725/6.

Task Force 17 continued north-westward at 20 knots during the night, and at 0530/7 was in latitude 13° 25.5' S., longitude 154° 48' E. Rear-Admiral Fletcher now detached the support group (17.3), under Rear-Admiral Crace, reinforcing him with a third destroyer, the *Farragut*, to proceed ahead to attack the enemy transports and light cruisers which has been reported heading for the Jomard Passage during the night. Rear-Admiral Crace increased speed to 25 knots and steered for a position off the southern exit of the passage.

Enemy Occupation Force Sighted off Misima

Meanwhile there had been no information of the movements of the Japanese carriers, the most important target for air attack, since the previous afternoon, when two of this type, correctly estimated by the Americans as the *Zuikaku* and *Shokaku* of the 5th Carrier Squadron, and therefore additional to the unidentified carrier reported with the Occupation Force, had been sighted near Bougainville Island. The morning air searches by the *Yorktown*'s reconnaissance aircraft were planned to cover two areas, namely the neighbourhood of Deboyne Island and also to locate the 5th Carrier Squadron, which was expected to run southward from Bougainville and to be within striking distance on the morning of 7 May.

At 0619 the *Yorktown* launched a search group of 10 scout bombers to conduct a single plane search for a distance of 250 miles over a 120 degrees arc, on a median bearing of 025 degrees, limiting bearings 325 degrees and 085 degrees. One scout, having the sector with median 067 degrees, went out only some 150 to 165 miles and returned on account of bad weather, and it is probable that the *Zuikaku* and *Shokaku* were in this unsearched bad weather area to the east-north-eastward. At 0735 another scout made contact with two heavy cruisers in latitude 10° 40' S., longitude 153° 15' E., 25 miles east of Misima Island, in the Louisiades; the enemy ships sighted and challenged him. Two other scouts each shot down one twin-float torpedo bomber, one near Misima Island and one in latitude 11° 35' S., longitude 156° 43' E.

Two hours after launching, the first anxiously awaited report of the Japanese carriers came in. At 0815 a sighting report was received of two aircraft carriers and four heavy cruisers in latitude 10° 03' S., longitude 152° 27' E., about 40 miles north of Misima Island, steering 140 degrees, speed 18 to 20 knots.

On receipt of this report, orders were given to launch the attack groups at the enemy carriers, which were estimated, not unnaturally, to be the *Zuikaku* and *Shokaku*. The *Lexington* began launching at about 0855 a group of 10 fighters, 28 scout bombers[4] and 12 torpedo aircraft, retaining eight scout bombers at the ship for anti-torpedo aircraft patrol. Ten of the bombers were armed with one 500-lb. and two 100-lb. bombs each, the remainder with 1,000-lb. bombs. The *Yorktown* launched, nearly an hour later, from 0944 to 1013, a total of 25 scout bombers, 10 torpedo aircraft, and five escort fighters[5]; the bombers carried 1,000-lb. bombs, and the depth setting of the torpedoes was 10 feet. The distance to the enemy was about 160 miles.

At 1022 a message was received in *Yorktown* from shore-based aircraft of the Australian Command, that a force consisting of an aircraft carrier (*Shoho*), 16 warships and 10 transports[6] was in latitude 10° 34' S., longitude 152° 26' E., a few miles north of Misima Island, course 285 degrees. A few minutes later, at 1030, the *Yorktown*'s search group began to land, and it was discovered that, owing to a fault in the reporting mechanism the report of two carriers at 0815 was in error; the pilot had sighted, and imagined he was reporting cruisers. The *Lexington* was informed (1123), and the attack group was re-directed to the enemy reported by shore-based aircraft an hour earlier, in latitude 10° 34' S., longitude 152° 26' E. There was little difference in the two positions. The message was apparently sent by voice transmission though the element of surprise does not seem to have been lost thereby, and no harm seems to have been done: on the contrary, some hours had been saved in sending off the strike, though it must have been a disappointment that the *Zuikaku* and *Shokaku* were still unlocated and that instead of two carriers the powerful attack group would have only one as its target.

Sinking of the *Shoho*

The *Lexington*'s group made contact with the *Shoho* about 1100. The Japanese Occupation Force was in an area of fine weather, with unlimited ceiling and visibility 20 miles or more.

The *Lexington*'s more lightly armed bombers attacked at once. The attack apparently came as a complete surprise to the enemy. One or perhaps two hits were made by this first wave, causing a small fire and possibly damaging the *Shoho*'s steering gear. This did not, however, prevent the enemy carrier from turning into the wind, directly a lull came, to launch her aircraft, 10 to 20 of which were seen on her flight deck. She had however chosen her moment for launching aircraft with bad judgment, for just as she was turning into the wind, about 1115, the *Lexington*'s dive-bombers (*i.e.* scout bombers, carrying 1,000-lb. bombs) and her 12 torpedo aircraft made a co-ordinated attack, followed almost simultaneously by the *Yorktown*'s bombers.

The target was a perfect one. The *Shoho* was steaming into the wind, making no attempt to manoeuvre. The four or five cruisers of her screen were on a 5,000 to 6,000 yard circle, a formation too loose to afford effective anti-aircraft gun support. The enemy fighters were drawn off by the *Lexington*'s first wave, giving the *Yorktown*'s aircraft a clear field. Dives were made from 18,000 feet, very steeply, bomb releases at about 2,500 feet.

The *Shoho* was completely overwhelmed by this mass attack. By the time the *Yorktown*'s slow torpedo aircraft arrived and made their attack the enemy carrier was listing to starboard and burning furiously. The torpedo aircraft, however, were unaware that the ship was already a wreck, for they had approached at less than 1,000 feet altitude, insufficient to enable the objective to be seen before deploying. The leader of the escort fighters for the torpedo aircraft, who was coaching the latter from a position above them, made an attempt to divert part of the group to another target, but was unsuccessful, for they were already in their approach. This was made from the starboard bow of the Japanese formation, between the two leading cruisers whose fire the aircraft encountered, then circling out and launching their attack on the starboard beam of the carrier, making use of the smoke which almost completely shrouded her and releasing their torpedoes at very close range. The *Shoho* was only a light carrier, and no unarmoured ship could have hoped to stand up to this terrible bombardment.

Approximately three minutes after the attacks were completed the ship capsized and sank in lat. 10° 29' S., long. 152° 55' E., taking with her some 500 of her crew. None of the American air crews had been able to identify her.

There was no officer in tactical command at the scene to divert the attack groups when it was apparent that the *Shoho* was a wreck, and consequently with one exception every bomb and every torpedo was aimed at the carrier, and the other Japanese ships escaped unscathed. The sole exception was the last *Yorktown*'s bomber, who, seeing the carrier enveloped in flames, attacked a cruiser, unsuccessfully.

The Americans reported 21 bomb and 19 torpedo hits on the *Shoho*. The official Japanese figures were 13 bomb and seven torpedo hits. Of the latter three were on the port and four on the starboard side.

Air cover from Rabaul had been arranged for the Japanese Occupation Force, but all the aircraft encountered during the battle were apparently launched by the *Shoho*, which had a fighter patrol of 10 or 12 aircraft overhead. Several of the *Lexington*'s attack group had encounters with them during the attack and withdrawal. One American scout bomber was shot down, and another made a forced landing on Roussel Island, in the Louisiade Archipelago, friendly territory whence the crew was later rescued by the Australians. Four Japanese fighters and a torpedo aircraft were shot down by the *Lexington*'s aircraft.

The enemy protective aircraft having been apparently drawn off by the *Lexington*'s attack group, the *Yorktown*'s aircraft encountered no opposition before the attack. After it was completed, however, some six Japanese fighters and three scout bomber types attacked the *Yorktown*'s dive-bombers and torpedo aircraft. The escorting American fighters shot down three of the enemy fighters. The ruse new to the American pilots of emitting smoke when heavily attacked, saved some Japanese aircraft. One *Yorktown* dive-bomber was lost, last seen on the return flight when it broke off to attack an enemy aircraft.

Japanese Attempts to Locate U.S. Carriers

Whilst the attack on the *Shoho* was in progress evidence of the efforts of the enemy's aircraft to locate the American carriers were continually seen on the radar screen. The Japanese airscraft operated, however, under the handicap of not being fitted with radar. At 0833, before the launching of the attack groups, the first enemy aircraft was picked up by radar, 30 miles to the north-westward, but *Yorktown* fighters were unable to make contact. The *Lexington*, when launching her attack group, retained at the ship eight scout bombers for anti-torpedo aircraft patrol; and at 1019 the *Yorktown* launched a combat air patrol, maintaining one throughout the day. All aircraft in the combat air patrol were controlled by the fighter director on board the *Lexington*.

Weather favoured Task Force 17. The ships were in an area of unsettled weather extending east and west. The wind was east to south-east, force 12 to 22 knots, and up to 30 knots in gusts. There were sufficient breaks in the clouds to allow aircraft to be launched and landed without undue difficulty. But visibility was generally limited to 10 or 15 miles, reduced during the day by frequent rain squalls to less than a mile and at sunset to 4 miles by pronounced haze. Actually, Rear-Admiral Fletcher's force was sighted by Japanese aircraft from Tulagi early in the forenoon of 7 May, and had he been attacked by the air groups of the *Zuikaku* and *Shokaku* before his strike groups had returned and been rearmed his situation would have been serious. The Commander of the Japanese Covering Force, Rear-Admiral Goto, ordered the *Shoho* to attack, but she was overwhelmed and sunk before she could do so.

Meanwhile, enemy aircraft were about continually. At 1044 an unidentified aircraft was picked up coming in on bearing 045 degrees, distance 41 miles. A section (4) of *Yorktown*'s fighters, vectored out, made contact with a Japanese four-engine patrol bomber and shot it down. Radio interceptions indicated that the position of Task Force 17 was known to the enemy. On the other hand, the position of the Japanese 5th Carrier Squadron was still not known to the Americans, and there was little likelihood of finding a suitable objective near the scene of the morning's attack. Rear-Admiral Fletcher decided to launch no further strike against the Japanese Occupation Force. The *Neosho* at 1021 had reported being bombed by three aircraft in lat. 16° 50' S., long. 159° 08' E., but the signal did not specify whether the attackers were carrier-borne type. With the probability that the Japanese 5th Carrier Squadron was in the neighbourhood it was considered the air striking force should not be squandered on any lesser target but should be held in readiness to counter-attack. C.T.F. 17 therefore decided to rely upon shore-based aircraft to locate the *Zuikaku* and *Shokaku*. The day wore on. At 1308 the attack groups returned from sinking the *Shoho*. Still there was no news of the enemy carriers. Fighters were continually being sent out to investigate contacts which proved to be the *Yorktown*'s fighters, who did not use radar identification. Rear-Admiral Fletcher decided to take his force westward during the night, in the expectation that the enemy would pass through the Jomard Passage by morning, making for Port Moresby, probably accompanied by carriers.

However, as night was coming on, a succession of events occurred, which rendered necessary a fresh appreciation of the situation. At 1629 an enemy seaplane came in sight of the *Yorktown* bearing 315 degrees, distance 9 miles, and escaped in the failing light despite the efforts of two sections of fighters to intercept it. At 1747 radar showed a large group of enemy aircraft to the south-eastward on a westerly course. The *Lexington*'s fighters in the air were vectored out, and the *Yorktown* launched 11 more in support. Some of the latter were kept over the ships, but seven went out and made contact in the haze and falling darkness with a group of Japanese Navy dive-bombers, one of which they shot down. This was apparently a force of about 27 bombers and torpedo aircraft from the *Zuikaku* and *Shokaku* which Rear-Admiral Hara sent out during the afternoon to make a dusk attack on the American force. They searched for 300 miles, but failed to find the U.S. carriers; and finally they jettisoned their bombs and were now making towards their own ships.

Meanwhile, the *Lexington*'s fighters were engaging successfully a formation of nine Zero fighters, part, no doubt, of the bombers' escort. When the *Yorktown*'s fighters arrived they saw four or five oil patches on the sea, marking aircraft which had been shot down. The *Yorktown*'s also claimed to have destroyed three of the enemy. One *Lexington* and two *Yorktown* fighters were lost.

It was deep dusk, or as some say, after dark, when the American fighters returned to their ships and commenced landing. At 1850, whilst they were in the landing circle three enemy aircraft, apparently mistaking the carriers for their own flew past on the starboard side with their running lights on and blinking in Morse code on an Aldis lamp. One of them gave an incorrect response to the landing signal and took a wave off. He was recognised as hostile, and as the group crossed over the bow to port one of the *Yorktown*'s fighters opened fire on them, but without visible effect.

At 1910, again, three enemy aircraft appeared, whilst the combat air patrol was still landing. Some ships opened fire, accidentally damaging one of the *Yorktown*'s fighters and possibly shooting down one of the enemy.

Twenty minutes later the *Lexington*'s radar showed aircraft circling and apparently landing on a carrier 30 miles to the eastward. The Japanese carriers at this time had neither radar nor homing devices, and the American radio telephone inadvertently jammed the frequency used by their aircraft, preventing the pilots from getting a bearing on their carriers; Admiral Hara switched on searchlights to aid the night recovery, but eleven aircraft came down in the sea.[7]

The *Yorktown*'s radar gave somewhat similar indications to the *Lexington*'s, of a single aircraft circling at 25 to 30 miles on bearing 60 degrees, but later plotted on course 310 degrees and believed to be one of her own fighters. On the other hand, radio interception on the homing of lost Japanese aircraft indicated that the enemy carriers probably were within 150 miles either to the eastward or westward; the aircraft were quite close to Task Force 17, but none of the American ships were equipped for taking bearings of the transmissions on the frequency employed.

It was now dark, and in the uncertainty of being able to locate the enemy carriers Rear-Admiral Fletcher dismissed the idea of sending a surface force to attack them. A force despatched during the night might fail to make contact with the enemy or to rejoin by daylight. He detached the destroyer *Monaghan* (0055/8) to search for survivors of the *Sims*, the oiler *Neosho*'s escort, which the Commander-in-Chief Pacific Fleet reported sunk; but apart from this, he decided to keep his ships concentrated and to prepare for a battle with the enemy carriers next morning.

The Japanese, too, had decided against a night attack, for although they believed the American force to be only 40 miles to the southward, they were uncertain of its size. The Port Moresby landing was postponed for two days and the invasion transports headed for Rabaul. The Japanese retreat had begun although nobody yet admitted the fact.[8]

Attack on the *Neosho* and *Sims*

Unfortunately, the *Monaghan*'s search was vain, for the position in which the *Sims* had been sunk was incorrectly worked out by the *Neosho*'s people.

During the attack on the *Shoho*, and in fact ever since the raid on Tulagi had revealed to the Japanese the presence of American carriers in the Coral Sea, land planes and seaplanes from Rabaul and Shortland Island had been searching without success to locate the Allied task force. Finally, on the morning of 7 May, their reconnaissance aircraft sighted what they took to be the American carriers and directed to the attack the bombers from the *Zuikaku* and *Shokaku* which with the remainder of the Moresby task force were to the north-eastward of the Occupation Force and still undiscovered by the Americans.

Unfortunately for the enemy, the identification of their reconnaissance aircraft was wrong, though this was not discovered until too late. The ships sighted were not the *Lexington* and *Yorktown*, but the oiler *Neosho* and her escort *Sims*.

After being detached from Task Force 17 at 1725 on 6 May these two ships had proceeded southward in accordance with the arrangements for fuelling (*see* Appendix A) and by about 0730/7 reached a position in latitude 16° 01' S., longitude 158° 01' E., when radar and visual contact with aircraft began to be made. It was at first thought the aircraft were American, but at 0859 a bomb suddenly fell about 100 yards from the *Sims*, released by an aircraft which came over at a height of 15,000 feet and was not seen before the bomb fell.

Both ships increased speed and ran south-eastward, and after one or more radar contacts two groups of 15 and seven aircraft respectively, coming from the northward in succession, examined without molesting the ships, and disappeared to the north-eastward, fired on without effect.

At 1003 another group of 10 aircraft approached from a bearing 140 degrees, and three of them, twin-engined bombers, made a horizontal run on the *Neosho* and dropped three bombs to starboard from a high altitude, two of which fell within 25 yards of the ship. Both ships opened fire, but the enemy made off to the north-eastward.

For an hour and a half no further attack took place, though aircraft continued to show on the radar screen, until 1131, when approximately 24 enemy dive-bombers were sighted at a considerable height, apparently manoeuvring into position to attack. The *Sims* thereupon took station on the port quarter of the *Neosho*. Of the actual attack which took place during the next quarter of an hour or more no clear picture was retained by the two doomed ships. The enemy aircraft dived from all directions and the sequence of events was lost in the ensuing confusion and destruction.

In a few minutes the destroyer *Sims* was a wreck, struck by at least three bombs, estimated at 500-lb., released by four enemy aircraft who pulled out of their dives at altitude so low that survivors of the *Neosho* averred that those which were not shot down were destroyed by the blast of their own bombs. Bombs exploded in both the forward and after engine rooms and wrecked the *Sims*. The ship lost all power and stopped. Her topside was a shambles. An effort to keep the vessel afloat was made by jettisoning all possible weight. A motor boat and two life rafts were launched, and the former was ordered to go aft and try to extinguish a fire in the after deck house and flood the after magazine. But before this could be done the *Sims* seemed to break amidships. She went down slowly, stern first. All hands began leaping into the sea and swimming clear, but as the water reached the top of the funnel a very heavy explosion occurred, followed a moment later by a second, causing heavy loss of life amongst the men in the water. Only 15 men, two of whom later died, reached the *Neosho* in the motor boat, during the early afternoon. The Commanding Officer, Lieut.-Comdr. Willford M. Hyman, was last seen on the bridge of the *Sims* giving orders in an attempt to save the ship.

Meanwhile, the *Neosho* was also in trouble. The majority of the Japanese bombers had concentrated on her, and although the crews of the 20-mm. guns are reported to have shot down three of the enemy and damaged others, the oiler received seven direct hits and a number of near misses. One of the three enemy bombers that was shot down, crashed in flames into No. 4 gun enclosure; intense fires broke out at once and spread aft over the stack deck. The time was about 1144.

Soon after the attack ended the Commanding Officer, Commander John S. Phillips, ordered all hands to prepare to abandon ship but not to do so until word was passed. Unfortunately, several men on the after deck began leaping into the sea without orders, and seven life rafts were cut adrift. Motor whaleboats were sent to pick up and bring back the men, but many were lost.[9] Wind and sea increased, and darkness came on before any of the rafts could be towed back to the oiler.

The latter was obviously doomed, for although the fires had been brought under control the pumps were unable to keep down the rising water, and the main deck was buckling and seemed likely to break in two at any time. Nevertheless, the ship remained afloat all night, though by the morning of 8 May she had developed a list to starboard of 26 degrees and the utmost endeavours could only reduce this by some 3 degrees.

8 and 9 May passed with the men employed in making rafts and rigging

masts and sails for all available boats. At 1012/9 the *Neosho*'s position was taken as latitude 15° 35' S., 156° 55' E. The signal codes had been destroyed, but wireless transmission in plain language was possible on the auxiliary transmitter.

At 1230 on 10 May an Australian Hudson bomber appeared, inquired if the ship was in distress, and on receiving an affirmative answer flew off to the southward after circling the ships several times. The *Neosho* gave her position but received no reply. By 11 May it was apparent that the ship had settled appreciably during the night and the distortion of her plates had increased alarmingly. About 1130, when the question of abandoning ship and making for the Australian coast was being considered, a Navy Catalina patrol bomber from the *Tangier* appeared from the east and within an hour and a half the U.S. destroyer *Henley* which had been despatched from Numea, was sighted approaching. By 1412 all survivors were taken off, and at 1522, at Commander Phillips' request, the doomed *Neosho* was sunk by two torpedoes and several rounds of 5-inch gunfire in lat. 15° 35' S., long. 155° 36' E.

The *Henley* searched the area until dark without finding any of the men who had abandoned ship, then headed for Brisbane, in order to get the wounded to hospital. Ordered at 0100/12 to return to the scene of the bombing, she went and made a wider, but still fruitless, search.

Meanwhile, it was discovered that the position of the *Neosho* at the time of attack had been incorrectly plotted and transmitted, and the U.S. destroyer *Helm* was sent from Numea, on 14 May, to make a search in the corrected position. On 17 May, in lat. 15° 16' S., long. 155° 07' 30" E., four of the *Neosho*'s survivors were rescued from a life raft; all were in a critical condition from exposure, and one man died soon after being taken aboard. They were the sole survivors of 68 men from four rafts lashed together, and they told a grim story of food and water becoming exhausted because neither was rationed, of men becoming crazed and leaping into the sea or dying on the rafts. The *Helm* searched until sunset on 17 May and aircraft from the *Tangier* maintained a search until 22 May, but no further survivors were found.

Attacks on the Support Group

The support group of cruisers and destroyers under Rear-Admiral Crace which had been detached at 0530 on 7 May, did not long remain undiscovered by the enemy. At 0810 radar indicated that three aircraft were shadowing the force, and one of the enemy, a twin-float monoplane, was sighted to the north-eastward by the *Chicago*, at a range of some 20,000 yards, and remained in view for about half an hour, circling well out of gun range.

No further enemy aircraft approached until the afternoon. At 1345, when the force was approximately 12° S., 151° 30' E., 60 miles south of the Jomard Passage, radar contact was made with a group of aircraft bearing 135 degrees, range 56,000 yards, and 12 minutes later a formation of some 12 single-engine monoplanes was seen coming up from astern on a parallel course, and was taken under fire at ranges of 6,000-12,000 yards. The enemy quickly retired unhit.

Half an hour later there was radar contact at 150,000 yards with a group of aircraft closing on a bearing 250 degrees. The weather was fine, wind eight knots from 120 degrees, sea slight, sun bearing 318 degrees, altitude 52 degrees, when at 1432 sunlight flashing on their wings revealed a group of aircraft, range 25,000 yards, approaching from right ahead. These were 13–14 Type 97 (Navy) Mitsubishi twin-engine torpedo aircraft, with fighter protection, from the 25th Air Flotilla at Rabaul.

Task Group 17.3 was steering 275 degrees, speed 25 knots at the time, in Formation V, with the flagship *Australia* as guide, the *Chicago* and *Hobart* bearing 135 degrees and 225 degrees respectively, distance 1,600 yards, and the destroyers *Farragut*, *Perkins* and *Walke* disposed as anti-submarine screen, thus:–

Perkins
X

Farragut   *Australia*   *Walke*
X   X   X

Hobart   *Chicago*
X   X

Within three minutes the enemy began their attack. Gliding down at 12 miles from 5,000 feet to 100 feet at eight miles they started their approach from the starboard quarter. The ships opened fire and almost immediately two of the enemy, including their leader, were seen to crash about 1,000 yards ahead, whereupon the remainder separated into groups. The larger group continued on their bearing, whilst one small group swung to the left to come in from the starboard bow and another group swung right to come in slightly later from the port quarter. With the exception of one of the enemy, which released its torpedo at a height of 100–150 feet, all the aircraft made their release at 40 feet, range 1,000–2,000 yards.

The next few minutes were crowded, torpedoes coming from all angles and enemy aircraft machine-gunning the ships. The latter put up a heavy curtain of fire and manoeuvred to avoid torpedoes. At least two more of the enemy were shot down by the ships' fire. Only five torpedo tracks were seen, all of which were successfully avoided by every ship, and at 1442 the engagement was at an end. The only damage suffered was by the *Chicago*, which had seven men wounded by machine gunfire, two of whom died later.

There was, however, no respite for Rear-Admiral Crace's ships, for almost immediately they came under attack by Navy Type 96 Mitsubishi high level heavy bombers which approached from astern and were sighted at 1443 at 14,000 feet after being picked up by radar at 45 miles. The ships opened fire, but none of the enemy was hit. Although observers reported the group to number 26 aircraft only one salvo of bombs was dropped near the ships. This straddled the *Australia* with a pattern 500 yards long, but all bombs missed and only two of the nearer shook the ship slightly. At 1501 the attack was over; the task group reduced speed to 20 knots and steered a southerly course until 2000 when Rear-Admiral Crace altered to the westward and proceeded on a course parallel to the New Guinea coast.

It was reported that a few minutes after the high level bombing attack three aircraft, subsequently identified as United States Army B.26 bombers, passed over and dropped a salvo of bombs close to one of the destroyers of the task group. However, not all of the ships witnessed the incident.

Although shadowed by enemy aircraft, the support group was not further molested; and the successful air battles in which Rear-Admiral Fletcher's attack group engaged next day, to the westward, destroyed any opportunity the force might have had of engaging the Japanese in a surface encounter.

Air Battles of 8 May

Japanese Carriers Sighted (Plan 2)

After the decision to defer action against the *Zuikaku* and *Shokaku* until daylight Rear-Admiral Fletcher continued to the southward during the night of the 7/8 May and at 0800/8 was in lat. 14° 25' S., long. 154° 31' E., course 125 degrees, speed 14 knots, the composition of his force being the carriers *Yorktown* (flagship) and *Lexington*, the five cruisers *Astoria, Chester, Portland, Minneapolis* and *New Orleans,* and seven destroyers *Phelps, Dewey, Aylwin, Morris, Anderson, Hammann* and *Russell.*

The weather was fine, clouds few, wind from 085 degrees to 112 degrees, 16–20 knots, sea smooth, ceiling almost unlimited, but horizontal visibility somewhat restricted through haze. These conditions held, with slight variations, throughout the entire day.

Intelligence reports received during the night had indicated that the enemy invasion force was retiring northward, but there was no news of the *Zuikaku* and *Shokaku*. In the uncertainty whether the Japanese carriers were to the eastward or westward it was necessary to carry out a 360 degrees search, and at 0625, about half an hour before sunrise, the *Lexington* launched a scouting group of 22 aircraft to cover a radius of 200 miles in the northern and 150 miles in the southern semicircle.

The enemy were located almost by chance. At 0820, just as one of the scouts was turning for home he sighted a carrier hidden in rain squalls.[10] The scout keyed the report to his ship on voice frequency, but a slipping generator clutch prevented receipt. However, the scout of the adjoining sector, to whom he had made a voice report, relayed the message to the *Lexington*, and also found the enemy himself, and reported their subsequent movements; and at 0828 the news was received on board the *Lexington* that a force of two carriers, four heavy cruisers and some destroyers had been sighted. Position was given at 0835, lat. 11° 51' S., long. 156° 04' E., bearing 28 degrees distant 175 miles from Task Force 17. The enemy carriers were standing south at high speed, and an intercepted radio transmission indicated that the Japanese, in their turn, had sighted Task Force 17 almost simultaneously.[11]

The force sighted was the Japanese Sixth Squadron, the so-called Port Moresby Task Force, containing, in addition to the *Zuikaku* (flagship of Rear-Admiral Hara) and *Shokaku*, the cruisers *Myoko* and *Haguro* reinforced by two of the Occupation Force cruisers, and six destroyers. The seaplane carrier *Kiyokawa Maru* which had been encountered at Tulagi on 4 May belonged to this force, but if she was in company with the force on 8 May she was not sighted.

Launching of attack groups by the carriers commenced at 0900, the *Lexington* launching 24 scout bombers, ten fighters, and 12 torpedo aircraft, and the *Yorktown* seven scouts and 17 bombers, all with 1,000-lb. bombs, six escort fighters, and nine torpedo aircraft with torpedoes set to run at 10 feet.

The *Yorktown*'s Group Attacks

The *Yorktown*'s attack group went first, the scouts and dive-bombers going ahead of the torpedo aircraft at 17,000 feet, escorted by two fighters. The bombers sighted the enemy at about 1,032, steering a course 190 degrees at 20 knots. The Japanese force had the protection of the area of bad weather that had concealed Task Force 17 on the previous day. The weather in the neighbourhood of the enemy was unsettled, with intermittent rain squalls; and a broken lower layer of clouds covered the area at 2,000 to 3,000 feet. Visibility varied from 2 to 15 miles.

At 1049 the bombers were near the enemy and commenced circling whilst waiting for the slower torpedo aircraft to arrive and take up position for attack. One enemy carrier, apparently the *Zuikaku*, now headed for a large rain squall, but the *Shokaku* turned into the east-south-easterly wind and began to launch her aircraft. Some of the enemy ships opened fire.

Nine minutes elapsed before the torpedo aircraft were in position and a co-ordinated attack by dive-bombers and torpedo aircraft began on the *Shokaku*. The bombers attacked down-wind, from 17,000 feet, altitude of release 2,500 feet, and as on 4 May, they were handicapped by the fogging of their telescopes and wind shields, which greatly reduced their bombing accuracy. They encountered considerable anti-aircraft fire and were attacked, both in the dive and on the pull-out, by Zero fighters, some 15 to

18 of which were over the Japanese formation, out-numbering the American fighters. The *Yorktown*'s scouts shot down four and the bombers seven of the enemy, besides damaging others. The Americans made good use of the low cloud cover, and had no losses. The fighters also attacked unsuccessfully two Japanese dive-bombers on the return trip, but the engagement had taken place near their extreme range and they were hampered by shortage of fuel, having had to climb to altitude with the bombers. The *Yorktown*'s bombers claimed six certain hits, three further possible hits, and several near misses. Actually they made two hits.

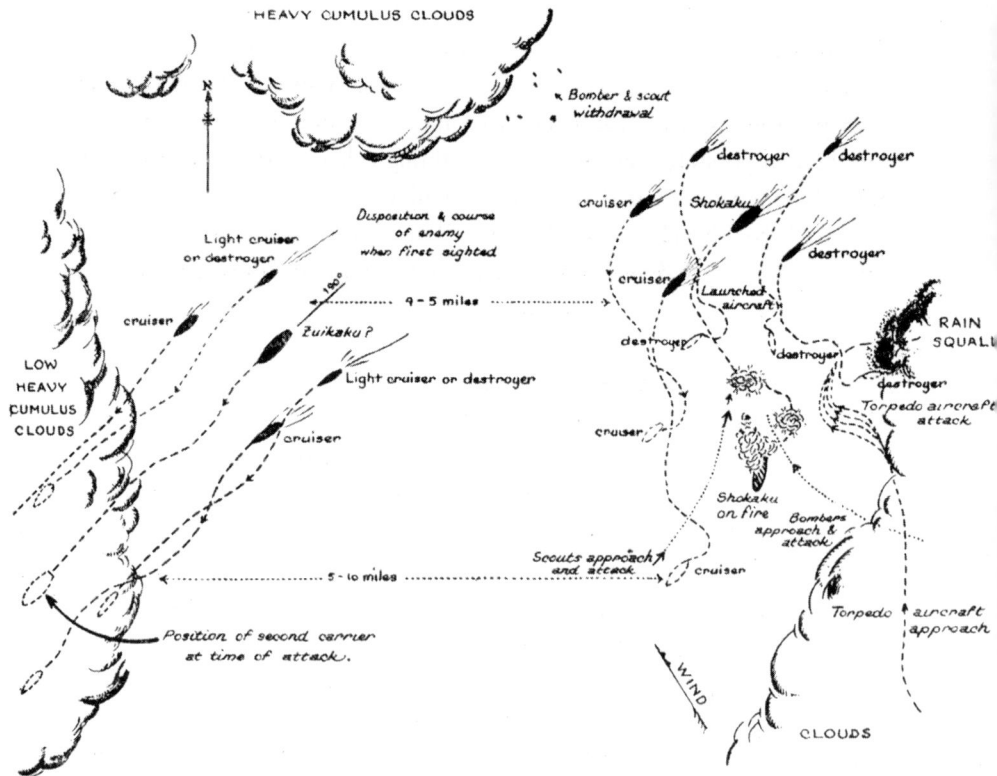

Fig. 1. Attacks by *Yorktown*'s aircraft on Japanese carriers, 8 May.

Meanwhile, the torpedo squadron made its approach from the southeast, the four escorting fighters driving off an attack by six Zero fighters, and thus permitting the torpedo aircraft to make their releases unmolested. As the dive-bombers made their attack the carrier had commenced a turn to port and then put her helm over and turned sharply to starboard; and it was during this turn that the *Yorktown*'s torpedo aircraft made their releases, under very heavy fire from the carrier and her four escorting cruisers, though the latter were on so wide a circle that the range was too great to be effective. As on 7 May, the Japanese ships escorting the carrier scattered, either in order to obtain sea room for themselves or to give the carrier plenty of sea room, although they materially reduced the effectiveness of their supporting anti-aircraft fire by doing so. This was the more fortunate for the American torpedo aircraft, compelled as they were, by the slow speed and low altitude of drop of their Mark 13 torpedoes, to come in low and slow. They reported that three or possibly four torpedoes hit, though all apparently made erratic runs.[12] The Japanese stated, however, that all were released at a range which permitted the *Shokaku* to avoid them.[13] Three Japanese Zero fighters and one scout were shot down during the torpedo attack; and during the return to the *Yorktown* one enemy torpedo aircraft was shot down.

Attack by the *Lexington*'s Group

The *Lexington*'s attack group had difficulty in finding the enemy in the prevailing very poor visibility. The three fighters escorting the dive-bombers lost contact with the latter en route and returned to the carrier. Eighteen bombers also returned without finding the enemy, and one torpedo aircraft turned back on account of engine trouble.

Four scouts and two fighters joined up with the 11 remaining torpedo aircraft and their four escorting fighters.

After flying to the end of their navigational leg without sighting the enemy, they began flying around a square. A few minutes later they entered a clear area, on the far side of which, some 20 miles away, were enemy ships. An unsuccessful attempt was now made to call up the lost bombers. Japanese fighters, Zeros and Me. 109s appeared. The American fighters engaged them, losing at least three of their number, without being successful, however, in shooting down any of the enemy.

As one of the survivors came out of cloud cover he found himself, at a height of 1,000 feet, directly above a Japanese carrier, presumably the

Zuikaku, accompanied by a cruiser and a destroyer. The carrier showed no sign of damage, and the fighter was apparently undetected, for he circled the ship twice, unmolested by either aircraft or A.A. fire. Fifteen miles away to the eastward another larger group of ships was visible, one large ship of which, apparently a carrier and no doubt the *Shokaku*, was on fire.

Meanwhile, the four scouts and 11 torpedo aircraft, leaving the fighters engaged in combat, had gone on and attacked a carrier, together. The time of the attack was given in the radio logs at 1057, *i.e.* approximately simultaneously with that by the *Yorktown*'s aircraft, but it is not known whether the clocks of the two groups were synchronised. Whether this attack was made on the *Zuikaku* or on the *Shokaku* is uncertain. The *Zuikaku*, although she reported being attacked at this time, was not hit or damaged: all bombs missed her, and owing to the long range at which the torpedoes were fired the ship was able to avoid them. The *Lexington*'s attack group reported that their target, when last seen, was on fire, and they claimed two 1,000 lb. bomb and five torpedo hits. Actually they made one bomb hit and no torpedo hits.

No less than seven of the *Lexington*'s fighters were shot down in this engagement and one torpedo aircraft and three scout bombers ran out of fuel on the return journey and were lost. Two enemy scouts were shot down by the fighters, and four enemy fighters were probably destroyed, two over the carrier by the fighters and two by torpedo aircraft on the return from the attack.

The *Shokaku* sustained in all three bomb hits, causing severe damage. Her position at the end of the engagement was reported by C.T.F. 17 as lat. 12° 00' N., long. 155° 50' E.

Preparations to Meet Japanese Air Attack

The Americans became aware that they had been sighted by the enemy almost simultaneously with the sighting of the *Zuikaku* and *Shokaku* by the *Lexington*'s scouts, for at 0832 a Japanese plain language wireless transmission was intercepted, giving the position, course and speed of Task Force 17, apparently sent by a 4-engine patrol aircraft which was sighted and shot down by the *Yorktown*'s combat air patrol.

Preparations were made to meet the attack which it was estimated would come about 1100. The *Yorktown* had launched first combat air patrol and eight scout bombers as anti-torpedo aircraft patrol about 0724; the fighters were brought in and at 0941 second combat air patrol was launched. The *Lexington* launched her returning scouts as anti-torpedo aircraft patrol and additional fighters were launched by both carriers up to 1102–04, at which time all serviceable aircraft were in the air, the fighters as combat air patrol, with scout bombers as anti-torpedo aircraft patrol. The cruisers' aircraft, which had been up as an inner air patrol, were recalled when the enemy attack appeared imminent.

In order to reduce signalling between carriers and to allow Commander Air (Rear-Admiral A. W. Fitch, U.S.S. *Lexington*) freedom of action for his carriers and air groups, C.T.F. 17 at 0908 ordered him to assume tactical command of the Fleet. The ships were in circular disposition with the carriers as centre, axis 350 degrees, cruisers on 3,000 yard circle, destroyers on 4,000 yard circle. An even tighter formation was subsequently adopted by the U.S. Pacific Fleet as the result of experience in the battle which took place on this day. Various courses were steered in launching and recovering aircraft but the general course was south-easterly and just before the commencement of the action was 125 degrees, speed 20 knots; speed varied up to 30 knots after the attack began. Before the action began the *Yorktown* adjusted her position on the *Lexington* so that the latter would not be between her and the sun and thus mask her fire should the enemy approach from that direction. The circular formation was not maintained, however, as the enemy attack developed, for in consequence of high speed manoeuvring to avoid torpedoes and bombs the two carriers gradually drew apart, and several miles separated them at the conclusion of the action. Five ships accompanied the *Lexington*; whilst seven remained with the *Yorktown*. Apart from her smaller escort the *Lexington* was handicapped by the fact that her new light guns (12 1.1-in. and 20 20-mm.) had only just been received and the guns' crews were not yet fully trained.

At 1000 the enemy's disposition and 0900 position were reported to Commander South-west Pacific Force in the hope of shore-based aircraft being available to attack and shadow; but although Army bombers of General MacArthur's Australian Command were actively engaged during 2–12 May in reconnoitring and bombing enemy bases in the area, weather conditions apparently prevented them from locating the Japanese carriers, though they attacked the retiring transport force.

Combat Air Patrol Goes Out
The Fighters
At 1008 an enemy four-engine patrol bomber was sighted by the *Yorktown*'s lookouts and was shot down by a section of fighters at 1015.

About three quarters of an hour later ships' radar indicated a large group of enemy aircraft approaching from the northward, distance 68–75 miles. The exact height of the enemy was uncertain, but was known to be over 10,000 feet. They approached on a steady bearing. All aircraft on combat air patrol were recalled to the vicinity of the carriers (1059) and at 1103 the *Yorktown* launched four additional fighters, making a total of eight fighters from that ship and nine from the *Lexington* on combat air patrol. Only three of these 17 fighters intercepted the enemy prior to delivery of his attack, 15 to 20 miles from the Fleet. Fighter direction for the aircraft of both carriers was carried out by the *Lexington*.[14]

At 1102 five of the *Lexington*'s fighters were vectored out on bearing 020 degrees, distance 30 miles, height 10,000 feet. Two of the aircraft were subsequently diverted to intercept torpedo aircraft coming in at a low altitude. The remaining three made contact with the enemy about 20 miles out, but were some 1,000 to 2,000 feet below the Japanese who apparently numbered about 60–70, disposed in layers extending from about 10,000 feet upwards. At the lowest level were the torpedo aircraft, then fighters, then dive-bombers stated to be at about 17,000 feet or higher, then more fighters. Approximately a third of the force were fighters, and the comparatively small number of fighters borne on board the American carriers, having to protect both their groups and their ships simultaneously, were outnumbered. At 15–20 miles the three *Lexington* fighters attacked the enemy bombers, but their performance was insufficient to enable them to gain enough altitude to prevent the enemy from making their bombing dives.

No other of the 17 fighters was in position to attack the enemy until after the latter had commenced or completed their attacks. The two *Lexington* fighters who were diverted to intercept torpedo aircraft attacked the latter at 1116, about four to five miles from the Fleet. Two more *Lexington* fighters were told to orbit overhead, climbed to 12,000 feet, and attacked the tail end of the enemy formation. What the remaining two *Lexington* fighters did, was not reported.

At 1108 four of the *Yorktown*'s fighters had been vectored out on bearing 020 degrees, distance 15 miles, height 1,000 feet, but they sighted nothing.

By this time, the American carriers were under attack, and the four fighters were ordered to return, climbing to 10,000 feet; they were able to shoot down one Zero fighter after the attack was over. The four remaining *Yorktown* fighters were kept over the ship at about 8,000 to 10,000 feet. One section was not able to intercept the enemy before they attacked, though they shot down one Zero fighter and one dive-bomber who had already released his bomb. The other section attacked a formation of dive-bombers as they commenced their dive, and went down with them, shooting down one dive-bomber before it dropped its bomb and another after release. In all, the *Yorktown*'s fighters shot down four Zero fighters and three dive-bombers, besides damaging others, without loss to themselves. Two of the *Lexington*'s fighters were shot down but both pilots were picked up.

The Scout Bombers

The eight *Yorktown*'s scout bombers launched at 0724 were still in the air and the *Lexington* had also eight scouts out as anti-torpedo aircraft patrol when the attack came. In default of sufficient fighters, scout bombers were employed as two seater fighters, without bombs, at low altitudes against the Japanese torpedo aircraft, being disposed in a protective screen at 3,000 feet outside the cruiser screen. This was recognised as a make-shift arrangement.

The enemy torpedo aircraft were already making their diving approach when sighted by the *Yorktown*'s scout bombers. These made a great effort to break up the attack, but the Japanese were high and too fast for them. The patrol was then attacked by a large number of Type 97 and Zero fighters, and a mêlée followed in which the scout bombers, though out-numbered by faster and more manoeuvrable machines, and losing four of their number almost at once, shot down at least four of the enemy fighters and damaged or destroyed several more. The four *Yorktown* aircraft which returned were all badly damaged.

The *Lexington*'s anti-torpedo aircraft patrol (eight scout bombers) was at 2,000 feet, about 6,000 yards out, *i.e.* somewhat further than its proper station, when the Japanese torpedo aircraft came in over them at high speed. The scout bombers, inferior in performance to the enemy fighters and faced with large numbers of the enemy were unable to do more than hamper the attacks. One Japanese torpedo aircraft was shot down. One American scout bomber was shot down by enemy fighters and one went over the side on landing.

The Attack Opens

At 1112–1113 the Japanese torpedo aircraft were sighted 15 miles off, approaching in a fast power glide from about 5,000 feet from the port beam. Some ships opened fire at once, but many were slow in starting, and throughout the earlier part of the action at least, A.A. fire particularly the 5-inch, was extremely erratic and relatively ineffective. There was no arrangement for controlled, co-ordinated fire of the screening ships' anti-aircraft batteries.

The attack began out of range of any guns smaller than 5-inch, and although it was reported that in the course of the action gunfire destroyed at least 17 of the enemy, most of them were apparently shot down after releasing torpedo or bomb, though American doctrine laid stress on the necessity of destruction before release. The American secondary A.A. armament consisted of 20 mm. and 1.1-inch guns. The former were not effective at ranges greater than 1,000 yards, which was insufficient against torpedo attacks and just barely effective against dive-bombers. As regards the 1.1-inch gun, there was a lack of directors, and the rate of training with the gears then fitted was slow, and during the early stages of the action there was a tendency to give insufficient lead and to shoot under the target. The Americans at this date did not possess an automatic lead computer; in fact, the problem of A.A. protection had not advanced very far. The *Chester* estimated that 30 per cent to 40 per cent of the U.S. 5-inch shells fired were blind. The executive officer of the *New Orleans* reported that the ship was more seriously "under fire" from the American ships than from the enemy.

The Japanese attacks appeared to be directed against the two American carriers, though in the circumstances of the moment one or two torpedoes and a few bombs appeared as if aimed at the screening ships. When the enemy were about 8,000 to 10,000 yards away it became clear that they intended to attack both the U.S. carriers simultaneously with torpedo and dive-bombers. The numbers, both of torpedo aircraft and dive-bombers, that attacked each carrier, were approximately equal.

It quickly became apparent that the American makeshift anti-torpedo aircraft patrol would be unable to prevent the enemy's torpedo attack from getting in. Their approach differed greatly from that employed in the attack on the *Prince of Wales* and *Repulse* a few months earlier, the only precedent on which the Americans could base their tactics. The approach against the British ships was made in squadron formation. Against Task Force 17, however, squadrons broke up into small groups which attacked from various directions. The standard procedure appeared to be a fast relatively shallow power glide from 5,000 feet to altitude of release, ranging from 100 to 200 or 300 feet, release being at relatively high speed. Some torpedo aircraft, however, delivered their torpedoes from heights of as much as 500 feet, either designedly or in consequence of being fired at.

Attack on the *Yorktown* (Appendix C)

The violent avoiding manoeuvres made by the American carriers soon caused them to draw apart, and the screening ships nearest to each carrier also separated into two groups without signal, to protect them. The cruisers *Astoria*, *Portland* and *Chester*, with four destroyers including the *Russell*, *Hammann*, *Aylwyn* and one other, formed a circular screen around the *Yorktown* at about 2,000–3,000 yards distance.[15]

During the engagement the *Astoria* kept the *Yorktown* as nearly as possible on bearing 073 degrees, distance 1,700–2,200 yards, and the *Chester* maintained an approximate bearing 350 degrees from the *Yorktown*, distance 2,300–3,000 yards. The *Portland* was stationed 045 degrees, 2,300 yards from the *Yorktown*, but the first eight point turn to starboard by the latter, at the beginning of the engagement, left her on the carrier's port side, a position in which she remained throughout. The latter, in her efforts to avoid torpedoes and bombs steered an irregular zigzag course, using full helm; but in spite of the difficulty of keeping station without signals the screening ships maintained throughout positions from which they were able to keep up heavy fire.

One group of Japanese torpedo aircraft attacked the *Yorktown* from the port quarter. Four of them were reported shot down, but three released torpedoes; their attack was closely followed by that of four aircraft on the port beam, one of which was set on fire and crashed after making his release, two others completed their release successfully, and one dived into the water without dropping a torpedo. The position of release was reported to vary from 500 to 3,000 yards from the *Yorktown*. As the first three torpedoes struck the water the *Yorktown* applied full starboard helm and orders were given to the engine room for emergency full speed.

The three torpedoes dropped on the port quarter were soon lost to sight, and the *Yorktown*, having turned about ten points, was steadied on a course parallel to the second three until these had run past her to port, close

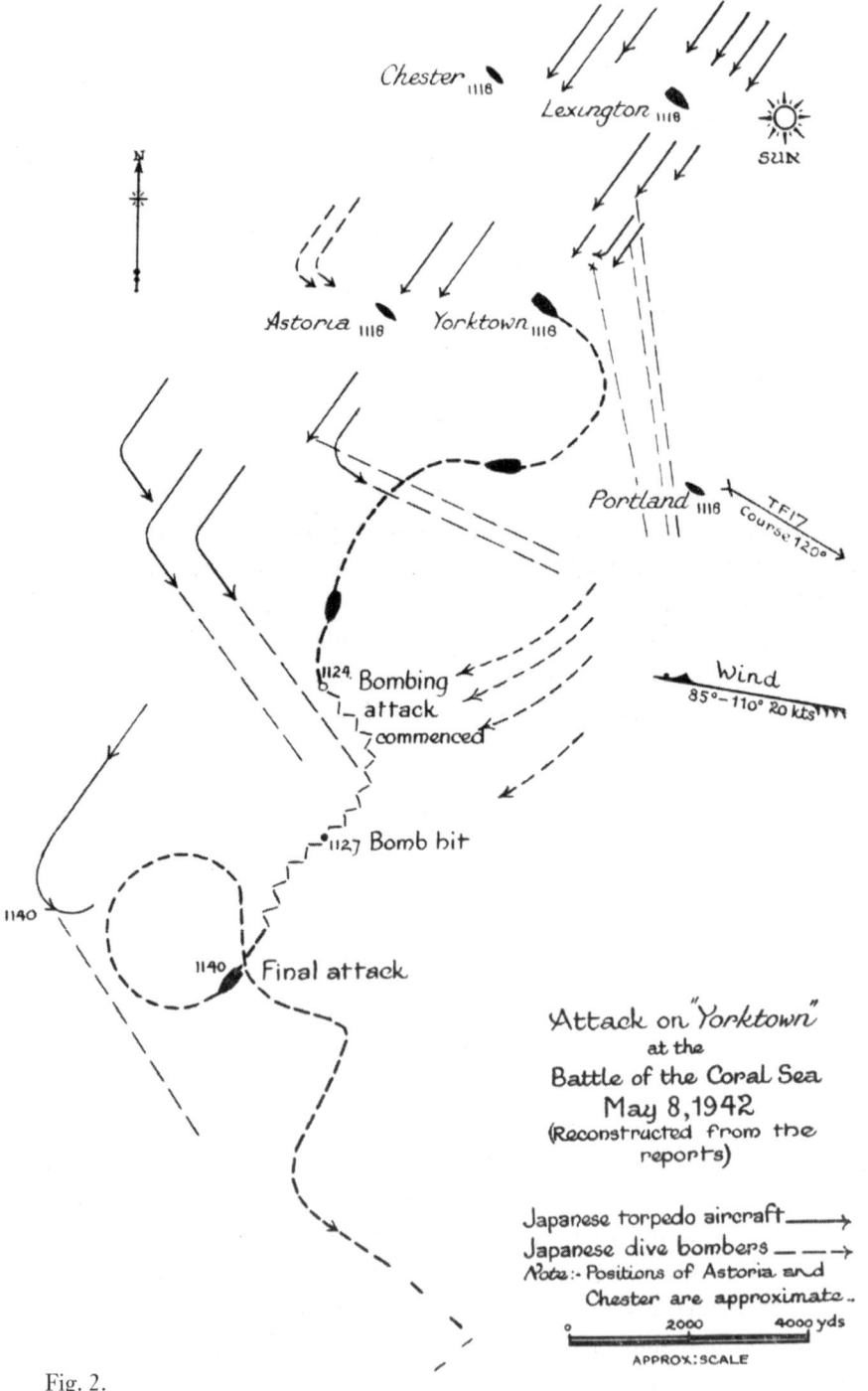

Fig. 2.

aboard. The remaining group of torpedo aircraft, making sharp left turns, rounded the *Yorktown*'s stern at a distance of about 8,000 to 10,000 yards. They were under heavy fire and released their torpedoes well out, from ranges varying between 1,500 and 4,000 yards, on the starboard quarter of the *Yorktown*. The ship at the time was steering about 215 degrees, and she turned to port and steadied with her stern to the point of release. Two of the torpedoes only were seen, both of which ran past on the starboard side. One of the attackers crashed.

After the torpedo aircraft began their high speed glide the dive-bombers continued at altitude for some minutes. At 1124 the dive-bombing attack commenced, the enemy, 10 or 12 in number, coming out of the sun and peeling off at about 6,000 feet, making their dives across the deck, generally from port to starboard with the bridge or island structure as point of aim. Dives were reported to be relatively shallow, perhaps not more than 45 degrees. Reports as to the bomb release point vary, some putting it at 2,000–3,000 feet, others no higher than 500–1,000 feet. The attackers were kept under heavy fire and course was changed under full helm, generally under the dive or towards the direction from which it started. The *Yorktown* received one bomb hit and a total of ten or 11 near misses; six on the starboard side, two very close (one touched the edge of the catwalk) between the bow and the bridge; at least two very near on the port quarter; and two or three on the starboard quarter which lifted the propellers clear of the water. All the bombs appeared to be of the same size and type as that which struck the ship, with two exceptions which were thought to approximate to the U.S. 1,000-lb. bomb.

The single direct bomb hit (at 1127) struck the flight deck about 23 feet before No. 2 lift and about 15 feet from the island. Fragments recovered indicated that it was probably a 12-inch projectile converted to an armour piercing bomb, similar to those used at the attack on Pearl Harbor in December 1941. It pierced the flight deck, making a hole 14 inches in diameter, passed through No. 3 ready room, the hangar deck, and second deck at an angle towards the starboard side, and after hitting a beam and a stanchion turned to port and pierced the third deck. Damage was not great, but the ship's speed was reduced to 24 knots through concussion damage necessitating the temporary securing of three boilers.

At 1131 the ship's radar went out of action, but began to function again without attention at 1222; the cause, namely action damage, was not discovered until next day. The Y E homing transmitter was put out of action by damage at 1150, and as a result, there was a period of several hours following the loss of communications in the *Lexington*, when no Y E homing means was available to either air group.

In the final phase of the attack which occurred about 1140, a single torpedo aircraft held on his course parallel to the *Yorktown* on her starboard side under continuous 5-inch and 1.1-inch fire until he was before the carrier's beam, when he turned towards the ship. Faced with the fire of every gun on that side, he released his torpedo at about 2,000 yards and by a violent manoeuvre escaped, apparently untouched. As he turned towards the *Yorktown*, the latter turned to starboard, and the torpedo passed harmlessly across her bows. The ship continued her turn through a complete circle, and resumed the approximate course she had been steering at the commencement of the engagement.

There is little doubt that brilliant manoeuvring was largely responsible for saving the ship from all but a single bomb hit and the avoidance of every torpedo fired at her; whilst the considerable volume of A.A. fire put up by the carrier and her screening ships, erratic though it was, contributed to her immunity by making the enemy hurry their torpedo and bomb releases. Expenditure of A.A. ammunition by the *Yorktown* was as follows:–

8 x 5-in./38 cal. guns	404 rounds
4 x 1.1-in. mounts	2,906 rounds
24 x 20 mm. guns	7,900 rounds
18 x 0.5-in. guns	15,800 rounds

The attack was then over and the *Yorktown* reduced speed to 18 knots and came into the wind (course 085 degrees) to land aircraft. She had sustained little damage and in less than two hours was capable of 30 knots. Her casualties were 40 killed (37 by the bomb hit) and 26 seriously wounded. None of her screening ships had been hit or damaged.

Turning the Tide

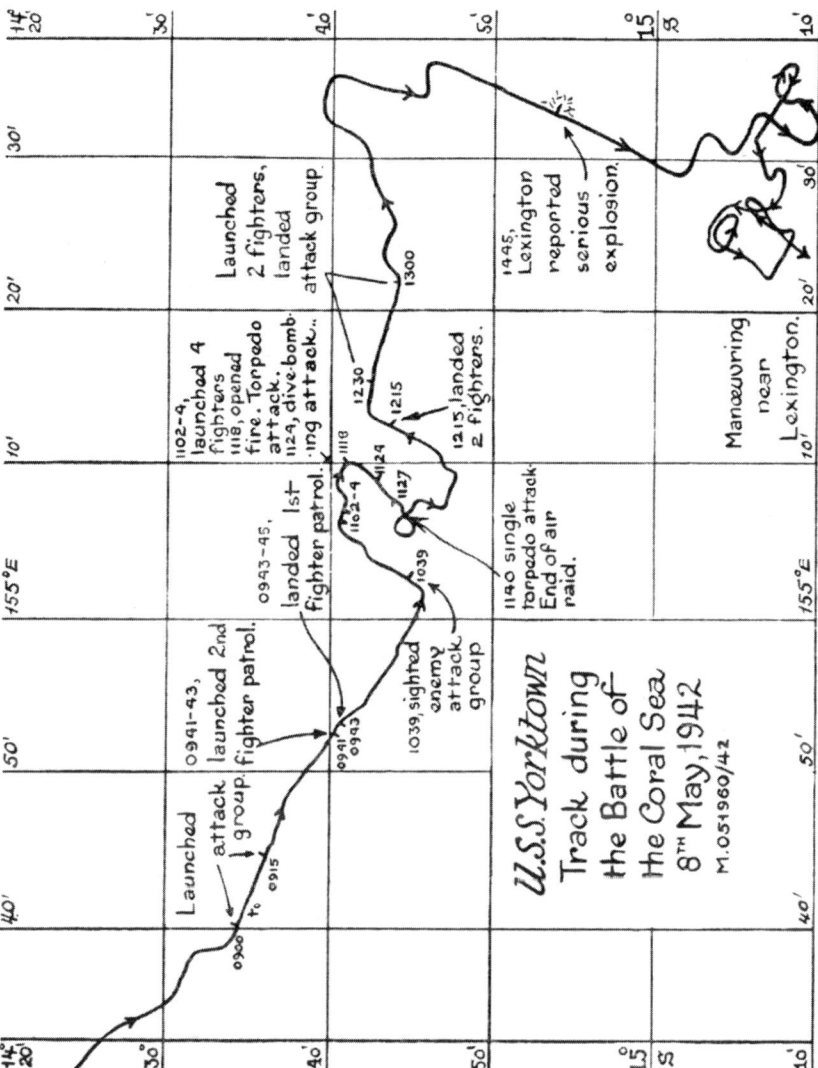

Fig. 3.

Attack on the *Lexington*

The attack on the *Lexington* was practically simultaneous with that on the *Yorktown*, or perhaps a minute or two earlier, since the former, being to northward of the Fleet flagship was nearer to the approaching enemy aircraft. A.A. fire was opened by the *Lexington* at 1113, and raggedly within the next few minutes by the ships near her, some delays being caused by the difficulty of aircraft identification. Her screening ships were both fewer and in general further out than the *Yorktown*'s; the *New Orleans*, for example, owing to the *Lexington*'s abrupt alterations of course and speed, found herself as much as 4,300 yards away from her at the start of the dive-bombers' attack. This was too far away to render effective A.A. fire support. The *Lexington* was, moreover, a less manoeuvrable ship than the *Yorktown*. The five ships which screened the *Lexington* were the cruisers *Minneapolis*, and *New Orleans* and the destroyers *Morris*, *Anderson*, and one other, probably the *Phelps*.

The first attacks were made by torpedo aircraft from two directions, port beam and starboard bow. The *Lexington* turned to port under full helm, to bring the first torpedoes ahead, but torpedoes soon began to arrive from both starboard and port, and though Captain Sherman manoeuvred as best he could to avoid them, the ship was struck just before the port forward gun gallery by a torpedo, released by an aircraft which reached a position a few hundred yards on the *Lexington*'s port beam without being taken under fire. At the time, the carrier had not long completed launching aircraft, which were still near, and the identity of the enemy machine remained undiscovered until it was on the point of releasing its torpedo, upon which firing commenced from all directions. One minute later a second torpedo struck the ship on the port side, abaft the first and level with the bridge.

In all, eleven torpedo tracks were seen; some from starboard crossed the *Lexington*'s bows; two were combed, one on each side; some from port ran ahead; and two ran under the ship without detonating. The *Lexington* reported four torpedo aircraft shot down by her gunfire.

Meanwhile, the dive-bombing attack, synchronised with the torpedo attack, had begun. Dive angles were reported to be about 70 degrees, much steeper, that is, than those of the aircraft attacking the *Yorktown*, and commencing at the high altitude of 17,000 feet. Making their approach, as they did, high in the sun and aided by a cloud, the enemy were not visible until in the final stages of their dive.

The first bomb, estimated at 1,000 pounds, struck the ready ammunition locker at the after end of the port forward gun gallery about the same time as the first torpedo. The explosion put out of action the entire battery, killed all the crew of one gun and caused a number of other casualties both in the battery and inboard, and started extensive fires. Two other very near misses on the port quarter which tore holes in the hull, were at first mistaken for torpedo hits. Another bomb, estimated at 500 pounds, struck the superstructure on the port side; and a much smaller bomb exploded inside the funnel. Fragments from near misses on the starboard quarter killed and injured a number of men. One apparent incendiary bomb was seen flaming as it fell, though it was not seen to hit.

The end of the action, which lasted only about 15 minutes, found the *Lexington* on fire in four places, and listing 6 degrees to port with three stoke holds partially flooded. But the fires were manageable, the list was already in process of being corrected by transfer of oil fuel, the pumps were keeping the water down, the steering gear was intact, and the ship was making 25 knots under good control.

No ship of the *Lexington*'s screen had received any damage, though the destroyer *Dewey* had six men wounded by machine-gun fire from torpedo aircraft, apparently whilst screening the *Yorktown*.

Sinking of the *Lexington*

The attackers had gone and the American force was apparently in good shape. About 1230 the attack group began to return from the attack on the *Shokaku* and *Zuikaku*, and commenced landing. In the case of the *Yorktown* this was completed at 1300 and she steered to close the *Lexington* which was some six to eight miles distant from her at the conclusion of the Japanese attack. Both the *Lexington*'s lifts were jammed, but as they were in the up position she was able to land her aircraft. There was at this time no doctrine in the U.S. fleet for obtaining maximum flexibility of handling returning aircraft by diverting them from one carrier to another. In any event, the ship was now on an even keel and all fires were either out or well under control, all damage was being cleared up, and so normal did she appear that many of the returning aircraft were unaware the ship had been hit. Certainly nobody foresaw the dreadful denouement which was about to occur.

Suddenly at 1247 a heavy explosion shook the ship. The explosion appeared to come from amidships, well down in the bowels of the carrier; the cause was not apparent, and it was at first thought to be a 1,000 pound bomb detonating after delay, though it was subsequently found to have been due to an accumulation of gasoline vapour near the central station. The primary explosion occurred in the motor generator room; the resulting damage to bulkheads enabled the fire to spread up through the ventilating system to the third and second decks. From this violent start the fire spread rapidly, above and below the armoured deck, constantly fed by oil, gasoline and other inflammables, and it was never actually got under control. At first her ability to operate was unaffected and she was able to land-on her air group about 1400. Seven of the torpedo aircraft were so short of fuel that they could not afford to spend time in recognition procedure and were fired on by the *Yorktown* for a short time, fortunately without result.

By 1422 all aircraft of both attack groups had either returned or been given up for lost. Consideration was now given to making another air attack or sending in the attack group of cruisers and destroyers for surface action. A returning *Lexington* pilot had reported that one enemy carrier was undamaged; and C.T.F.17 informed the Commander-in-Chief Pacific Fleet and Commander South-west Pacific Forces that there were strong indications that an additional carrier had joined the enemy forces. Although the *Shokaku* was erroneously believed sunk wireless interceptions indicated that at least some of her aircraft had been landed on board the *Zuikaku*. The *Yorktown* had only eight fighters, 12 bombers, and eight torpedo aircraft (with seven torpedoes) serviceable; and the idea of making another air attack was consequently rejected. The idea of surface attack was also rejected on account of the probability of the force being detected and subjected to strong carrier air attack before dark. C.T.F.17 decided to retire to the southward to investigate further the damage to the carriers and get aircraft in condition to renew the air attack next day. At 1510 Rear-Admiral Fletcher reassumed tactical command. He intended to take the *Lexington*'s serviceable aircraft aboard the *Yorktown* and despatch the *Lexington* to Pearl Harbor.

However, the decision had no sooner been taken than events compelled a reversal. For some reason, no report of the internal explosion had been made from the *Lexington* until 1445, nearly two hours after its occurrence, and throughout the afternoon matters had gone from bad to worse with the ship. The fire gradually put out of action more and more communications. All lights forward went out. The fire main pressure dropped to 30 or 40 pounds. Steering control was lost, and about 1630 the order had to be given to evacuate the engine and boiler rooms, and preparations were made to abandon ship. Fire fighting was no longer possible with all pressure gone, but at Captain Sherman's request Rear-Admiral Fitch directed the destroyer *Morris* to go alongside, pass over fire hoses and also take on board the *Lexington*'s superfluous personnel. But the fire was beyond control, additional explosions were occurring and there was danger of the ship blowing up at any moment. At 1707 Rear-Admiral Fitch ordered Captain Sherman to abandon ship.

Rear-Admiral Kinkaid was put in charge of the rescue operations which were carried out by the cruisers *Minneapolis* and *New Orleans*, and destroyers *Phelps*, *Morris*, *Anderson* and *Hammann*. Owing to the carrier's heavy list to port destroyers could not lie alongside and most of the crew had to take to the water or to life rafts; and with the ship in the trough of the sea, drifting to leeward with the wind, the men in the water on her lee side found difficulty in getting clear. Nevertheless the rescuing destroyers worked with skill and care in the growing darkness, and thanks to this and a high state of discipline on board it is believed that no man was lost by drowning when the ship was abandoned. Out of the *Lexington*'s total complement of 2,951 a preliminary check accounted for all but 26 officers and 190 men.

At 1750 a heavy explosion rocked the listing and burning carrier and threw aircraft from her deck high in the air. A final inspection by Captain Sherman and the executive officer, Commander M. T. Seligman, who both escaped injury in this explosion, showed that no man was left on board and the destroyer *Phelps* was detailed at 1853 to sink the ship by torpedoes; and after five torpedoes had been fired at her singly the *Lexington* sank suddenly at 1952 in 2,400 fathoms of water in Lat. 15° 12' S., Long. 155° 27' E. With her she took 35 of her aircraft. The remaining survivors of the day's battles, five fighters, eight scouts, and six bombers were landed aboard the *Yorktown*, which with the remainder of Task Force 17 withdrew southward.

Japanese Plan Abandoned

The Battle of the Coral Sea was the first set-back suffered by the Japanese since the raid on Pearl Harbor, and this set-back can be attributed directly to the escape of the U.S. carriers which were at sea when the raid took place. The outcome of the battle completely disorganised the Japanese Moresby expedition. One carrier was sunk and one was put out of action and had to withdraw to Kure for repairs, heavy losses had been incurred by both carrier- and land-based air groups, and there was a shortage of fuel for aircraft on board the *Zuikaku*, the only carrier remaining operational. The Japanese support force was no longer capable of fulfilling its function, and although the approaches to Port Moresby now lay open, the invasion force retired and the date of the projected operation was postponed until July. In June, however, the door to expansion shut by the Allies at the Battle of the Coral Sea, was finally bolted by the Battle of Midway, and the plan to invade Port Moresby by sea was abandoned.

The turning back of the Port Moresby expedition at the Battle of the Coral Sea put an end to Japanese southward expansion by sea, and saved for the Allies a base on which their subsequent progress to the final recapture of New Guinea was founded.

Lessons of the Battle

The Battle of the Coral Sea showed the aircraft to be the principal offensive weapon of both the U.S. and Japanese fleets. At the same time, it was clear that some method must be found of increasing the capacity of aircraft carriers for sustained operations. The answer was found in the development of the technique of fuelling, rearming, and storing at sea.

The Americans gained in the battle some valuable experience, of which they took immediate advantage.

On the tactical side, the outnumbering of the U.S. fighters resulted in the complements of the carriers being increased from an average of about 17 to 27, bringing them to numerical equality with the Japanese. As a protection for carriers against torpedo air attack a very tight disposition was in future adopted in the Pacific Fleet, the screening ships being stationed on a 1,500 to 2,500-yard circle. The desirability of close co-ordination between torpedo aircraft and dive-bombing attacks was considered to have been demonstrated.

Certain faults in material were brought to light. Fogging of sights and windshields received attention; and Admiral Nimitz pressed for more effective aircraft bombs and torpedoes, for too many hits were at present required to destroy an enemy carrier. Steps were taken to replace the existing torpedo aircraft by machines of greater speed and longer range.

Annex

Commander Task Force Seventeen Operation Order, No. 2-42
Enemy Forces and Dispositions (Extracts)
1. AERODROMES AND ANCHORAGES USED BY ORANGE (Enemy)
- (a) Rabaul. This port is the most important where shipping concentrates. The present estimated strength of shore-based aircraft at Rabaul is:–

Fighters	Bombers	Patrol aircraft	Small seaplanes	Total
12	20	17	4	53

    The Genzan Air Squadron is due at Rabaul. Air searches from Rabaul are up to 600 miles.
- (b) New Ireland. Kavieng airfield is used by enemy bombers. Its protection is unknown. The Strait between New Ireland and New Hanover is used as an anchorage and rendezvous for convoys. Convoys en route Rabaul may be routed to the northeast or the southwest of New Ireland. Kavieng Harbour is used as an anchorage by naval craft.
- (c) Queen Carola Harbour (Kessa). This harbour is at the northern end of Buka Island. It has been frequently used by men-of-war and is possibly mined. At the Southern end of Buka is Buka Passage. An aerodrome is located here and may be used by Orange aircraft. Light bombers and fighters can use this field. Anchorage is available for men-of-war and has been used.
- (d) Watom Island is off the southeast coast of New Ireland. Transports have been seen anchored here.
- (e) Dyaul Island is south of the northwest end of New Ireland. It is believed that Palmer Harbour is used by convoys.
- (f) Gasmata aerodrome is used as an advanced field from Rabaul.
- (g) Kieta, Bougainville. The land plane field at Kieta is not satisfactory

for military operations. Orange has not used this field so far. Orange has no aerodromes further south in the Solomon Islands.
(h) Buin. There is a satisfactory anchorage at Buin.
(i) Faisi Island has been occupied. A satisfactory anchorage exists here. So far only small ships have been noted in the harbour. Buoys are installed here. It is possible that this harbour may be used in the near future by patrol seaplanes.
(j) Salamoa. This port has a poor deep water anchorage but it is used by patrol seaplanes. The aerodrome, which is suitable for light bombers and fighters, is not used.
(k) Lae aerodrome is used by heavy bombers and fighters. The anchorage is used only while unloading supply ships. The estimated enemy air strength in New Guinea is as follows:–

Fighters	Bombers	Patrol aircraft	Total
30	15	4	49

The routine plane procedure at Lae is as follows: Warm up engines at 0530. Take off 45 minutes later. Patrol 5,000-8,000 feet until 1815 except for one 45 minute period some time between 1130 and 1345. No patrols are sent out on days of low visibility.
(l) Air reinforcements to the Rabaul area are being expedited from Marianas and Marshalls.
(m) Orange air attacks on Horn Island, Port Moresby and Tulagi (Solomons) indicate early operations in southeast New Guinea and probably Tulagi.

2. ORANGE SHIPPING IN NEW BRITAIN AREA
(a) Lae and Salamoa are only used for unloading supply vessels.
(b) Rabaul is the principal port for convoys. In considering the convoy routes to Rabaul, Orange does not use a set route. Some convoys round the southwest end of New Ireland and others round the northeast end of the same island. Units of these convoys often diverted, a few each to different harbours. Of the harbours so used, the following are known: Kavieng, Duke of York Island, New Hanover Island, the Strait between New Hanover and New Ireland,

Watom Island, Dyaul Island (Palmer Harbour), and Ulu Island. It would appear that most naval units remain at sea and not in Simpson Harbour as was previously the custom. However, merchant shipping uses the harbour extensively. An estimate of the number of ships to be found in Rabaul at any time would average 15 ships. Of these one or two would be of or greater than 10,000 tons, 5 to 7 would average about 7,500 tons, and the remainder would be considerably smaller. However, present indications are that a large number of transports and cargo ships are massing apparently for a movement toward southeast New Guinea.

(c) Kavieng. It can be expected that an average of two medium transports or cargo ships will be found in this harbour. Present data show about 20 additional transports or cargo ships underway in this area.

(d) Watom, Ulu, Dyaul Islands. If the number of Orange ships in Rabaul reaches about 15, it may be expected that new convoys will use these anchorages or the passage between New Ireland and New Hanover until some ships depart from Simpson Harbour.

(e) Faisi. No ships larger than fair sized schooners may be expected in this harbour.

3. ORANGE MEN OF WAR IN RABAUL AREA

(a) Rabaul. The only warships observed in the entire area recently are:

> One submarine tender and three or more submarines.
> An occasional aircraft carrier transporting planes.
> *Kamikawa Maru* which indicates that part of Air Squadron Six is present.
> A few destroyers patrol outside of Rabaul and the entrance to Simpson Harbour.
> *Fujikawa Maru*, also of Air Squadron Six, is en route and due at Rabaul
> Occasionally a light cruiser or two are seen in Simpson Harbour and Kavieng.
> Destroyer Squadron Six and Gunboat Division Eight.

(b) Major operations are predicted to commence in the New Britain area about April 28. It would appear that appreciable Orange strength has been concentrated around Truk and Palao. The units at Truk have been reported to have moved to the southward. A convoy has been reported under way 90 miles south of Kavieng. This convoy could be headed for Rabaul or further into the Solomons. A well armed 2,500-ton well deck cargo ship was reported near (west) of New Georgia.

(c) Units known to be at Truk or to the southward are:–
Carrier Division Five
Zuikaku – fighters–21; bombers–21; torpedo aircraft–21
Shokaku – fighters–21; bombers–21; torpedo aircraft–21
 Note:–three of each type are spares.
Desdiv Three (part of Cardiv 5)
Hokaze, Namikaze, Shiokaze, Numakaze

Crudiv Five (less *Nachi*)
Myoko, Haguro

Atago at Palao. Gunboat Division 8 at Truk.
Ryukaku at Truk

Commander Submarine Force and submarines at Truk

Desdiv 34	Desron 6	Yubari (F)
Natori (F)	Desdiv 29	Desdiv 30
Hakaze	Oite	Mutsuki
Akikaze	Hayate	Kisaragi
Yukaze	Asanagi	Yayoi
Tachikaze	Yunagi	Mochitsuki

Kasuga Maru en route Truk
Kamikawa Maru, Fujikawa Maru, and AirRon Six at or near Rabaul (apparently relieved *Kamoi* and AirRon Twenty-four).

Summary (minimum)
2 carriers with 42 fighters, 42 bombers, 42 torpedo aircraft (three spares each type)
1 carrier with 21 fighters, 42 bombers, 21 torpedo aircraft (three spares each type)

- 16 destroyers
- 3 (heavy) cruisers
- 1 submarine tender and probably 6 submarines
- 2 auxiliary seaplane tenders (large) with one air squadron
- 2 (light) cruisers
- 8 auxiliary gunboats
- 8 merchant vessels
- 9 transports or cargo ships
- 2 minelayers
- 2 or 3 battleships (south of Truk)

Appendix A

U.S. Operation Order No. 2-42
(Effective 0730 Z – 11½, 6 May 1942)
U.S.S. *Yorktown*, at Sea, 1 May 1942

Task Organisation
(Task Force 17, Rear-Admiral F. J. Fletcher, U.S.S. *Yorktown*)
(a)   17.2   *ATTACK GROUP* Rear-Admiral T. C. Kinkaid
         17.2.1
            Cruisers   *Minneapolis*   (Flagship) Capt. F. J. Lowry
                       New Orleans   Capt. H. H. Good
         17.2.2
            Cruisers   *Astoria*   Flagship of Rear-Admiral W. W. Smith
                                       Capt. F. W. Scanland
                       Chester   Capt. T. M. Shock
                       Portland   Capt. B. Perlman
         17.2.4
            Destroyers   Capt. A. R. Early
                       Phelps   Lieut.-Cdr. E. L. Beck
                       Dewey   Lieut.-Cdr. C. F. Cillingworth, Jr.
                       Farragut[16] Cdr. G. P. Hunter
                       Aylwin   Lieut.-Cdr. R. H. Rogers
                       Monaghan[17] Lieut.-Cdr. W. P. Burford

(b)   17.3   *SUPPORT GROUP* Rear-Admiral J. G. Crace
         17.3.1
            Cruisers   H.M.A.S.   (Flagship) Capt. H. B. Farncomb,
                       Australia[18] R.A.N.

			Chicago	Capt. H. D. Bode
			H.M.A.S. *Hobart*[18]	Capt. H. L. Howden, R.A.N.
		17.3.4 Destroyers	*Perkins*	Flag of Cdr. F. X. McInerney
				Lieut.-Cdr. W. C. Ford
			Walke	Lieut.-Cdr. T. E. Fraser

(c) 17.5   *AIR* Rear-Admiral A. W. Fitch
(U.S.S. *Lexington*, Commander Carrier Division One)

		17.5.1 Carriers[19]	*Yorktown*	(Fleet flagship) Capt. E. A. Buckmaster
			Lexington	(Flagship) Capt. F. G. Sherman
		17.5.4 Destroyers	*Morris*	Captain G. C. Hoover
				Commander H. B. Jarrett
			Anderson	Lieut.-Cdr. J. K. B. Ginder
			Hammann	Com. A. E. True
			Russell	Lieut.-Cdr. G. R. Harting

(d) 17.6   *FUELLING GROUP* Commander J. S. Phillips

		Oilers	*Neosho*	Capt. J. S. Phillips
			Tippecanoe	
		Destroyers	*Sims*	Lieut.-Cdr. W. M. Hyman
			Worden	

(e) 17.9   *SEARCH GROUP* Commander G. H. de Baun
Tangier (Seaplane Tender (Large))
12 patrol aircraft (operated from Numea, New Caledonia)

1. INFORMATION

(a) Task Force Seventeen, including Task Force Eleven and some ships of the Southwest Pacific Force, is operating under Commander-in-Chief, U.S. Pacific Fleet and in accordance with Commander-in-Chief, U.S. Pacific Fleet despatches 142027 (April) and 220541 (April).

(b) Allied air searches from Australia, Port Moresby and Tulagi in accordance with Commander Southwest Pacific Force despatch 270840 (April). Frequent bombing raids are conducted against enemy bases at Rabaul, Lae and Salamaua.

(c) Six United States submarines (Task Force 42) operating out of Brisbane are patrolling the New Guinea–Solomon area. They may be expected to remain between longitudes 154–30 E. and 155–00 E. when passing to their patrol areas. They have been told that this force would operate east of 155–00 E. between latitudes 6–00 S. and 20–00 S. and west of 154–30 between New Guinea–Louisiade Archipelago and latitude 20–00 S.

(d) Commander-in-Chief, U.S. Pacific Fleet has stated that Australian Commonwealth Naval Board is issuing a directive that the Commander of a Pacific Fleet carrier task force shall command combined force of United States–Australian ships.

(e) *Achilles, Leander, Flusser, Henley, Helm* and convoy arrive at Efate May 5 for the reinforcement of that place.

(f) Attention is directed to Commander Task Force Seventeen serial (034N) enclosing Operating Procedure.

(g) The enemy is constantly increasing his strength in this area and the disposition of his forces is constantly changing. The task force is referred to daily radio intelligence promulgated by Commander Southwest Pacific Force. A summary of the more recent reports appears in Annex A.

2. This force will destroy enemy ships, shipping and aircraft at favourable opportunities in order to assist in checking further advance by enemy in the New Guinea–Solomon area.

3. (a) *ATTACK GROUP*

    (i) Locate and destroy enemy surface forces reported, by Allied reconnaissance aircraft or other source, to be advancing southward in the New Guinea–Solomon area.

    (ii) Destroy enemy forces encountered and defend carriers against

air and submarine attack while this force is concentrated.
  (iii) Furnish air patrols as requested by Commander Air.

(b) *SUPPORT GROUP*
  (i) Defend carriers against air, surface and submarine attacks by destroying enemy forces encountered.
  (ii) Be prepared to support the *Attack Group* as directed or to operate tactically with that group.
  (iii) Furnish air patrols as requested by Commander Air.

(c) *AIR*
  (i) Locate and destroy, by bombing and torpedo attack, enemy forces reported, by allied reconnaissance aircraft or other source, to be advancing southward in the New Guinea–Solomon area.
  (ii) Co-ordinate air attack with *Attack Group*, if directed; be prepared to use smoke.
  (iii) Provide daily air searches and patrols; defend this force against enemy air attack; request *Attack Group* and *Support Group* Commanders to augment carrier air patrols as desired.
  (iv) Destroyers defend carriers against air, surface and submarine attack.

(d) *FUELLING GROUP*
  (i) Unless otherwise directed pass through Point Rye one hour after sunrise on local odd days and Point Corn one hour after sunrise on local even days. At other times operate to southward of a line joining these points.
  (ii) If operating tactically with this force and an enemy surface or air attack develops, proceed without signal and operate in accordance with the preceding paragraph.

(e) *SEARCH GROUP*
  (i) *Tangier* base at Noumea; service patrol aircraft and control flights.
  (ii) Six aircraft make daily search, covering sector from Noumea between bearings 305 and 360 as far to the northwest as the boundary of the Southwest Pacific Area and as far north as

latitude 11–30 S. plus a triangle within the points, latitude 15–00 S. longitude 168–40 E., latitude 16–30 S. longitude 171–40 E. latitude 18–15 S. longitude 168–45 E. Modify these searches if later developments indicate a need therefor and keep the Task Force Commander advised.

(iii) Trail any enemy surface units encountered, reporting contact promptly.

(iv) This force will operate generally about seven hundred miles south of Rabaul. Upon receiving intelligence of enemy surface forces advancing to the southward, this force will move into a favourable position for intercepting and destroying the enemy. The *Attack Group*, possibly with all or part of the *Support Group*, may be detached.

(v) While *Air* and *Support Group* are operating together, Task Units 17.3.4 and *17.5.4* are combined under the command of the senior destroyer commander in order to co-ordinate screening duties, plane guarding, developing submarine contacts, etc.

(vi) Damaged ships proceed to such friendly port as the Commanding Officer deems expedient; report arrival to Commander-in-Chief, U.S. Pacific Fleet, Commander Southwest Pacific Force, Task Force Commander.

(vii) Ships becoming separated rendezvous at Point Rye one hour after sunrise on local odd days and Point Corn one hour after sunrise on local even days. At other times operate to the southward.

(viii) This order effective on signal.

4. Fuel oil and aviation gasoline in *Neosho* at Point Rye one hour after sunrise on odd days and Point Corn one hour after sunrise on even days. *Tippecanoe* will fill from *E. J. Henry* at Noumea about May 10 and thereafter will be at Points Rye and Corn as above. *Platte* is expected at Noumea May 13; *Cuyama* and *Kanawha* May 17; *Neosho* June 3.

5. (a) Maintain absolute radio silence except for enemy contact reports.
   (b) Communications in accordance with Task Force Seventeen Communication Plan 5–42.
   (c) Use zone zero time when separated from this task force, otherwise local zone time.

(d) The following special reference points are effective in addition to those prescribed by higher authority:–

Corn	Lat. 15–00 S., Long. 160–00 E.
Rye	Lat. 16–00 S., Long. 158–00 E.
Barley	Lat. 11–00 S., Long. 157–00 E.
Wheat	Lat. 17–00 S., Long. 153–00 E.
Oats	Lat. 15–00 S., Long. 151–00 E.
Moon	Lat. 19–00 S., Long. 167–00 E.

(e) Commander Task Force Seventeen in *Yorktown*.

Appendix B

Japanese Naval Forces
Kashima (light cruiser) Vice-Admiral Inoue (at Rabaul)

SUPPORT FORCE
SIXTH SQUADRON
  Carrier Division 5 Rear-Admiral Hara
    Zuikaku (flagship)   (Normal aircraft load:–27 fighters, 18 bombers, 18 torpedo, total 63)
    Shokaku   (Normal aircraft load:–27 fighters, 27 bombers, 18 torpedo, total 72)
  5th Cruiser Squadron Vice-Admiral Takeo Takagi
    Myoko   10 7.87-in., 8 4.7-in. H.A. guns
    Haguro   10 7.87-in., 8 4.7-in. H.A. guns
    Ashigara   10 7.87-in., 8 5.1-in. guns
  Destroyer Division 27   (*Shigure, Yugure, Ariake, Shiratsuyu*)
  Destroyer Division 8   (? 7) (*Ushio, Akebono*, oil tanker *Higashikimi Maru*)
    Tokiwa (minelayer)
    Kiyokawa Maru (seaplane carrier)
    Toho Maru (oiler)

OCCUPATION FORCE
  6th Cruiser Squadron
    Aoba (flagship)
    Kinugasa
    Kako   6 7.87-in., 4 4.7-in. H.A. guns
    Furutaka

18th Cruiser Squadron
    Tenryu (flagship)   4 5.5-in., 1 3.15-in. H.A. guns
    Tatsuta   4 5.5-in., 1 3.15-in. H.A. guns
    Shoho (light carrier) (load, 12 fighters, 9–12 torpedo aircraft)
    1 Destroyer

Destroyer Flotilla 6
    Yubari (light cruiser) 6 5.5-in., 1 3.15-in. H.A. guns
    6 destroyers
    Kamikawa Maru (auxiliary seaplane tender)
    Tsugaru (minelayer)
        Five transports carrying 144th Infantry Regt., one bn. Mountain Arty., attached Cavalry, Engineer, transport and A.A. companies, under command of Major General Horii.

Submarine Flotilla 8
    6 submarines

Japanese Naval Losses (Japanese Figures)

Sunk: Light carrier *Shoho* (off Misima 7 May in 10° 29' S., 152° 55' E.)

          Old destroyer *Kikuzuki* (at Tulagi 4 May in 9° 07' S., 160° 12' E.)

          4 landing barges (at Tulagi 4 May)

Damaged: Carrier *Shokaku* (8 May)

          Minelayer *Okinoshima* (at Tulagi 4 May) (Subsequently sunk (11 May) by a U.S. submarine in 5° 06' S. 153° 48' E.)

          Destroyer *Yuzuki* (Captain and others killed by strafing at Tulagi 4 May)

          Aircraft – 80 lost

          Personnel about 900 lost

Appendix C

U.S. and Japanese Aircraft Losses, 4–8 May 1942

U.S. Lost			Japanese (shot down, U.S. claims)
	4 May		
Yorktown			
2 fighter (pilots saved)	At Tulagi	by *Yorktown*'s aircraft	5 single-float seaplanes
1 torpedo aircraft			
All force-landed			
	5 May		
	Whilst cruising	by *Yorktown*'s aircraft	1 4-engined flying boat
	7 May		
	ACTION OFF MISIMA		
Yorktown			
1 dive-bomber missing	(Sinking of *Shoho*)	by *Yorktown*'s aircraft	2 scout bombers, 3 fighters, type 97
Lexington			
1 scout bomber shot down		by *Lexington*'s aircraft	4 fighters, type 97, 1 torpedo aircraft
1 scout bomber force-landed (crew saved)		Lost on board *Shoho*	15[20]

DURING SEARCHES BY U.S. AND JAPANESE

| | by *Yorktown*'s aircraft | 2 twin float aircraft, 1 4-engine patrol bomber |

ATTACK ON U.S. CARRIERS

Yorktown
2 fighters lost
Lexington
1 fighter lost

by *Yorktown*'s and/or *Lexington*'s aircraft — 6 Zero type fighters

ATTACK ON ALLIED SUPPORT GROUP

by Allied ships (T.G. 17.3) — 4 torpedo aircraft

8 May
ON PATROL

by *Yorktown*'s aircraft — 1 4-engine patrol aircraft, type 97, 1 torpedo aircraft

ATTACK ON ZUIKAKU AND SHOKAKU

Yorktown
2 dive-bombers lost,
1 fighter lost

by *Yorktown*'s aircraft — 14 Zero fighters, 1 scout

Lexington
7 fighters shot down,
1 torpedo aircraft,   Ran out of fuel.
3 scout bombers,   Lost.
1 fighter

by *Lexington*'s aircraft — 2 scouts, 1 fighter

ATTACK ON TASK FORCE 17

Yorktown

1 fighter landed on board *Lexington* and sunk,
4 scout bombers shot down

Lexington

2 fighters shot down (pilots saved),
1 scout bomber shot down,
1 scout bomber crashed on landing,
35 aircraft sank with ship

Total 68[21]

by *Yorktown*'s combat air patrol,
Anti-torpedo aircraft patrol

by *Lexington*'s combat air patrol

By ships of T.F. 17

Total 91[22]

4 Zero fighters, 3 dive bombers

4 fighters

1 torpedo aircraft, 3 fighters, 12 or more

Endnotes

1. A comprehensive review of the situation is given in *Battle Summary No. 25, Naval Strategy in the Pacific, December 1941–February 1943*, B.R. 1736 (18), Chap. III.
2. 144th Infy. Regt., 1 Bn. Mountain Arty., attached Cavalry, Engineer, Transport and A.A. companies, under command of Maj. Gen. Horii.
3. The *Secret Information Bulletin No. 1*, p. 17.
4. These are the figures given in the *Lexington*'s Report (M.051960/42, p. 21). The U.S. Combat Narrative *The Battle of the Coral Sea*, p. 15, says that there were 10 S.B.D.s (Douglas Dauntless Scout Bombers) armed with 1 x 500 and 2 x 100 bombs each, and 16 dive-bombers armed with 1,000-lb. bombs.
5. Figures taken from 'Action Reports of *Yorktown* Air Group during Coral Sea Engagement' (M.051960/42, p. 426). Different figures are given in the report (in the same paper, p. 63) titled 'Air Operations of the *Yorktown* Air Group against Japanese Forces in the vicinity of the Louisiade Archipelago on 7 May, 1942.'
6. This appears to have been mistaken identity, since there were only six transports in the Occupation Force.
7. S. E. Morison, *History of U.S. Naval Operations in World War II*, Vol. IV.
8. *Ibid*.
9. The U.S. Combat Narrative, *The Battle of the Coral Sea*, p. 51 states: 'A muster upon return to ship of the whaleboats show 16 officers and 94 men accounted for; 1 officer and 19 men known dead, and 4 officers and 154 missing, besides the 15 men from the *Sims*. Many were wounded and several later died.'
10. In view of the general impression that the American forces were lavishly equipped, it is of interest at this date apparently only the Commanders of scouting squadrons were equipped with binoculars, an item of equipment very difficult to obtain in U.S.A. as in the U.K.
11. A Japanese Intelligence Unit was borne on board each U.S. carrier.
12. The *Yorktown*'s report (M.051960/42), p. 87, says that three torpedoes were seen to make erratic runs. On p. 100 the report states that all nine Mark 13, Mod. 1 torpedoes fired during the operations of 4–8 May made erratic runs; but the report also shows that the only Mark 13 Mod. 1 torpedoes fired were these nine fired in this attack on the Japanese carriers on 8 May.
13. The American reports do not state at what range the torpedoes were released in this attack.
14. The U.S. *Combat Narrative* states: 'The failure of a large number of our fighters to intercept the enemy planes, despite the fact that ample radar warning of their approach was available, has resulted in criticism of the tactics of the Task Force fighter director. ... It should be noted, however, that no criticism of the *Lexington* fighter director was contained in any of the official action reports of 8 May.' A severe criticism of the fighter director by an officer in one of the carriers is appended as a footnote on p. 26 of the *Combat Narrative*. On the other hand, the U.S. Secret Information Bulletin No. 1, *Battle Experience from Pearl Harbor to Midway*, p. 8, seems to ascribe the failure fully to exploit the radar and fighter director system to failure to train in peace-time with equipment to be used during war.

15. It is not possible to give with certainty, the name of the fourth destroyer which accompanied the *Yorktown*. The latter reported it was probably the *Dewey* (M.015960/42, p. 78). S.I.B. No. 1 *Battle Experience from Pearl Harbor to Midway* pp. 7–14, gives it as the *Phelps*, but the report of Commander Destroyer Squadron One, of which *Phelps* was leader (M.015960/42, p. 265) makes it clear that she was with the *Lexington*. It is at any rate certain that in this action, which occupied only 15 minutes in all, seven ships accompanied the *Yorktown* and five the *Lexington*.
16. Detached at 0700/7 May to join the support group.
17. Detached at 0100/8 May to search for survivors of the *Neosho*.
18. H.M.A.S.
19. Aircraft available (operational).

	Yorktown			*Lexington*		
	4 May	7 May	8 May	7 May	8 May	
	12	10	9	12	12	Torpedo bombers (Douglas Devastator).
	17	17	14	?10	19	Fighters (Grumman Wildcat = British Martlett, II, IV).
	15	18	17	28 } 24	{ Bombers (Douglas Dauntless).
	15	17	15	8		Scout Bombers (Douglas Dauntless).
	59	62	55	58	55	

20. Japanese *Report on the Battle of the Coral Sea*, No. B.l. O.S./J.A.P./P.R./693.
21. In addition, the following *Yorktown*'s aircraft were 'damaged – no longer serviceable': 4 dive bombers, 4 fighters, 5 scout bombers, 3 torpedo aircraft, total 16.
22. The offical Japanese figure of losses was 80.

Part II

C.B. 3305 (1)   BR 1736 (47)

RESTRICTED – Attention is called to the penalties attaching to any infraction of the Official Secrets Acts

NAVAL STAFF HISTORY
SECOND WORLD WAR

BATTLE SUMMARY No. 46

BATTLE OF MIDWAY
3 – 6 June, 1942

This book is invariably to be kept locked up when not in use and is not to be taken outside the ship or establishment for which it is issued without the express permission of the Commanding Officer.

This book is the property of H.M. Government.
It is intended for the use of Officers generally, and may in certain cases be communicated to persons in H.M. Service below the rank of Commissioned Officer who may require to be acquainted with its contents in the course of their duties. The Officers exercising this power will be held responsible that this information is imparted with due caution and reserve.

T.S.D. 30/51
Training and Staff Duties Division (Historical Section),
Naval Staff, Admiralty, S.W.1

Chapter I
Situation after Battle of Coral Sea

U.S. Inferiority in Carriers	109
The Objective	110
Japanese Plan to Occupy Midway	112
Organisation of the Japanese Expedition	113
Operations of the Japanese Submarines	115
The Aleutian Diversion	117
Japanese Preparations for the Operation	117
Organisation of the U.S. Forces	118
Preparations at Midway	119

Chapter II
Preliminary Movements

Japanese Expedition Sails	126
Occupation Force Sighted	127
B.17s Attack Transport Unit	127
Night Attack on Transport Unit by Patrol Bombers	129

Chapter III
Air Attack on Midway

Japanese Attack Group Takes off from Carriers	132
Discovery of the Japanese Carriers	133
The Air Battle	133
Bombing of Midway	134
Japanese Cancel Second Air Attack on Midway	135

Chapter IV
Midway Aircraft Attack Japanese First Air Fleet

Army (B.26) and Navy Torpedo (TBF) Aircraft Attack	140
Douglas (SBD) Marine Scout Bombers Attack	142
Army B.17s Attack the Carriers	143
Vought-Sikorsky (SB2U) Marine Scout Bombers Attack	145

Chapter V
Destruction of First Air Fleet by U.S. Carrier Aircraft, and Attacks on *Yorktown*

Situation After the Attack on Midway	146
Task Forces 16 and 17 Launch Attack Groups	146
Enemy Alters Course	148
Hornet's Torpedo Squadron Attacks	149
Enterprise and *Yorktown* Torpedo Groups Attack	149
Enterprise Dive Bombers Attack	151
Yorktown Dive Bombers Attack	153
Sinking of the *Soryu*	153
Kaga Sinks, *Akagi* Scuttled	154
Bombing Attack on *Yorktown*	155
Torpedo Attack on *Yorktown*	156
Attack on the *Hiryu*	158
Attack by *Hornet*'s Bombers on the *Tone* and *Chikuma*	159
B.17s attack Japanese Striking Force	159
Midway Aircraft Attempt Night Attack	161
M.T.B.s Attempt to Attack	162
The *Hiryu* Sinks	162

Chapter VI
Pursuit of the Enemy

Movements of the U.S. Force	163
Japanese Movements	164
Mogami Damaged; Japanese Abandon the Operation	166
I-168 Bombards Midway	167
Contact with the Enemy	167
Marine Aircraft Attacks *Mikuma* and *Mogami*	168
Attack on *Mikuma* and *Mogami* by B.17s	169
B.17s Attack *Tanikaze*	169
Carrier Aircraft Search for Japanese Striking Force	171
Attacks on Japanese Destroyers	172

Chapter VII
Last Contacts and Sinking of the *Yorktown*

Mikuma and *Mogami* Sighted	174
First Attack on *Mikuma* and *Mogami* by *Hornet* Group	175
Enterprise Group Attacks *Mikuma* and *Mogami*	175
Second Attack by *Hornet*'s Group; Sinking of *Mikuma*	176
B.17s Bomb *Grayling* in Error	177
Escape of the Japanese	177
Sinking of the *Yorktown* and *Hammann*	178

Chapter VIII
Lessons and Effects of the Battle

Experience Gained	180
Effects of the Battle	181

Appendices

Appendix A	183
Appendix B	188
Appendix C	191
Appendix D	197
Appendix E	219
Appendix F	220
Endnotes	226

U.S. NAVY AND ARMY AIRCRAFT

Navy

Types
- F2A *Buffalo*. Single engine fighter, manufactured by Brewster.
- F4F *Wildcat* (Br. *Martlet*). Single engine fighter, manufactured by Grumman.
- SBD *Dauntless*. Single engine scout bomber, manufactured by Douglas.
- SB2U *Vindicator* (Br. *Chesapeake*). Single engine scout bomber, manufactured by Vought-Sikorsky.
- PBY *Catalina*. Twin engine patrol bomber (flying boat), manufactured by Consolidated-Vultee.
- TBF *Avenger*. Single engine Navy torpedo bomber, manufactured by Grumman.

General terms
- VF   Fighter.
- VPB Patrol bomber.
- VSB Scout bomber.
- VTB Torpedo bomber.

Army

- B.17 Heavy bomber, 'Flying Fortress', originally manufactured by Boeing.
- B.26 Medium bomber, 'Marauder', originally manufactured by Martin.

Notes:-

Times in this Battle Summary are local (Zone + 12), *i.e.*, 12 hours slow on Greenwich. Dates are West longitude.

The various forces engaged in the battle kept, and employed in their reports, the following times, which have where necessary been converted to Z + 12.

U.S. (West Longitude Dates).	C.-in-C., Pacific Fleet	Z + 12
	Midway Island	Z + 12
	Midway aircraft	Z + 12 and G.C.T. (= G.M.T.)
	B.17s from Oahu	Z + 10 ½ (apparently) and G.C.T.
	Task Forces 16 & 17	Z + 10
Japanese (East Longitude Dates)	All Forces	Z – 9

Bearings and courses are true unless otherwise stated. The spelling of place names is in accordance with the Admiralty Sailing Directions.

Notes on Sources:-

The U.S. reports on the Battle of Midway are bound up in Admiralty Record Office Case W.H.S. 8401, as follows:–

> M.051642/42. *Official Report by C.-in-C., United States Pacific Fleet on the Battle of Midway, 3–6 June* 1942. The track chart of the battle (Enclosure (A)) is in R.O. Enclosure Box 557. The remaining Enclosures (B)–(F) are not forthcoming; these included the Report of C.T.F.17.
>
> M.051432/42. *Report by U.S. Marine Corps of Midway Battle, June 4–6, 1942.*
>
> M.051772/42. *Battle of Midway. Second Supplementary Report by C.-in-C., U.S. Pacific Fleet* forwarding the Report of the Commander Naval Base Air Defence, including that of the 7th Air Force; *Enterprise* air report; and summaries of the air operations in the battle.

U.S. Secret Information Bulletin No. 1, *Battle Experience from Pearl Harbor to Midway*, contains an account of the battle based on the report of the C.-in-C. U.S. Pacific Fleet with comments by the C.-in-C. U.S. Fleet.

A secondary source is the Combat Narrative entitled *Battle of Midway June* 306, 1942; prepared by the Office of Naval Intelligence, U.S. Navy.

Japanese information on the battle is fairly complete. The operations of the striking fleet are contained in *The Midway Operation B.I.O.S./Jap/Docs.*/1602 (N.I.D. 0052799/47), and in *C.-in-C. First Air Fleet detailed Battle Report No.* 6 which has been reprinted in the O.N.I. Review May 1947 (U.S. Office of Naval Intelligence). The operations of the Occupation Force are contained in records (orders, reports, etc.) of the seaplane carrier *Kamikawa Maru*, (U.S. *Central Intelligence Group Intelligence Report* 00-*W-6*, N.I.D. 4576/47).

In *The Campaigns of the Pacific War* (U.S. Govt. Printing Office, Washington: 1946), the U.S. Strategic Bombing Survey (Pacific), Naval Analysis Division, have prepared a short summary of the battle, based on the report of the C.-in-C. First Air Fleet and the O.N.I. Combat Narrative referred to above and the U.S. Interrogations (listed), which latter are published in the same series as *The Campaigns of the Pacific War* under the title *Interrogations of Japanese Officials* (Vols. I, II).

Situation After the Battle of Coral Sea

U.S. Inferiority in Carriers

After the Battle of the Coral Sea the Americans found themselves in a serious situation in the Pacific. It is true that a valuable base for the reconquest of New Guinea had been saved for the Allies, and there were indications that the Japanese had, temporarily at least, renounced any designs they might have had on Australia.

This was the interpretation which the Americans put on the absence from southern waters of Japanese warships other than occasional submarines, and a husbanding of Japanese air strength so marked that during the weeks following the battle the shore-based aircraft of the Allies delivered against enemy bases in the Solomons and New Guinea a total weight of attacks two or three times as heavy as those of the Japanese on Port Moresby and other Allied bases. But the victory had been dearly bought with the loss of one carrier and damage to a second so severe as might require a considerable period of repair and possibly even a visit to a West Coast Navy Yard; and in a region where the air was now clearly demonstrated to be of paramount importance the Americans found themselves outnumbered in the Pacific as to fleet aircraft carriers by two to one: with naval aircraft which the Battle of the Coral Sea had shown to be inferior in performance to those of the enemy; and with screening forces insufficient in number to enable their battleships to be operated in support of their carriers.

This was the difficult situation of the Americans in the Pacific during the lull following the repulse of the enemy attempt on Port Moresby. Most of the available carriers were in the South Pacific, as the Americans knew the Japanese were well aware; for although the *Enterprise* and *Hornet* which with their supporting cruisers and destroyers composed Task Force 16, had arrived too late to take part in the battle, they had been sighted by a Japanese reconnaissance aircraft in southern waters about the middle of May, a fact to which the immunity of Nauru and Ocean Islands[1] from occupation by the enemy was ascribed. With regard to the two carriers of Task Force 17, although the Japanese could have no certainty that the *Lexington* had sunk after the battle, they could not fail to be aware that both this carrier and the *Yorktown* had been damaged. The remainders of the air groups of these two carriers were on board the *Yorktown* and urgently in need of reorganisation and rest. The force had been at sea continuously since 16 February.

The only other important American naval force in the Pacific was Task Force 1 containing battleships and a small destroyer screen, which was on the west coast of the United States.

The concentration of United States naval strength in the South Pacific seemed to invite a blow against the U.S. positions in mid-Pacific, and when before long it became evident that Japan was concentrating her fleet for movements of major importance, the Americans correctly appreciated that Midway Island and the Aleutians would be the threatened areas.

The Objective, Midway

Midway (see Fig. 1), westernmost but one of the Hawaiian Islands, acts as a sentry for Hawaii, as the Commander-in-Chief of the Japanese First Air Fleet succinctly stated in his appreciation. Its importance as an American outpost was further enhanced after the seizure of Wake Island by the Japanese on Christmas Eve 1941. The Japanese intended to use it after capture as a base for long-range reconnaissance aircraft and submarines.

It consists of an atoll on which are two small islands, Eastern Island and Sand Island. There is anchorage for deep draught ships, and the islands could support an air force of about the size of a carrier group. They were defended by fixed defences.

About 56 miles westward of Midway Islands is the atoll Curé or Ocean Island, where the Japanese planned to establish a seaplane base.

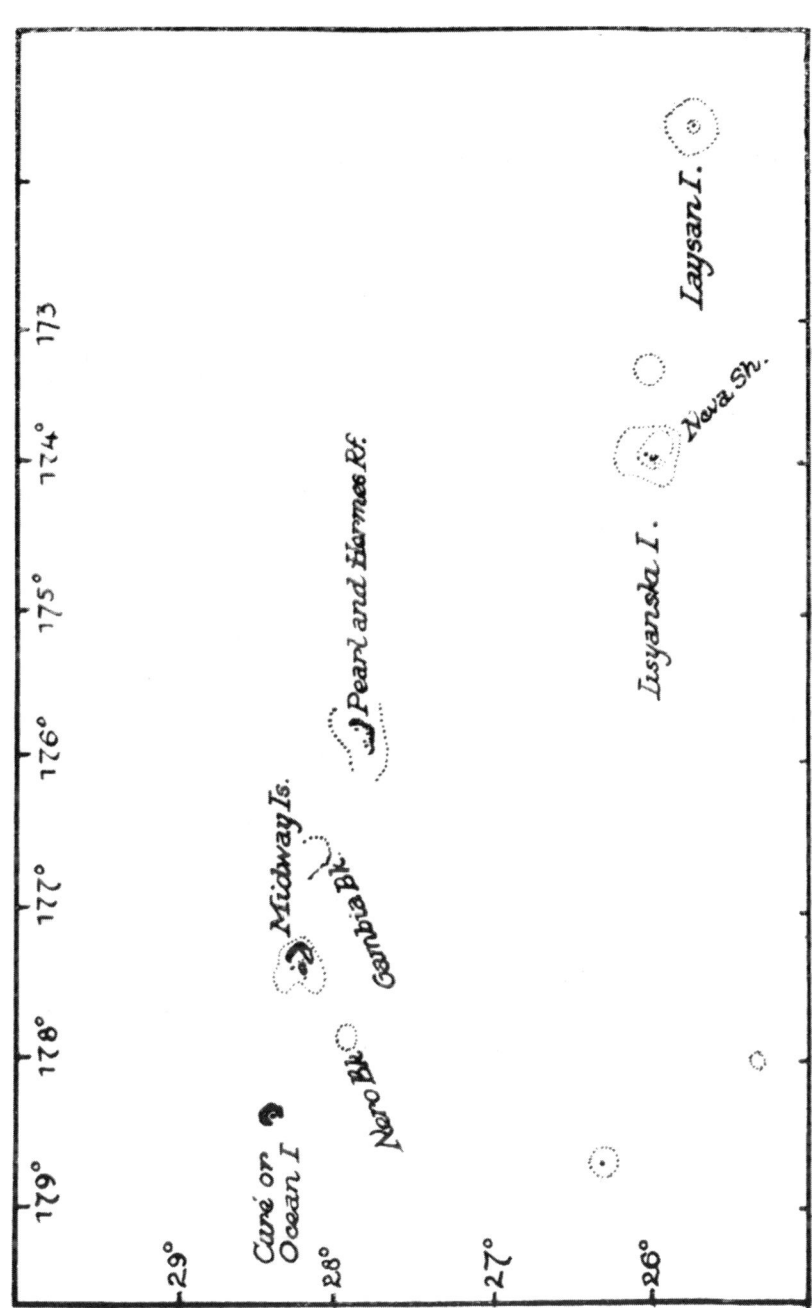

Fig. 1. Midway Islands.

Japanese Plan to Occupy Midway

The occupation of Midway Islands and establishment of a base in the Aleutians were an integral part of the plan of expansion of the defensive perimeter of which the seizure of Port Moresby was to have been the first instalment. Though foiled in the latter object, the Japanese refused, even in their secret reports, to regard the battle of 7/8 May as anything other than a victory for themselves; and certainly from a material point of view their losses were both lighter that those of the Allies and had proportionally far less effect on their all-important carrier strength.

Japanese intelligence of the disposition of the American carriers was far from complete. They knew of the presence of the *Enterprise* and *Hornet* in the Pacific, and placed them in the Hawaiian area.[2] They believed the *Ranger* was in the Atlantic, but could get no reliable information as to the whereabouts of the *Wasp*. Some of the prisoners taken in the Battle of the Coral Sea stated that the *Lexington* had been sunk, though others claimed that she was under repair on the west coast of the United States. The two or three American auxiliary (escort) carriers which were placed in the Pacific were known to be slow and were not considered by the Japanese to be capable of effective employment in offensive operations. The Japanese did not expect that the Americans had any powerful unit, built round aircraft carriers, in the neighbourhood of Midway.

A sortie by the American naval forces in the Hawaii area, in the event of an attack on Midway, was expected. The strength of these forces was estimated as follows:–

Aircraft carriers	2 to 3
Escort carriers	2 to 3
Battleships	2
Cruisers	7 to 9
Light cruisers	4
Destroyers	about 30
Submarines	25

Unburdened with the problem of two-ocean warfare the Japanese felt no doubts as to their ability to defeat this or any other force with which the Allies might be able to counter-attack.

The reinforcement of the air strength of Midway which was undertaken by the Americans after the Battle of the Coral Sea, did not escape the notice of the Japanese, who made a fairly close estimate of the American air forces on the island, as follows:–

Reconnaissance flying boats	2 squadrons
Army bombers	1 squadron
Fighters	1 squadron

(The actual strength is given in Appendix B.)

They believed that strict air patrols were maintained both day and night to a distance of about 500 to 600 miles from Midway and that about three fighters were kept over the islands at all times. Air reconnaissance was believed to be conducted mainly to the west and to the south, and to be less strict to the north-west and north. It was also thought that patrols by surface vessels were maintained, with submarines active to the west.

Air strength in the Hawaii area, which could be used for the speedy reinforcement of Midway, was estimated at the following:–

Flying boats	about 60
Bombers	about 100
Fighters	about 200

It was considered that combat air patrols and ships' A.A. fire could deal successfully with any attempt to counter-attack by U.S. shore-based aircraft.

Midway was believed to be very strongly defended, with powerful fixed defences and high angle guns, and a garrison of marines. The Japanese intended to land on Curé, Eastern and Sand Islands.

Organisation of the Japanese Expedition

The Japanese force for the M.I. (Midway) Operation comprised the main strength of the Japanese Combined Fleet and was organised in three groups; the Main Body, Striking Force, and Occupation Force, under the command of Admiral I. Yamamoto.

Occupation Force. Midway Island is very small, and no more than six transports were needed to carry the special naval landing force, consisting of some 1,500 marines for Sand Island and 1,000 Army troops for Eastern

Island, together with engineers and ancillary units. Two sea-plane carriers conveyed the 11th Air Flotilla which was to establish the seaplane base at Curé Island. Close escort of this transport unit was carried out by the 2nd Destroyer Flotilla, consisting of the light cruiser *Jintsu*, flagship of Rear-Admiral R. Tanaka who commanded the unit and its close escort, and 11 destroyers. A tanker was in company.

The assault forces apparently were ill-supplied with landing boats. They carried many different kinds, but were not sanguine as to the ability of most of them to cross the reefs, in which case rubber boats were supposed to be used.

Distant cover for the force was provided by the 2nd Fleet, formed at this date by part of the 3rd Battle Squadron (*Kongo*–flagship of Vice-Admiral Kondo, Commander-in-Chief of the Occupation Force–and *Hiyei)*, the 4th Cruiser Squadron (*Atago* and *Maya),* 5th Cruiser Squadron *(Myoko* and *Haguro)* and the 4th Destroyer Flotilla (light cruiser *Yura* and seven destroyers). A supply group and tankers accompanied the 2nd Fleet. The four cruisers of the 7th Cruiser Squadron (*Kumano*, Flagship of Rear-Admiral T. Kurita, *Suzuya, Mikuma* and *Mogami)* constituted a fast support force which took up a position between 75 and 100 miles ahead of the transports during the approach to Midway. It was intended that this force should shell Midway prior to the landing.[3]

Striking Force. The landing on Midway Island was to be preceded by an air attack carried out from the four carriers *Akagi* (flagship of Admiral C. Nagumo, Commander-in-Chief 1st Air Fleet), *Kaga, Hiryu* and *Soryu*, which had also the dual role of attacking the U.S. Fleet if located, and supporting the invasion force. The carriers were supported by the 2nd Division of the 3rd Battle Squadron (*Haruna* and *Kirishima),* 8th Cruiser Squadron *(Tone* and *Chikuma),* and the 10th Destroyer Flotilla (light cruiser *Nagara* and 16 destroyers). Two supply groups accompanied the force, which was under the command of Admiral Nagumo.

Main Body. A powerful force under Admiral I. Yamamoto, Commander-in-Chief Combined Fleet, consisting of the 1st and 2nd Battle Squadrons (three and four battleships respectively), the 9th Cruiser Squadron (two cruisers) and the 3rd Destroyer Flotilla (light cruiser *Sendai* and 12 destroyers), together with the light carrier *Zuiho* and two supply groups, was in support.

Operations of the Japanese Submarines[4] (Fig. 2)

In connection with the Midway Operation the Japanese intended to carry out a reconnaissance of Pearl Harbor by submarines of the 6th Fleet based on French Frigate Shoal, half-way between Midway and Honolulu, about the end of May.[5] However, when the submarines arrived at French Frigate Shoal they found that the Americans were using it as a seaplane base, and the plan had to be abandoned.

French Frigate Shoal was also to have been a land-based aircraft refuelling station and two submarines of the 13th Submarine Flotilla *(I-121, I-123)* carried supplies of aviation spirit to refuel aircraft of the 24th Air Flotilla which had the duty of giving air cover and carrying out reconnaissance from the Marshall Islands during the operation. This plan, too, had to be abandoned.

The submarines reported by radio the changed situation at French Frigate Shoal, and proceeded to carry out a patrol between the Shoal and Midway, keeping to the southward of Lisyanski Island.

In the hope of intercepting the U.S. Fleet a patrol was established by submarines of the 3rd Flotilla off Hawaii and of the 5th Flotilla between Midway and Hawaii. Only one of these boats encountered any ships. This was *I-168*, which was ordered by wireless to search for a damaged aircraft carrier, and on 7 June discovered and sank the damaged *Yorktown*. This submarine, whose patrol line ran close to Midway, kept the Commander-in-Chief informed as to the air strength and absence of U.S. surface craft at the island, and reconnoitred and reported on Curé Island, and at 0130/5 it shelled Midway.

Two submarines of the 3rd Flotilla were stationed in the Hawaii area on life-saving duty. Japanese aircraft were unable to communicate direct with the submarines.

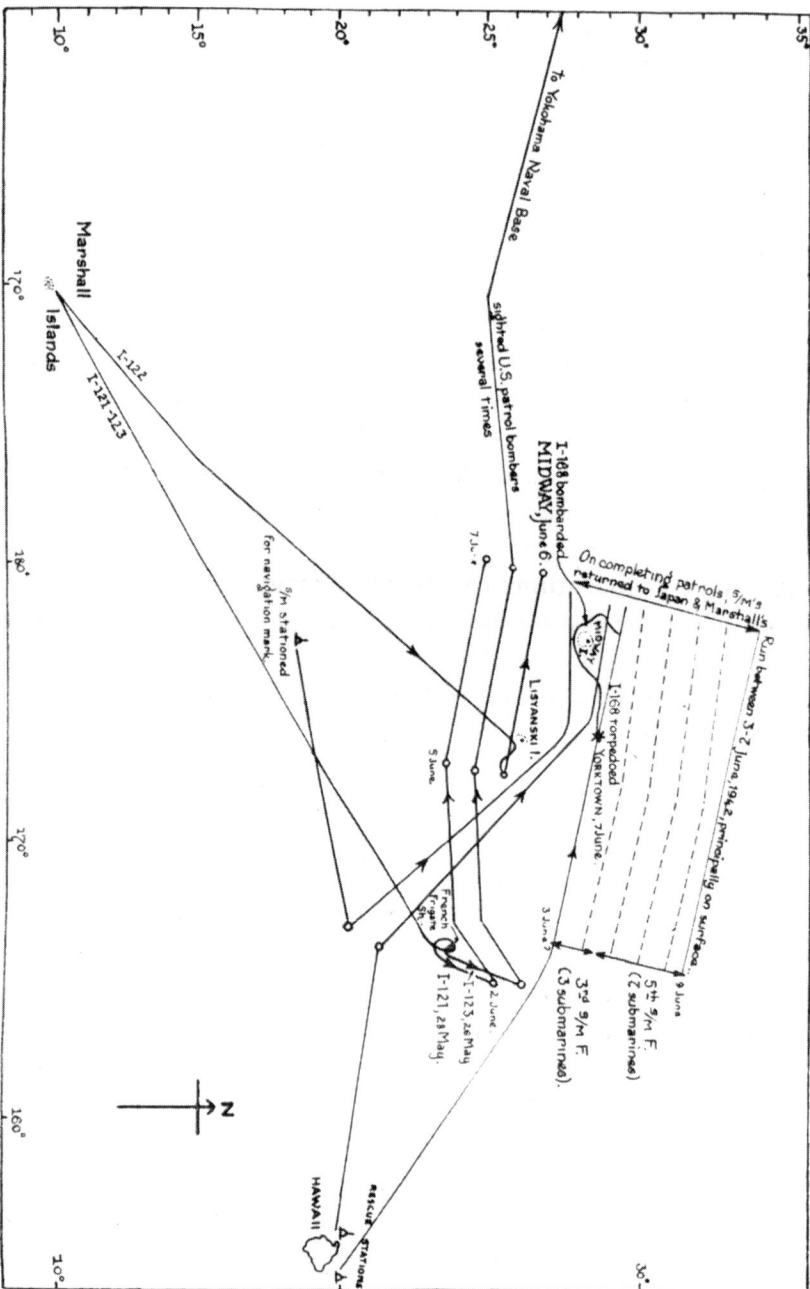

Fig 2. Tracks of Japanese submarines, 3–7 June.

The Aleutian Diversion

Intimately connected with the Midway operation and acting as a diversion for Operation M.I. the Japanese planned an attack on the Aleutians, Operation A.L. This was carried out by a small but powerful force consisting of two aircraft carriers, two heavy cruisers, and three destroyers, termed the Second Mobile Force or Second Task Force.

On 3 June (West longitude date), the day before the carrier attack on Midway, an air attack was carried out on Dutch Harbour, followed on 6 and 7 June respectively by the occupation of Kiska and Attu.

The Americans appreciated the likelihood of an attack on their Aleutian bases concurrently with an operation against Midway. To meet the threat, a new Task Force 8 was formed out of the five cruisers and four destroyers which were the only spare ships within reach. This was despatched to reinforce the sea frontier forces being assembled in the Alaskan area.

Japanese Preparations for the Operation

The carriers detailed for the Midway operation returned to their home ports from the raid on Ceylon, on 22 and 23 April, and immediately set about repair and maintenance and urgently needed flight training.

During the operations which had lasted for more than five months there had been a considerable turn-over in flight personnel, and there was time for no more than basic training for most of the airmen. Some experienced flyers had lost much of their skill. Only one carrier was available for take-off and landing drills. The Commander-in-Chief of the Japanese 1st Air Fleet, in his Battle Report, paints a picture of rudimentary conditions of training almost incredible in a power which had presumed to challenge the might of the United States. Inexperienced flyers barely reached the point where they could make daytime landings on carriers, and only the more experienced pilots carried out about one dusk landing apiece. No opportunity was available for joint training, thus precluding co-ordinated action between contact units, illumination units, and attack units. Consequently, night attacks were practically ruled out. There was no opportunity for bomber leaders to participate in formation level bombing drills. The only target ship, the old battleship *Settsu*, was limited to waters in the western Inland Sea, causing waste of time by flyers in coming and going, to the prejudice both of their dive-bombing and of their basic training. Even this minimum practice could not be conducted satisfactorily since the men were kept busy with maintenance work. In air combat tactics only the more experienced got further than lone air combat training and even they were limited to about a three-plane formation. Only the fundamentals of night flying were learnt by the inexperienced.

The need for replacements and transfers of personnel had greatly lowered the fighting efficiency of the ships of the striking force. Maintenance and repair work went on until a few days before departure, which affected the men's efficiency. The ships did not assemble from their home ports until a few days before the scheduled date for sortie, and the squadron as a whole had no opportunity to carry out joint drills. Limitations in time prevented satisfactory training in group formations. This was particularly true of the newly formed 10th Destroyer Flotilla, some of the units of which underwent training as A.A. screening ships, others as A.S. screens; but the squadron as a whole had no opportunity to carry out joint drills.

Organisation of the U.S. Forces

The Americans were well aware that if their appreciation of a Japanese intention to attack Midway was correct, the situation was most serious. Midway was unable to defend itself without support; their carriers were far away, and perhaps only two would be fit in time to fight. Task Force 17 had already been recalled to Pearl Harbor for replenishment and for repair of the *Yorktown*. Task Force 16 was now immediately ordered north; it arrived at Pearl Harbor on 26 May and sailed on 28 May under Rear-Admiral R. A. Spruance, for a rendezvous north-east of Midway. Task Force 17 reached the base on 27 May and excellent work by the Navy Yard, the Service Force, and supporting services placed the *Yorktown* and her aircraft in reasonable fighting condition in three days; and the force sailed on 30 May for the rendezvous, under Rear-Admiral F. J. Fletcher.

Task Forces 16 and 17 made rendezvous at 1530 on 2 June as arranged in 32° 04' N., 172° 45' E., about 350 miles north-east of Midway, having fuelled at sea en route; and the combined force, under the command of Rear-Admiral Fletcher, moved to an area of operations north of Midway, Task Force 16 operating about 10 miles to the southward of Task Force 17.

Task Force 17 contained now the single carrier *Yorktown*, two heavy cruisers, and five destroyers. The *Yorktown*'s aircraft were made up by the addition of squadrons from the *Saratoga*, to a total of 36 scout bombers, 12 torpedo bombers, and 25 fighters. The *Enterprise* and *Hornet* in Task Force

16 each carried 35 scout bombers, 14 torpedo bombers, and 27 fighters. The lesson of the Battle of the Coral Sea, when the American fighters were outnumbered at every encounter, had resulted in a 50 per cent increase in the number of fighters borne, bringing them to numerical equality with the Japanese, ship for ship.

Consideration was given to the employment of Task Force 1 in the defence of Midway. It was not moved out from U.S. waters, however, because of the undesirability of diverting to its screen any units which could add to the long range striking power of Task Forces 16 and 17 against the enemy carriers; and events proved that none of the air units which were employed could have been spared from the purpose for which it was used.

The Commander-in-Chief, United States Fleet, Admiral E. J. King, believed that the Japanese plans were designed to trap a portion of the U.S. fleet. For this reason he gave orders that only strong attrition tactics were to be employed, and that the U.S. carriers and cruisers were not to be unduly risked. This, and the fact that the Americans were defending a fixed point against a superior enemy force, dictated the American tactics.

A submarine cordon was established to cover the approaches to Midway on an arc from 240 degrees to 000 degrees (see plan 1) on 3/4 June. Six submarines patrolled sectors of the 150 miles circle[6] and three were stationed on the 200 miles circle from Midway.[7] The *Flying Fish* and *Cachalot* were on station patrols some 60 miles north-north-west and north-west of Midway respectively, and the *Cuttlefish* 700 miles west of Midway. Three were placed in support on the 800 mile circle north west of Oahu,[8] and four 300 miles north of that island,[9] and the last ones to become available on the 100 miles circle from Oahu. Nineteen of the 26 submarines in the Central Pacific, all that could reach the Oahu–Midway area by 3 June, were employed, the consequent cessation of their offensive patrols being accepted.

Admiral C. W. Nimitz, Commander-in-Chief, United States Pacific Fleet, retained in his own hands the broad tactical direction of all forces in the Midway area.

Preparations at Midway

Measures were taken to strengthen Midway to the maximum extent possible.

The problem at Midway for the Americans was to hit the enemy before they were hit. The danger against which they had to guard was that their aircraft might be surprised on the ground and destroyed, and their runways put temporarily out of action by bombing, before the enemy was damaged. There were two essential requirements to prevent this; effective search and long-range striking power.

For long-range search 30 Navy patrol bombers (Catalinas) were sent to the island and for long range strikes 17 B.17s of the Seventh Air Force and four Army B.26s fitted with torpedoes were sent to Midway from Hawaii, in spite of the difficulty of protecting these aircraft on the ground. Major-General C. L. Tinker, U.S. Army, Commander of the Army Air Force in Hawaii, himself came to the scene of action.[10] To provide close-in air striking power the marine air group was brought up to a strength of 28 fighters and 34 scout bombers,[11] though only 30 pilots were available for the latter type. This group was augmented by six new Navy torpedo bombers. Because of overcrowding of the facilities at Midway there was considerable interchange between that island and Hawaii, so that the number of aircraft available varied from day to day. The figures given above were those for 3 June. The radio and communication personnel at Midway were reinforced for the control of the additional aircraft.

All Navy and Army aircraft sent to Midway, and all B.17s of the 7th Bomber Command whose duties involved landing on or basing at Midway, operated under the control of the Commanding Officer, Naval Air Station, Midway, Captain C. T. Simard; but there was no co-ordinating authority for the operations of the aircraft based at Midway and those of the U.S. carriers respectively; moreover, the carriers normally operated under conditions of radio silence.

In the belief that the Japanese planned a rendezvous about 700 miles west of Midway B.17s flew searches to a distance of 800 miles on 31 May and 1 June, and on 2 June a B.17 without bombs searched 800 miles to the west without making any contacts. From 30 May to 3 June Catalinas searched 700 miles from bearing 200 degrees through west to 020 degrees.[12] Cover was good except beyond 300 miles to the north and north-west, where visibility was very poor.[13] It was precisely this area of low visibility and fog that concealed the approaching Japanese carriers from the Americans for some 30 hours, until they came within 650 miles of Midway.

On account of this unsearched area it was thought possible the enemy would escape detection on the day before reaching attacking range if they approached from that direction, though it was appreciated that the same weather would no doubt affect accuracy of navigation and prevent the

Japanese from launching a night attack. It was thought that on passing from the bad weather area early in the morning they would fix their position at dawn before sending off an attack. This would occur between 0430 and 0500, and Midway could consequently expect to be attacked about 0600. In the event, the American appreciation was correct: Midway was attacked at 0630.

To counter the threat of dawn attack, search aircraft were sent off as early as possible each day, usually about 0415. To safeguard them from destruction and to ensure that a striking force would be available immediately if a target was located, the B.17s took off directly afterwards. They remained in the air for about four hours, by which time the progress of the search and the reduction of their fuel load rendered landing possible and desirable. The four B.26s, the six TBFs and the other aircraft remained on the ground but fully alert until the search had reached a distance of 400 miles.

The garrison of Midway was increased to the maximum. The Marine Sixth Defence Battalion was reinforced by part of the Second Raider Battalion, with special equipment for opposing a mechanised landing, and by the A.A. and Special Weapons Group of the Third Defence Battalion. The troops worked day and night to strengthen the defences of the islands. Underwater obstacles were installed and anti-tank and anti-personnel mines planted.

For the local defence of Midway Motor Torpedo Boat Squadron One, consisting of 11 M.T.B.s, was sent from Hawaii and placed under the direction of the Commanding Officer, Midway. These boats assisted in meeting the enemy air attack on the islands and carried out rescue work of airmen down at sea. Rescue boats were also stationed at Pearl-Hermes-Lisyanski, Gardner, Laysan, and Necker Islands in the Hawaii Group.

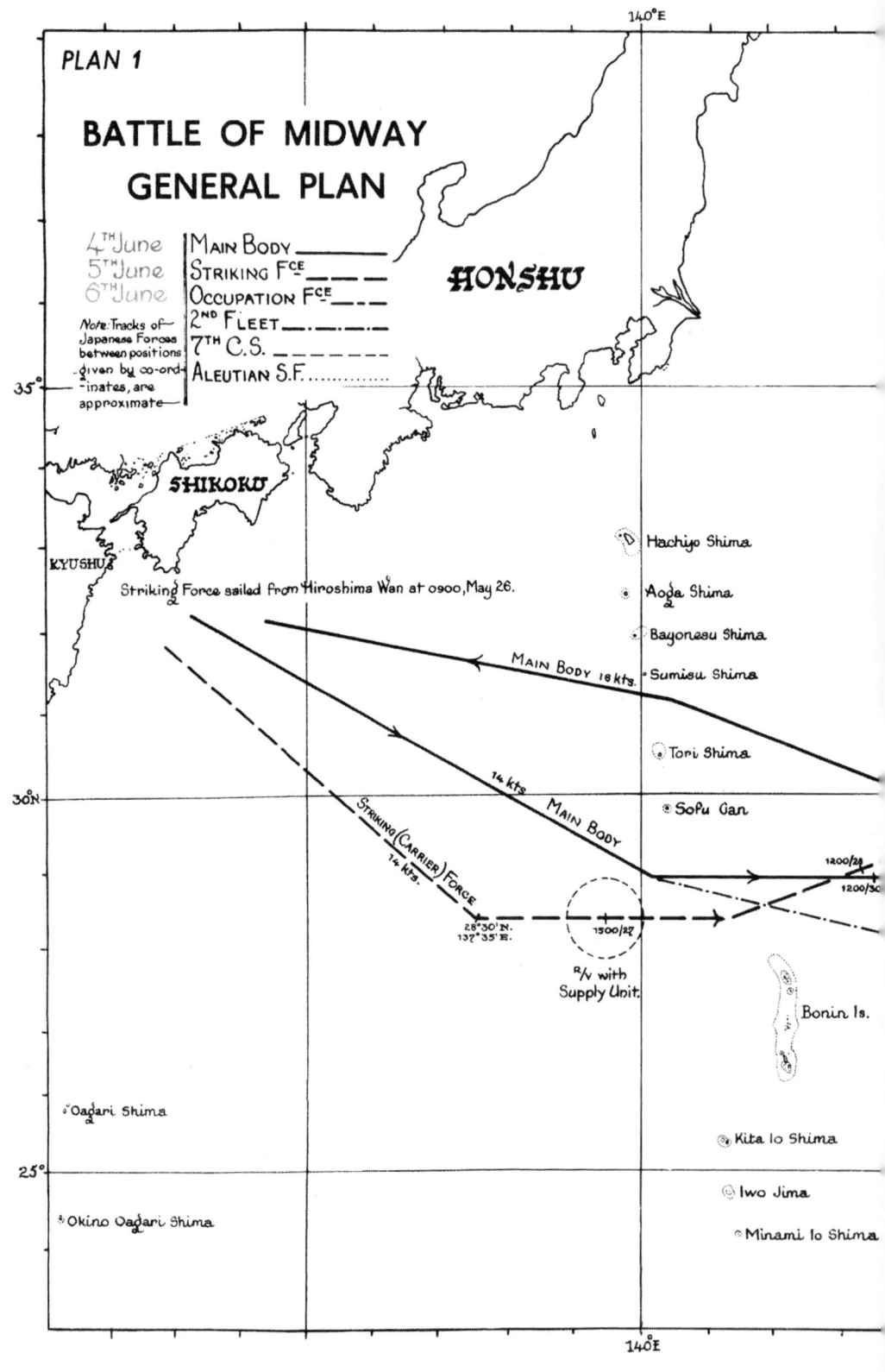

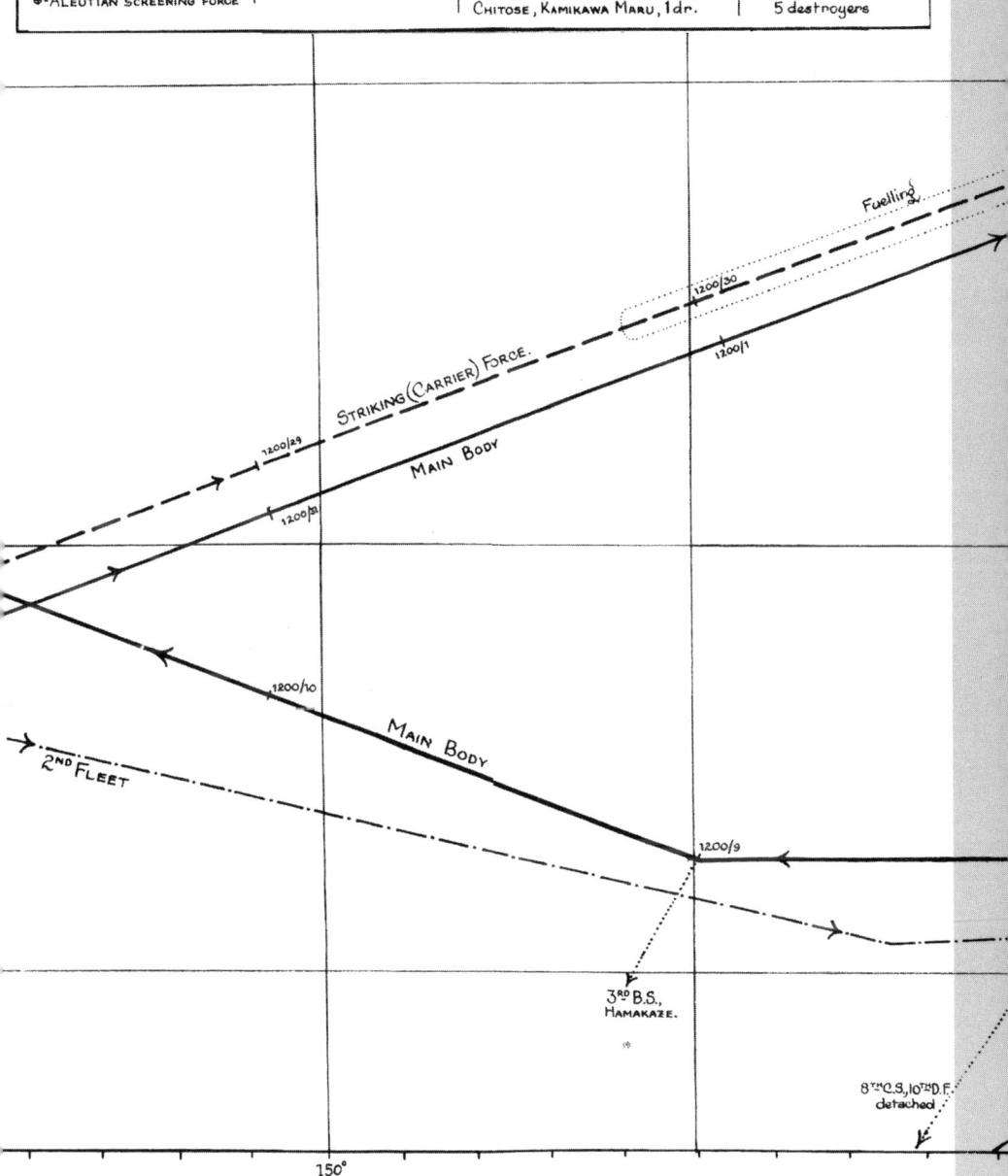

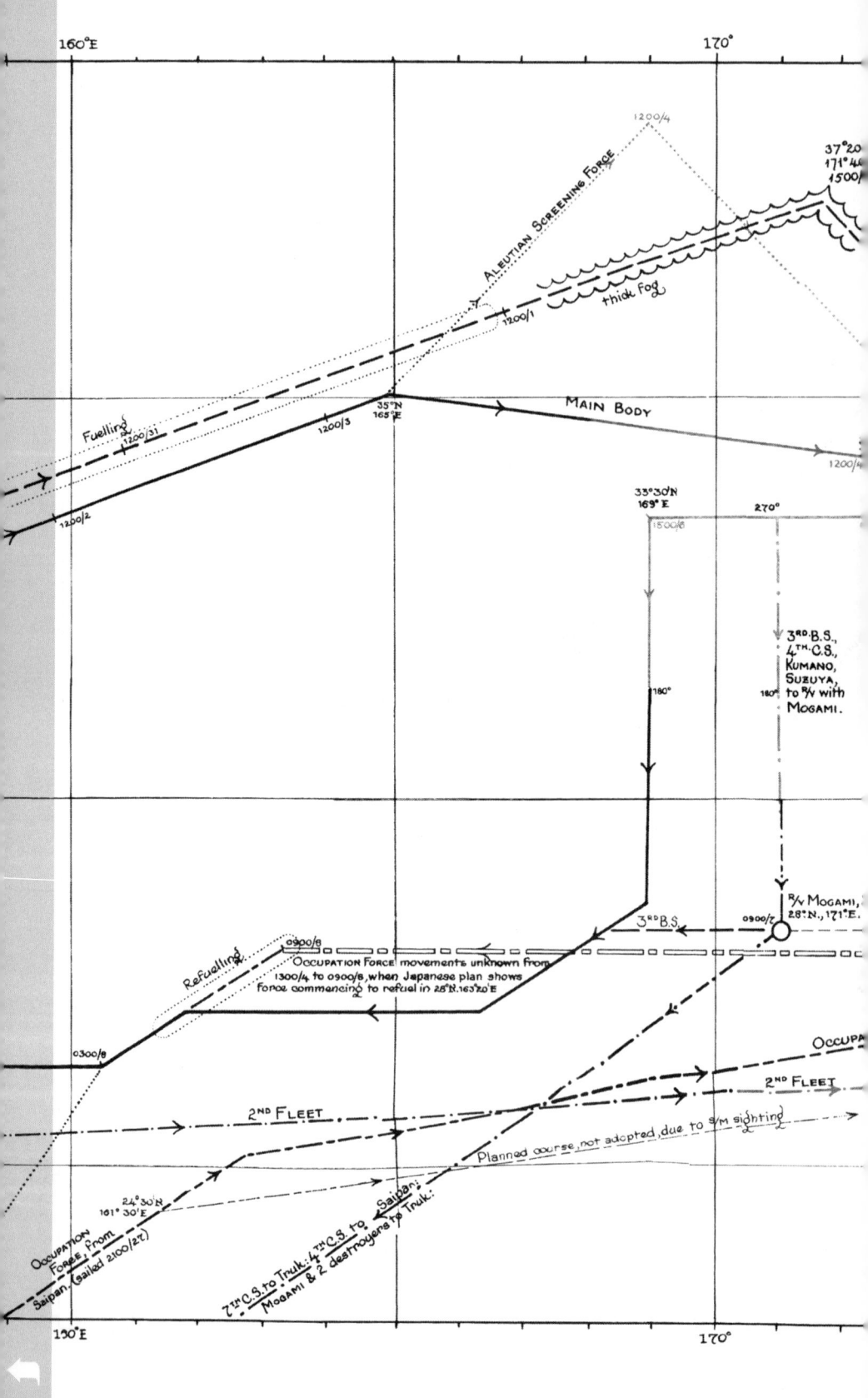

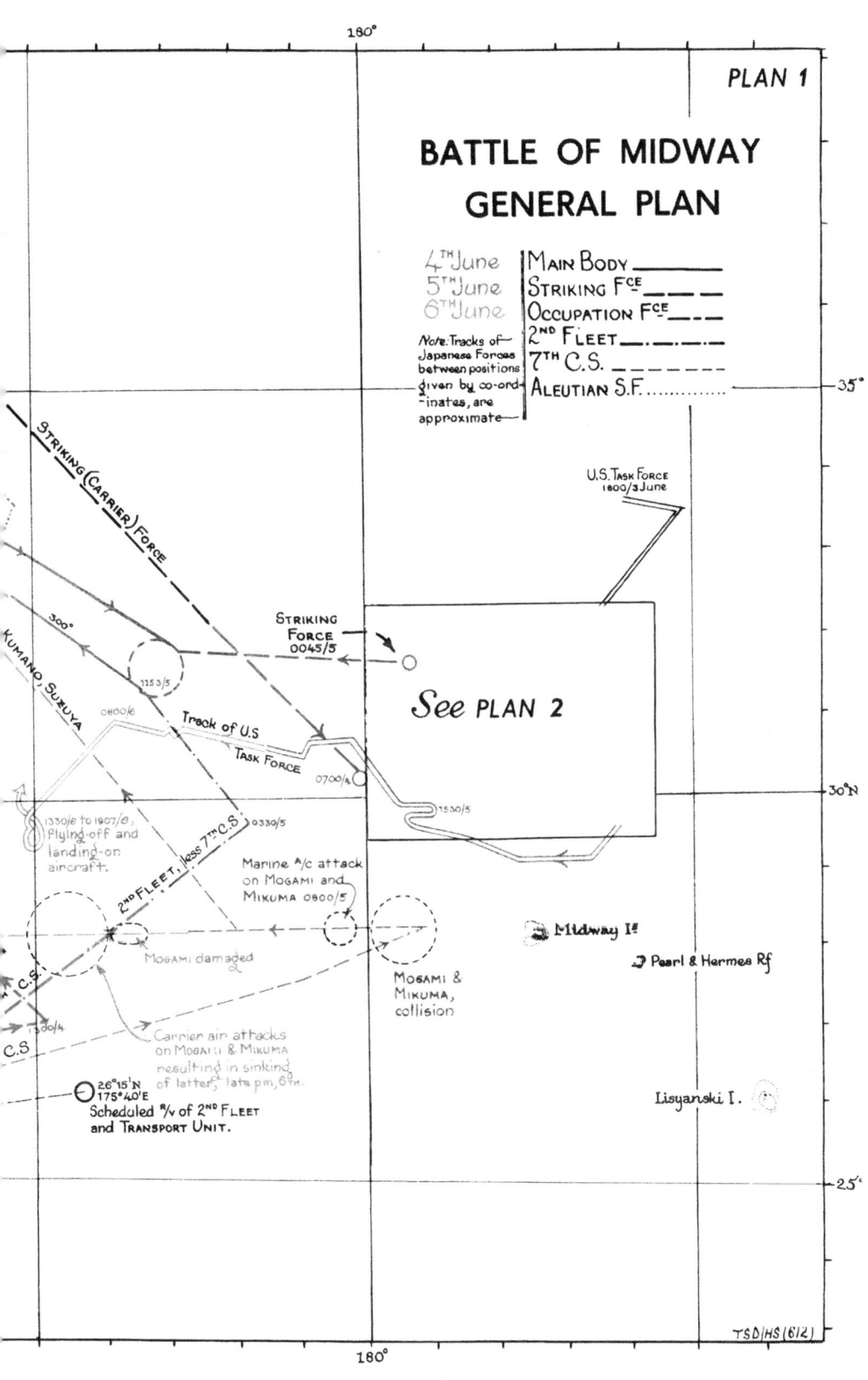

Preliminary Movements

Japanese Expedition Sails (Plan 1)

The striking force sailed from Hashira Jima in Hiroshima Wan (Inland Sea) at 0900 on 26 May (Z + 12). The supply unit was met at 1500 on 27 May in about 28° 30' N., 139° 30' E., and the force turned north-eastward and headed for the area to the north-west of Midway. The ships fuelled at sea on 31 May and 1 June. Visibility steadily decreased from about 1300 on 1 June, so that fuelling had to be broken off before all ships had completed. By 1400/1 the force was completely closed in by fog. Course was altered to the south-eastward at 1630 on 2 June in 37° 20' N. 171° 40' E., for the run down towards Midway, but visual signalling was impossible and radio silence had to be broken at 1300, the orders for alteration of course being made on long wave. By the morning of 3 June, however, surface visibility had improved greatly, though there were scattered clouds overhead.

The main body was apparently about 30 hours astern of the carriers and took a shorter route towards the operating area. At 1500 on 3 June in 35° N., 165° E., Admiral Yamamoto detached a considerable portion of his force, termed the Aleutian Screening Force, to screen him to the northward. Simultaneously, the main body altered course to the eastward, to be within supporting distance of the carriers coming down from the north. The Aleutian screening force steered to the northeastward till 1200/4, when it altered course to rejoin, though it did not make junction until the operation had been abandoned and all detachments had turned for home.

The reinforced Second Fleet (distant cover and screening force for the Occupation Force) sailed from the Inland Sea with the main body and continued to the south-eastward to close the transport unit at the appointed rendezvous in 26° 15' N., 175° 40' E., when the main body turned north-easterly.

The transport unit with its close escort sailed from the Inland Sea and was serviced at Saipan whence it sailed at 2100 on 27 May with the intention of assaulting Midway from the south. Passing west of Tinian, it picked up some of the slowest transports[14] which had sailed from Eniwetok, the westernmost of the Marshall Islands, and proceeded towards the rendezvous with the Second Fleet, in 26° 15' N., 175° 40' E. Owing to a submarine report, however, the unit, which should have altered course to the eastward when in 24° 30' N., 161° 30' E., continued on course 058 degrees until reaching the 165 degrees meridian in 26° 30' N. The naval units zigzagged, but the transports, unless under attack, steered a steady course at their maximum speed of 10 knots. Air cover was given by the 24th Air Flotilla from the Marshall Islands and the 26th from Marcus Island.

Occupation Force Sighted

The air searches which had been carried out from Midway for the past few days were rewarded on 3 June. On that day the usual search was made. By 0430 all aircraft fit for service were in the air, in order to clear the runways. As on the previous days, coverage was good except beyond 400 miles to the north-north-west. A few hours later reports began to be received at the island from the Catalinas, indicating that an enemy surface force was approaching from a bearing of 265 degrees. This was the Japanese Occupation Force.

First contact was made with the transport unit at 0904 by an American patrol bomber which reported two cargo ships in 25° 08' N., 174° 30' E. At 0924 a large number of ships, later reported as 11, was sighted by a Navy patrol aircraft bearing 261 degrees, distant 700 miles from Midway, steering an easterly course at 10 knots.[15] Several smaller groups of ships were reported about the same time and were correctly interpreted as belonging to the Occupation Force and its escort, converging on a rendezvous for the final advance on Midway.

The reporting Catalina was ordered to return to base on account of shortage of fuel and the probability of its being shot down if it attempted to shadow;[16] and at 1230 a special long-range B.17, which it was thought could look after itself, with no bombs, but with a Naval observer on board, took off to shadow the enemy forces now reported 500–600 miles S.W. of Midway, and to direct a striking force out.[17] The B.17 sighted only two transports and two destroyers bearing 261 degrees distance 700 miles at 1640.

B.17s Attack Transport Unit (Fig. 3)

None of the sighting reports included the enemy carriers,[18] consequently the Commanding Officer of the Midway defence forces was unwilling to commit his long-range striking force of B.17s pending the receipt of more definite news. About noon the enemy reports crystallised into positive information, and at 1230 the striking force of nine of the 17 B.17s of the Seventh Air Force at Midway was despatched to attack.

Interception was effected at 1623 of a force reported bearing 265 degrees 570 miles from Midway. The actual position was probably about 60 miles further to the south-eastward, viz., approximately 26½° N., 17½° E.[19] The bombers estimated the force to contain five battleships, cruisers or destroyers with about 40 transports and cargo ships, but in point of fact no battleships or cruisers (other than the light cruiser *Jintsu*) were present, for the enemy that had been sighted was the Occupation Force and its close escort; and the particular formation which the bombers attacked comprised the transport unit, viz., six transports and the tanker *Akebono Maru* escorted by the *Jintsu* and six destroyers, proceeding in the formation shown in Fig. 3. The seaplane carriers had quitted the force about 1½ hours earlier and proceeded at 17 knots for Curé Island, and if they were sighted they were apparently not recognised for what they were.

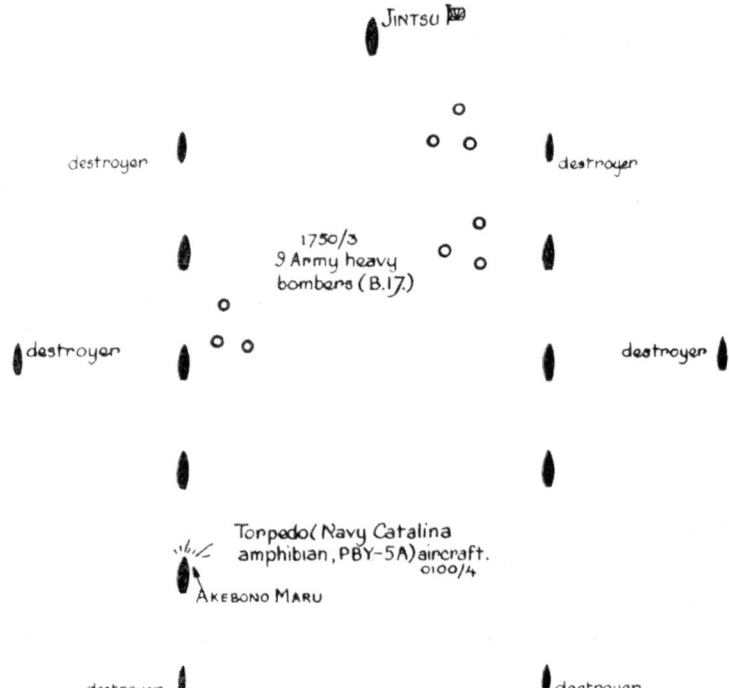

Fig. 3. Air attacks on Japanese transport unit, 3/4 June.

The B.17s were loaded with demolition bombs, seven with 4 x 600 lb. and two with 4 x 500 lb. They carried out a high level horizontal bombing attack in flights of three aircraft at altitudes of 8,000 and 10,000 and 17,000 feet respectively, dropping their bombs with 1/10 seconds delay. Three 500 lb. failed to release.[20] No enemy aircraft opposed them, but at the bomb release line very heavy but inaccurate anti-aircraft fire was encountered throughout the attack. Bursts were from 5,000 to 18,000 feet, but in this as in practically all future attacks in the battle the fire was mainly behind the attacking aircraft, none of which was hit.

The attack came as a surprise to the enemy, who were not fitted with radar, and their first warning was when the first bombs fell. Nevertheless, the A.A. fire they put up was so heavy that the bombers did not consider it wise to remain in the area for close observation. They estimated the damage caused as follows:–

- 1 heavy cruiser or battleship hit, burning.
- 1 transport hit, burning.
- 1 heavy cruiser believed hit at the stern, no evidence of damage except some smoke from the stern.

The attack demonstrated the relative ineffectiveness of high level horizontal bombing against ships which retain speed and manoeuvrability, for the Japanese reported that no ship was hit and no bomb fell nearer than 200 yards, despite the fact that the transports steered a steady course without zigzagging until it was recognised that they were under attack.

The B.17 flights returned individually to Midway, landing at 2040. On that day, as throughout the operation, owing to the lack of space at Midway and the short time available for preparation the Seventh Air Force crews had had to reservice their own aircraft and carry out essential maintenance, and as a result in some cases they went into the air in an exhausted condition.

Night Attack on Transport Unit by Patrol Bombers   (Fig. 3)

At 2115 four Navy patrol bombers (Catalinas), three of which had flown from Pearl Harbor, a ten-hour flight, that afternoon, were despatched to make a night torpedo attack on the Japanese force approaching from the westward. The night was clear, with broken cumulus clouds at 1,000 feet. The third and fourth aircraft were lost from the formation in passing through cloud about 2400 and 0100 hours respectively, though one of them succeeded in finding the target alone and attacking, but the other turned back and eventually landed in the sea near Lisyanski Island, short of fuel, the crew being rescued 53 hours later.

At about 0015/4 radar indicated a group of some ten ships 10 or 12 miles to port of the group, and soon the silhouettes of, apparently, ten or more large ships (actually seven or eight including the *Jintsu*) in two columns, escorted by six destroyers became visible in the moonlight. This was the transport unit which had been attacked by B.17s during the afternoon, and the reported position was about 261 degrees 500 miles from Midway. There were indications of another large group nearby, close to Midway.

The attackers approached down moon with engines throttled back. At 100 feet altitude the leader launched his torpedo at 800 yards range at the largest ship, which was leading the northern column. The second aircraft dropped his torpedo at 200 yards and opened machine-gun fire on his target, causing some casualties. The result was not observed, but it was apparently this torpedo which made the only hit obtained in the attack; it struck the tanker *Akebono Maru* forward, killing 11 men and wounding 13; but the damage merely caused the tanker to slow down, and she was able to keep with the unit, and was capable of 13 knots after the battle.[21] The third aircraft found the target visually; he was attacked by a fighter directly after releasing his torpedo, and escaped in the clouds. The Americans estimated that one transport or cargo ship has been sunk and one severely damaged. 'This night attack by Catalinas was a daring and historical feat,' wrote the Commander-in-Chief, U.S. Pacific Fleet in his Report.

The three patrol bombers returned from the attack individually, and landed at Laysan, being warned by radio that Midway Island was under air attack.

At 0700 the *Cuttlefish* reported contact with an enemy tanker bearing 260 degrees 600 miles from Midway. Commander Submarines Pacific Fleet ordered her to shadow, but she was forced down and lost contact. Two hours later all submarines were given the position, course and speed of the Occupation Force, as reported by aircraft, and were ordered to close the enemy. This attack on the Japanese transport force was the prelude to the Battle of Midway itself which may be taken as beginning at dawn on 4 June. The battle fell into three well-defined phases:–

(a) Air attack on Midway Island by the Japanese striking force and attempts of the Midway shore-based aircraft to halt the enemy advance (0430–0830, 4 June).
(b) Sinking of the four carriers of the Japanese striking force by U.S. carrier-borne aircraft, and Japanese counter-attacks on the *Yorktown* (0900–1800, 4 June).
(c) Attacks on the defeated Japanese during their withdrawal, by U.S. shore-based and carrier-borne aircraft (5–6 June).

These successive phases of the battle will be described in the following chapters.

Air Attack on Midway

Japanese Attack Group Takes Off from Carriers

While the Occupation Force was approaching Midway from the westward the Japanese striking force, 650 miles to the northward, had altered course to the south-eastward at 1630 on 2 June in 37° 15' N., 171° 07' E. From 1500/2 to 1500/3, however, only some 220 miles were made good, and consequently the force never emerged from the unsearched area of low visibility during the daylight hours of 3 June (see Plan 1). Some doubtful sightings of American aircraft were made by the force in the evening and early part of the night of 3/4 June, causing fighters to take off from the *Akagi* at 1940/3, whilst at 2330 ships went to action stations, in each case for false alarms.

At dawn on 4 June the Japanese forces were converging on Midway Island according to plan, their striking force about to fly off its air groups to attack the island from a position some 230 miles to the north-westward. About 200 miles to the north-east of this force was the American carrier force, steering to the south-west. Neither carrier force had been located by its opponents, and the Japanese were unaware of the strength the Americans had been able to concentrate. The Americans knew the approximate position of the Japanese transport force, and the attacks of the night before had revealed to the Japanese that they could not hope for tactical surprise. On Midway Island, all aircraft were standing by and the dawn reconnaissance was just taking off.

At 0430 on 4 June, an attack group of 36 naval fighters, 36 bombers, and 35 torpedo aircraft (armed with bombs), made up as follows:– *Hiryu* – 17 torpedo, 9 fighters; *Soryu* – 18 torpedo, 9 fighters; *Akagi* – 9 fighters, 18 bombers; *Kaga*, 9 fighters, 18 bombers, under the command of the flight officer of the *Hiryu*, Lieut. Tomonaga, took off for Midway from the Japanese carriers which were then some 210 miles to the northwestward of Midway, in approximately lat. 30° 45' N., long. 179° 40' E.[22]

Discovery of the Japanese Carriers

Meanwhile the Americans had not succeeded in locating the Japanese carriers, and at about the same time the usual search group of Naval Catalinas took off from Midway, covered by a Marine fighter patrol. Their orders were to search to 425 miles for the four enemy carriers which the Americans evidently appreciated were riding the weather front to the north-west, after which they were to return to Laysan and Lisyanski, to avoid exposing them unnecessarily at Midway where attack was now believed to be imminent.

The Catalinas made contact with the Japanese attack group about an hour after it had taken off from the carriers. One or more of the American flying boats was shot down[23], but at 0545 they sent a report to Midway of many aircraft heading for the island, bearing 320 degrees distant 150 miles, and five minutes afterwards the Midway radar picked up aircraft at a distance of 93 miles, altitude about 10,000 feet. Only seven minutes later, at 0552, the impatiently awaited news of the enemy carriers arrived, when another flying boat sighted two carriers and a number of supporting ships, including battleships, on the same bearing as the enemy aircraft, distant 180 miles, coming in at 25 knots on course 135 degrees.

The Air Battle

The alarm was sounded at Midway at 0555, and in a few minutes every serviceable aircraft was in the air. Bombers and torpedo bombers made for the enemy carriers (*see* Section 19), while between 0556 and approximately 0620 the 1st, 4th and 5th Division of Marine fighters (eight F2A Brewster and six F4F Grumman) were vectored towards the target, and the 2nd and 3rd Divisions (ten F2A Brewster) were vectored out on 310 degrees for 10 miles and instructed to orbit, being temporarily withheld in case another group of enemy aircraft should appear on another bearing. As none appeared, they were shortly after ordered to join in the interception of those aircraft already reported. The group was also joined by two fighters (F4F) which for some reason had remained in the air from the early morning covering patrol, and now landed, refuelled, and took off again. One fighter returned with engine trouble, leaving a total of 25 which proceeded to meet the Japanese attack.

Contact was made at 12,000 to 15,000 feet, at 0616, about 30 miles from Midway. The Japanese bombers were in a tight 'V' formation, with the fighters apparently at a lower altitude, for they were not at first seen by the Americans[24] who consequently attacked the bombers in separate divisions from 17,000 feet. These Marine fighters, although shore squadrons, were of the carrier type, and found themselves not only outnumbered by the Japanese Zero fighters, but markedly outclassed in speed, manoeuvrability and climb, though superior in armour, armament, and in the possession of leak-proof tanks. Each American fighter, after one or two passes at the bombers, found himself attacked by Zero fighters which outmanoeuvred him, and from which there was little possibility of escape other than in cloud cover, though it is reported that in two cases pilots successfully led the enemy into the fire from light A.A. guns ashore and on board the M.T.Bs. It is clear from the reports that the individual American pilots fought gamely, single aircraft going after Zero fighters even though the hunter inevitably became the hunted. To repulse or break up the attack on Midway was not in their power, however.

Their losses were heavy. Of 27 fighters of the Marine air group that intercepted the Japanese, including interceptions over the island during the attack, only 12 returned in answer to the message broadcast at 0715, 'Fighters land, refuel by division, Fifth Division first', and of these seven were severely damaged.[25] They estimated they had destroyed eight fighters and 25 bombers, but the Japanese reported that they lost no more than one fighter, one bomber and three torpedo aircraft.[26] They too, greatly overestimated the number of American fighters destroyed, which they put at 41.

Bombing of Midway

Meanwhile, at Midway, despite the efforts of the American fighters, considerable damage had been done. The weather was good, with excellent visibility, though there appears to have been a small amount of cloud above 1,600 feet.[27] The first battery got on to the target at 50,000 yards range, and at 0631 the observation post reported that all A.A. batteries had opened fire.

The attack was opened about 0630 by the torpedo aircraft from the *Hiryu* and *Soryu* which each dropped one 805 kg. (1,700 lb.) land bomb from 3,400 m. (11,150 feet), followed by the dive-bombers from the *Akagi* and *Kaga*, which each dropped one 242 kg. (550 lb.) land bomb. Targets were reported by the Japanese to have been as follows:–

> *Hiryu* and *Soryu*   Neutralization of A.A. fire, attacks on airfield and installations on Sand Island, though the *Soryu*'s aircraft also attacked the Eastern Island airfields;

Akagi and *Kaga*   Enemy aircraft both in the air and on the ground.

Most of the structures above ground were considerably damaged, the most serious at the time being the destruction of the power plant on Eastern Island, necessitating fuelling of aircraft by hand from tins and drums. Little damage was caused to the runways, and it was thought the Japanese wished to leave these intact for their own future use, though the available evidence suggests that the opposite was the case.

The attack lasted for about 17 minutes, though at 0701 two batteries opened fire again for a few seconds on a single aircraft appearing to the south. Smoke from the burning oil tanks interfered with A.A. fire. The Americans reported that ten enemy aircraft were shot down by their guns, but the Japanese reported only three so lost.

Japanese Cancel Second Air Attack on Midway

After the take off of the Midway attack group, the remaining torpedo aircraft of the Japanese striking force were ordered to arm and stand by in readiness to attack any surface vessels located by the searches then being made.

The striking force had launched altogether seven reconnaissance aircraft shortly before dawn, between 0430 and 0500, to search to the east and south as follows[28] (see Fig. 4):–

Akagi and *Kaga*	One ship-based torpedo aircraft each.
Chikuma	One seaplane.
	One seaplane.
Tone	One seaplane.
	One seaplane.
Haruna	One seaplane.

All aircraft were ordered to go out 300 miles, then turn left-handed for 60 miles, except the *Haruna*'s, which went out 150 miles and 40 miles to the left. One of the *Chikuma*'s seaplanes turned back at 0635 on account of bad weather, when 350 miles from her launching point.

At 0715 the command aircraft of the attack group (Air Officer, *Hiryu*) reported that a second attack on Midway would be necessary; this was decided upon, and the attack aircraft were ordered to remove torpedoes and replace them by 805 kg. land bombs.

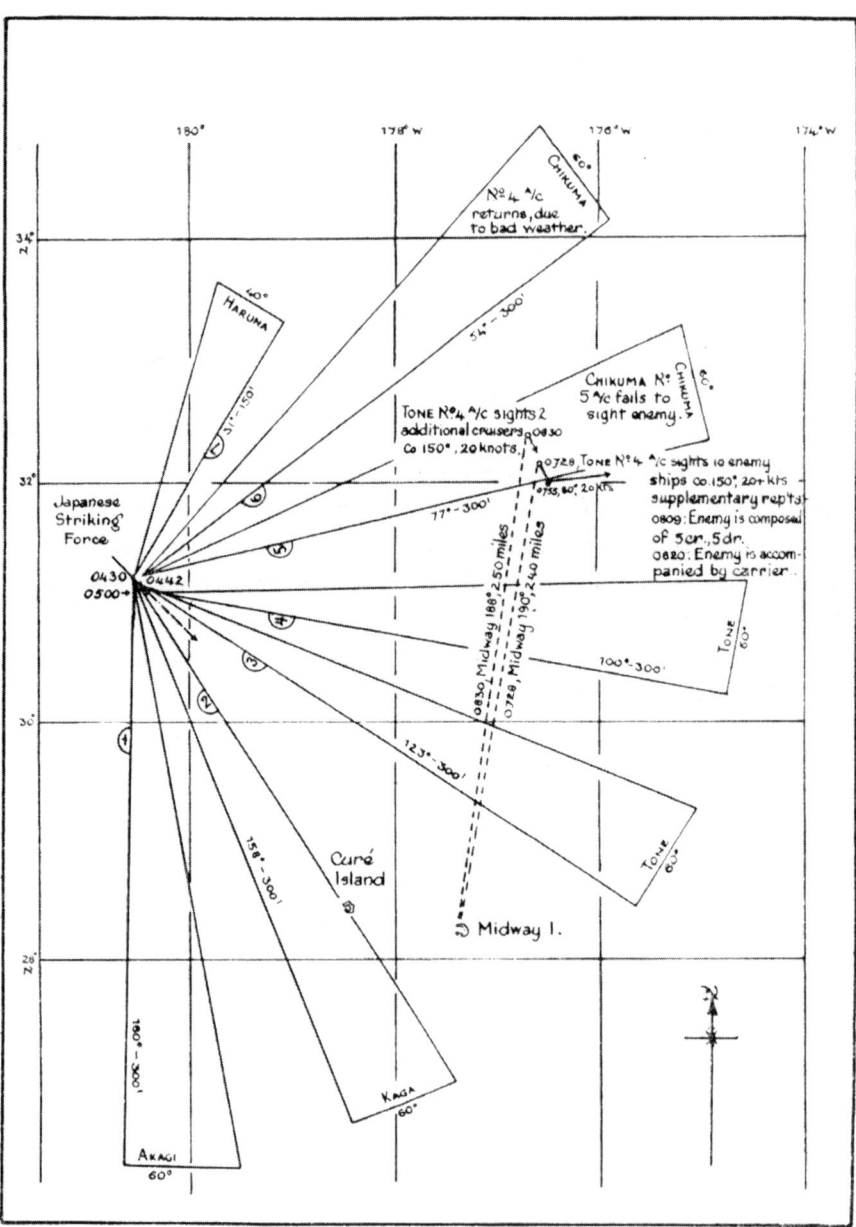

Fig. 4. Japanese air search chart, 4 June.

The order had barely been given, before a report came in from the pilot of one of the *Tone*'s reconnaissance aircraft that he had sighted what appeared to be a force of ten enemy surface ships, in position bearing 010 degrees distant 240 miles from Midway, steering a course of 150 degrees at a speed over 20 knots. The weather was cloudy, and the *Chikuma*'s first aircraft (No. 5) through whose sector of search the U.S. force was passing, failed to sight the Americans. The aircraft was ordered to report the enemy types, and meanwhile preparations for air attack were made, those attack aircraft which had not yet exchanged their torpedoes for bombs being ordered to retain their torpedoes. Half an hour later, the reply from the *Tone*'s aircraft arrived: 'Enemy is composed of five cruisers and five destroyers,' followed, at 0820, by 'The enemy is accompanied by what appears to be a carrier'. This was the *Yorktown*. Two additional cruisers were reported a few minutes later, astern of the larger force, steering a similar course. The shore-based American aircraft had been attacking Admiral Nagumo's force at intervals for over an hour, and an air attack was in progress at the moment, but directly a lull occurred the Admiral altered course and headed for the enemy.

The second wave of attack on Midway gave place to the new and more important object of attacking the American carriers. Owing, however, to the necessity for re-equipping the torpedo aircraft it was not immediately possible to send off a strike against the *Yorktown*. The Midway attack group was expected back very shortly, and it was therefore decided to await their return and then to despatch the strongest possible group to attack the reported carrier.

Before this could take place, however, the situation underwent a dramatic and, for the Japanese, a disastrous change. The last aircraft of the Midway attack group was safely on board and it was confirmed that substantial results had been obtained; preparations were hastily going forward for a 'grand attack' by 93 aircraft on the *Yorktown*. Though the striking force had been under attack since 0710, first by American Army, Navy and Marine shore-based torpedo aircraft and bombers, followed at 0920 and again at 1020 by carrier-based torpedo aircraft, it had suffered no hits or damage whatever (see next section). Then, at 1022, antagonists of a very different calibre appeared – the American carrier-borne dive-bombers. Seldom in war can a situation have been more swiftly and suddenly reversed; within a few minutes three out of four of the carriers had been reduced to flaming wrecks and Japanese sea power had suffered a blow from which it never recovered for the remainder of the war.

Before describing these devastating attacks, however, it is necessary to give an account of how the American shore-based air attacks had fared.

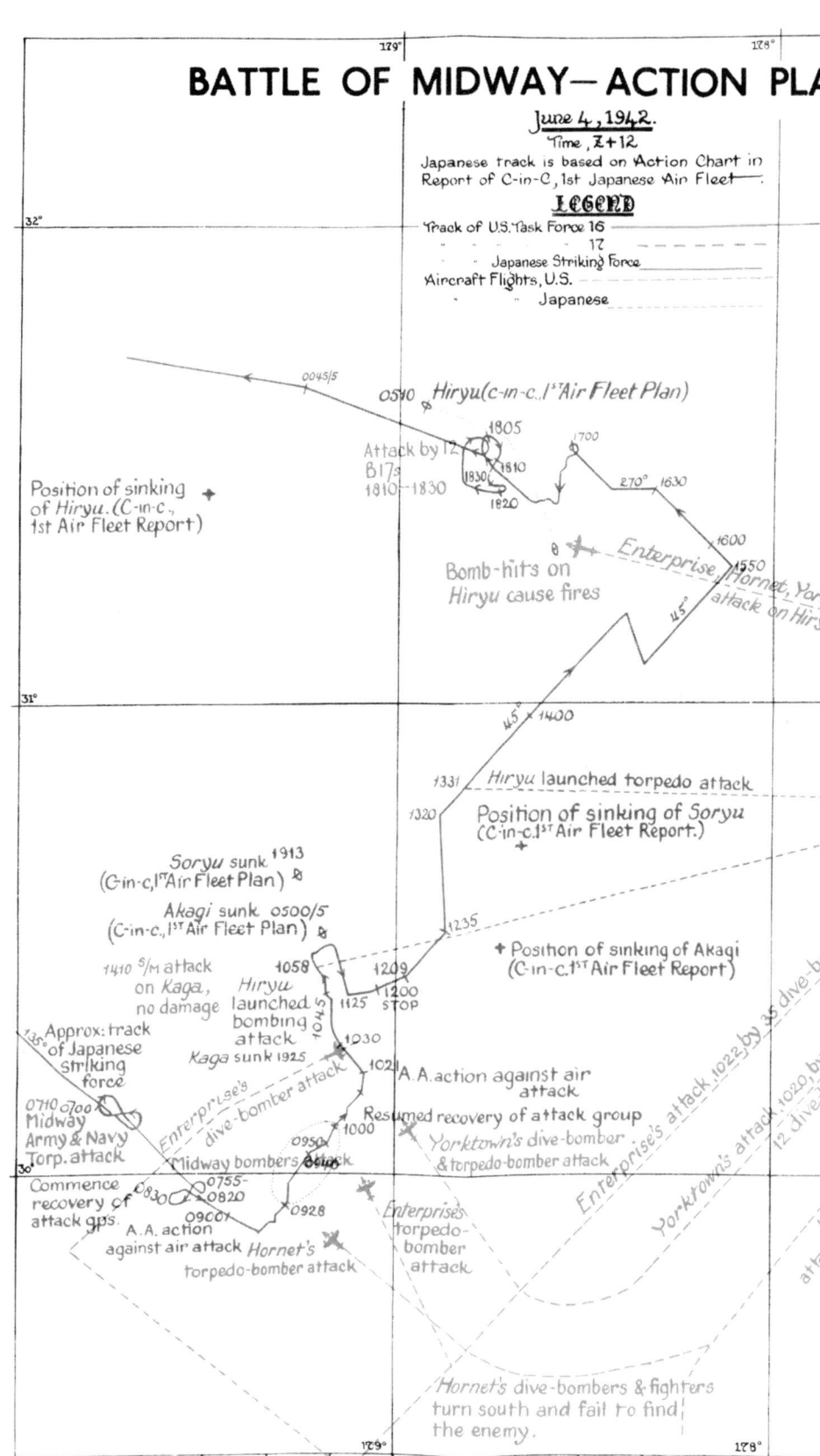

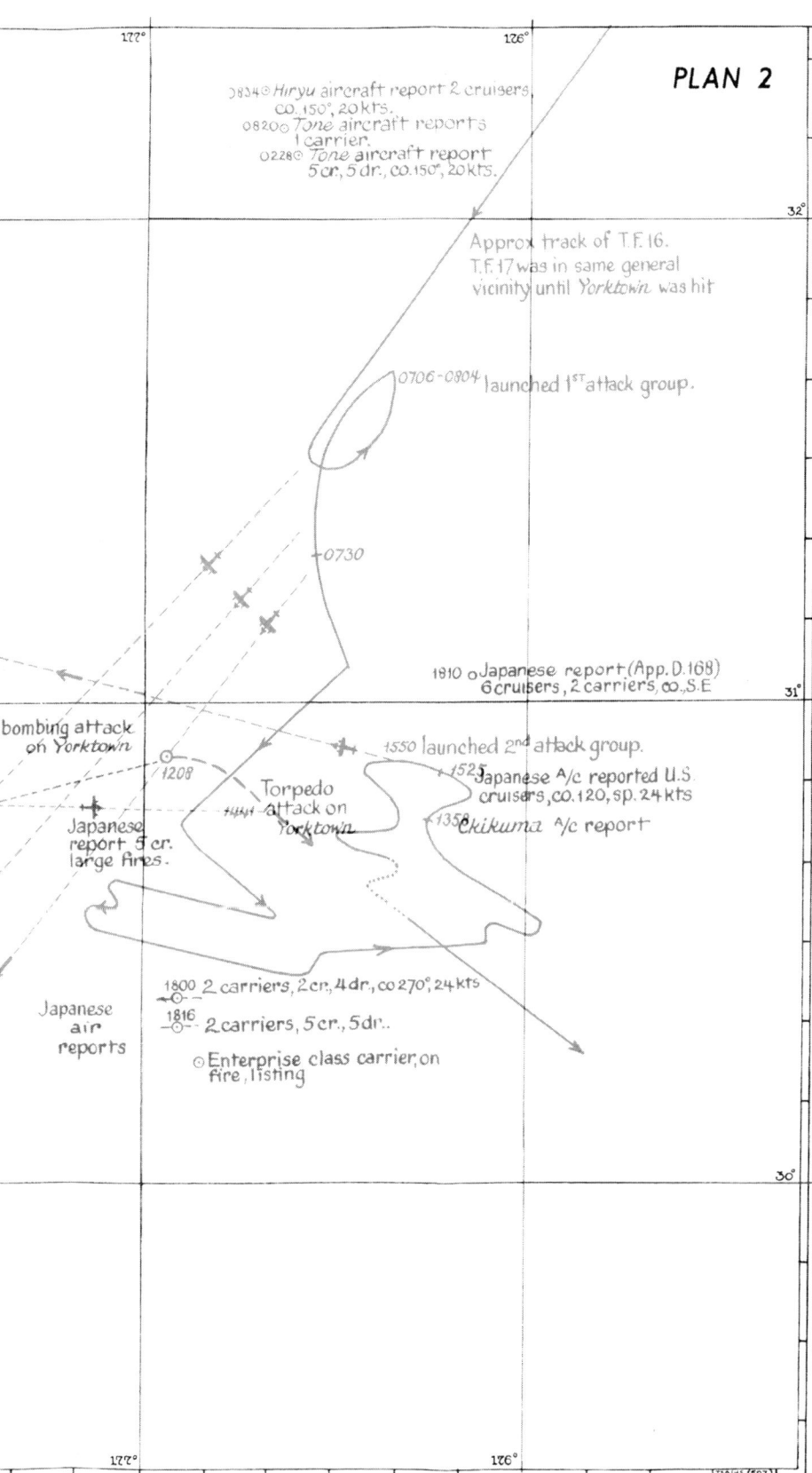

Midway Aircraft Attack Japanese First Air Fleet

Army (B.26) and Navy Torpedo (TBF) Aircraft Attack (Plan 2)
To return to Midway Island. When the Japanese carriers were sighted at 0552, the four Army B.26s, under Captain J. F. Collins, Jr., and the six Navy torpedo bombers under Lieut. F. K. Fieberling, were already manned, with engines warmed, and they were at once despatched to attack. History was made by the fact that for the first time the B.26s each carried a torpedo.

The Army aircraft took off at 0625, and at 0705 they sighted the Japanese striking force which they reported as three carriers, one battleship, several cruisers, and about six destroyers. Sighting by the Japanese was simultaneous at about 27,000 yards range and all carriers flew off fighters. Approaching from the south-east, the Americans were met by heavy anti-aircraft fire from the Japanese striking force, which steered directly towards them; and just before reaching the enemy formation six Zero fighters were met head on at 700 feet. As Captain Collins manoeuvred, first to the left and then to the right, to find the best path through the enemy's A.A. fire, he caught sight of six Navy torpedo aircraft which had left Midway fifteen minutes earlier than his own group; they were just going in for their attack, approaching from his right and across his course. To avoid the Japanese fighters the B.26s dived steeply to 200 feet, and most of the enemy's fire passed overhead. It was probably at this point that two of the Americans were shot down.

Captain Collins chose as his target the carrier *Hiryu*, in the centre of the formation, releasing his 2,000 lb. torpedo, with depth setting 12 feet, at 200 feet and 200 m.p.h. from 25 degrees off the bow, range 800 yards, as the carrier turned across his path. His No. 4 slightly below and to his left, released at about 450 yards from 150 feet, and then pulled up over the carrier. One of the two B.26s shot down was reported to have launched its torpedo, and was then thought, though incorrectly, to have struck the *Hiryu*'s flight deck and hurtled into the sea. None of the three torpedoes fired by the B.26s found their mark, and the only damage reported by the

Japanese was two men killed by strafing aboard the flagship *Akagi*. The last of the Japanese fighters, 50 of which were reported to have been disposed over the enemy ships,[29] at altitudes from 20,000 feet downwards, was not shaken off until the B.26s entered cloud cover on the way home, 15 to 20 minutes later. In both the surviving American aircraft the machine guns gave trouble, and Captain Collins reported that all his guns were unsatisfactory during the entire fight. One of the two machines crashed on landing, and both were so badly damaged as to be unserviceable.

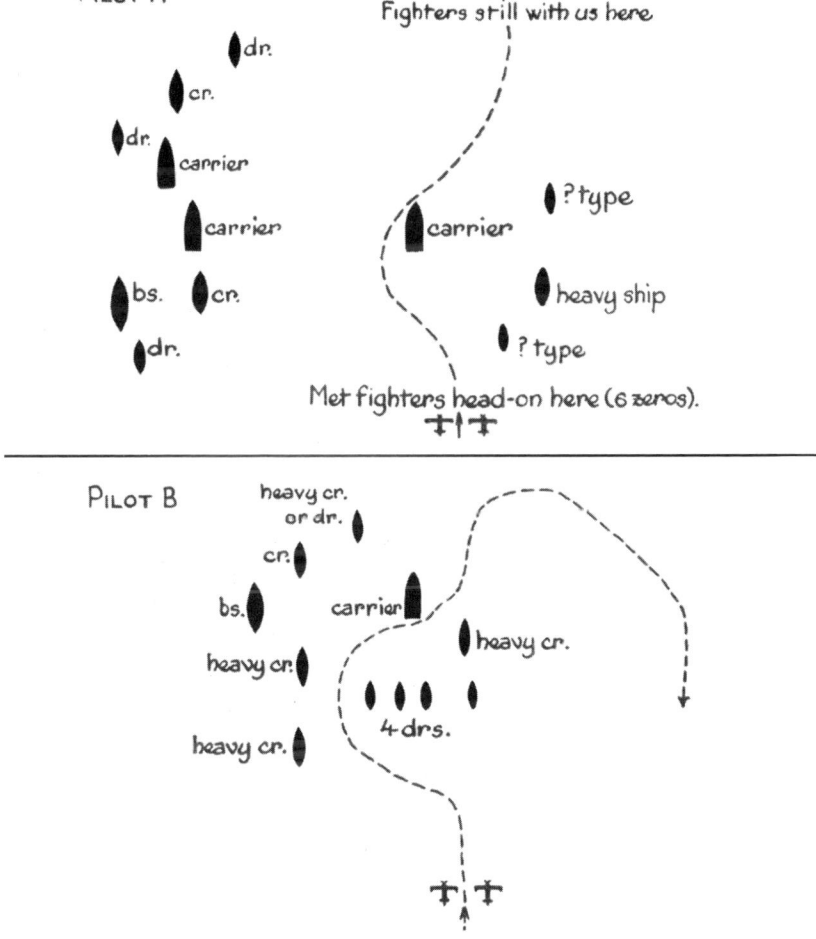

Fig. 5. Attack on *Hiryu* and *Akagi* by Army and Navy torpedo aircraft, 0710 on 4 June.

The six Navy torpedo aircraft attacked simultaneously with the Army bombers. Both the *Akagi* and *Hiryu* reported being attacked, the former by four and the latter by 13 aircraft. The Navy aircraft, like the B.26s, encountered heavy A.A. fire and an overwhelming number of fighters, for which the unescorted TBFs, despite their excellent armament, were no match, particularly since they had to slow down to limiting torpedo releasing speed. Two were shot down before they could release their torpedoes; it was estimated that the remaining four fired torpedoes but none of them hit, their slow speed enabling the Japanese ships to avoid them. Only a single badly damaged aircraft survived to make a landing with one wheel retracted, and the pilot could give no clear account of the attack.

Douglas (SBD) Marine Scout Bombers Attack

Fifty minutes later, the Marine scout bombers of squadron VMSB–No. 1 at Midway attacked. Thirty took off on signal, and were already in the air orbiting, 20 miles east of Eastern Island, when the report of the Japanese carriers came in; instructions to attack were sent but no acknowledgment was received, and the orders were repeated periodically for over an hour, though as events proved they had been acted upon at the first transmission. The scout bombers proceeded in two groups, the one commanded by Major L. R. Henderson, with 18 SBD-2[30] aircraft, the second under Major B. W. Norris with 12 SB2U-3s.[31] Two of the SBDs developed engine trouble and one SB2U was forced to return with a loose cowling. Ten of the pilots had joined the squadron only a week before, and there had been very little opportunity for training flights.

As only three of his pilots had experience of the SBDs, the Commander decided to make a glide bombing attack, for although less effective and more hazardous than dive-bombing it permitted lower pull outs.

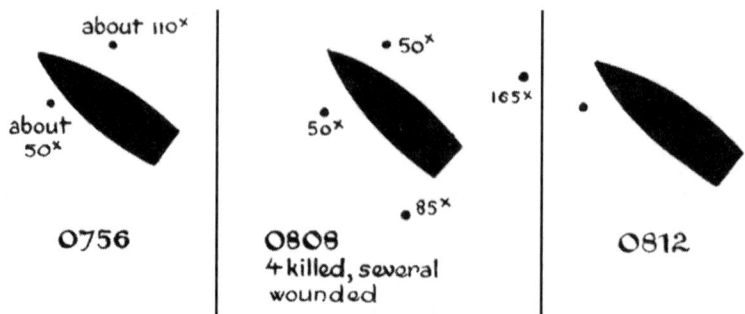

Fig. 6. Attack on *Hiryu* by S.B.D.s, 0755 4 June – fall of bombs.

The SBDs sighted the enemy striking force at approximately 0755, and began to come down in a wide circle from their height of 9,000 feet to get into position for glide-bombing attack from 4,000 feet. The squadron was at once attacked by several enemy fighters, and the enemy ships opened violent anti-aircraft fire. Major Henderson's own aircraft, on which the Japanese fighters apparently concentrated, was quickly set on fire and he himself was put out of action; the fighter attacks were so heavy that Captain E. G. Gliddon, Jr., who then took charge, led the squadron into a heavy layer of cloud from which it emerged at 2,000 feet and dived in close formation on the *Hiryu* under heavy A.A. fire and renewed attack by fighters. Bombs were released at 500 feet or less, and it was thought three direct hits were made, but the Japanese subsequently stated that there were no hits. The *Hiryu* had a number of casualties from near misses, but no damage was reported. Eight of the American bombers returned to base, but only six remained fit for service. 'Two were seen to go down in flames, and one went out of control before reaching Midway. The pilot jumped and was picked up by a P.T. boat. Another was forced down 100 miles west of Midway, but both pilot and gunner were rescued two days later.'[32]

Army B.17s Attack the Carriers

About 20 minutes after Major Henderson's attack, and before Major Norris's group of Marine scout bombers reached the target, Army B.17s of Flight 92 under the Commanding Officer of the 431st Bombardment Squadron, Lieut.-Col. W. C. Sweeney, Jr., attacked the Japanese striking force.

The 16 available Fortresses had taken off directly after the reconnaissance group, and cleared Midway about 0415. To occupy them usefully during the four hours before they could safely land they were ordered to attack the Japanese Occupation Force to the westward, which it was estimated they would find at a distance of about 480 miles. There had been no report of the latter since the night attack by patrol bombers; and it was not until five hours after the Army aircraft took off that the force was again picked up. At 0916 three cruisers in column were sighted in about 28° 00' N. 176° 35' E.; at 0945 a force of four heavy cruisers, two oilers, and two cargo ships with destroyers in about 27° 35' N., 175° 10' E.; and at 0952 large vessels, including perhaps a battleship, in 26° 30' N., 176° 30' E. All were proceeding on course about 077 degrees towards Midway.[33] The B.17s had the benefit of prolonged experience with naval forces obtained during co-ordinated patrol operations. They had been warned to be prepared for a change of objective if the enemy carriers should be discovered; and orders to this effect were sent to them as soon as the report of the carriers came in. The Fortresses were about 200 miles from Midway when they received the message, in plain language, stating that another enemy task force, including many carriers, was approaching Midway on a bearing 325 degrees, distance 145 miles.

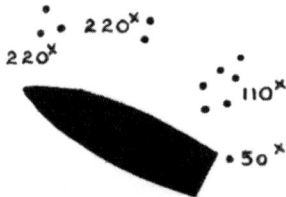

Fig. 7. Attack on *Soryu* by B.17s, 0814 4 June – fall of bombs.

Climbing to 20,000 feet, the Americans altered course for the carriers. The enemy were met at 0732, but it was not until 0810 that two carriers were seen through the broken clouds. The circling of the Fortresses had brought them to the north-westward of the Japanese fleet, and they attacked from astern from 20,000 feet.

The attack was made by flights of three aircraft (only two aircraft in flight 5). The first two flights dropped a total of 40 x 500 lb. demolition bombs and reported one hit on the stern of a carrier. The third and fifth flights attacked a second carrier, the third flight reporting one hit on the port bow, one waterline hit, one possible hit and five near misses; and the fifth flight one hit, one possible hit and two near misses. The fourth flight reported one hit and two near misses on a third carrier.[34] In all, 16 x 600 lb. and 92 x 500 lb. bombs were dropped; the remainder hung up through failures of releasing gear. No Japanese ship appears to have noticed any bombs, except the *Soryu* which reported about 11, the nearest 50 yards away. No ship suffered any damage, and the relative ineffectiveness of high altitude horizontal bombing on ships which retained freedom of manoeuvre was again amply demonstrated.

The enemy A.A. fire was heavy and at the proper altitude, but generally behind the target. The Japanese fighters did not display anxiety to close their formidable antagonists though the Fortresses reported that they were able to shoot down two Zeros.

Vought-Sikorsky (SB2U) Marine Scout Bombers Attack

The second unit of the Marine group, eleven SB2Us under the command of Major Norris, flying at 13,000 feet, sighted the Japanese striking force at 0820, just as the Fortresses were finishing their attack. Japanese fighters were encountered at 13,000 feet, before the unit was in position to attack, and their opposition was so severe that the Americans were unable to search for the main objective, the carrier; and consequently a secondary target, the battleship, *Haruna*, was chosen. The unit attacked in a long flat glide through the clouds at 2,000 feet and pulled out at a very low altitude. One aircraft which was out of position attacked a destroyer and the bomb of one machine hung up. The Americans estimated that two bombs hit the *Haruna* but this was not the case, though two fell very close. The *Haruna* reported that only five or six bombs in all fell near her, and it is possible that the three bombs which the carrier *Kaga* reported dropped by carrier-based bombers at 0830, the nearest no more than 20 yards from her stern, were dropped by the SB2Us. However, the carrier was not damaged.

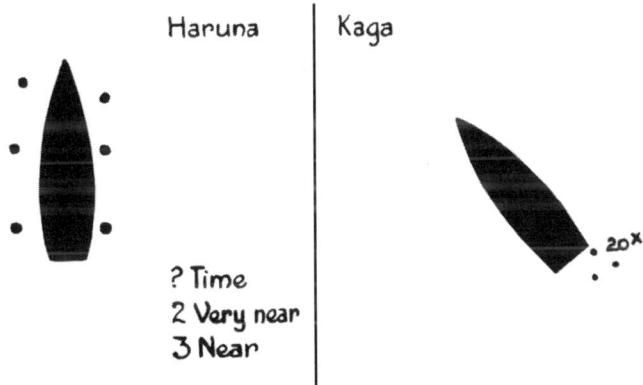

Fig. 8. Attacks on *Haruna* and *Kaga* by S.B.2Us, 0820 4 June – fall of bombs.

Two of the S.B.2Us were lost through forced landings in the sea before reaching Midway, the two pilots and a gunner being rescued: the other gunner was apparently killed early in the attack.

Destruction of First Air Fleet by U.S. Carrier Aircraft and Attacks on *Yorktown*
(Plans 1 and 2)

Situation After the Attack on Midway

The outlook on this June morning, as the last of the Midway aircraft withdrew from the scene of the attacks on the carriers, was most unfavourable to the Americans. Indeed, had they known, it was even more serious than they supposed; for in place of the ten or so ships which they believed their air attacks to have damaged, actually only a single ship, a tanker, had suffered slight damage. On the island, nearly everything above ground had been destroyed or badly damaged by the Japanese air attack. The Midway bombers and torpedo bombers had struck with full strength, but had not checked the great force of about 80 ships, including three (actually four) undamaged carriers, reported to be converging on the island base. Most of the American fighters, as well as the torpedo aircraft and dive-bombers which were the only types capable of making a high percentage of hits on ships, were destroyed or out of action.

This was the situation when the United States aircraft carrier force rode into the battle.

Task Forces 16 and 17 Launch Attack Groups

The American carrier Task Forces 16 and 17,[35] after making rendezvous on 2 June north-east of Midway in 32° 04' N., 172° 45' W., had moved westward during the night 2/3 June, Task Force 16 being about 10 miles south of Task Force 17. On 3 June they turned north, and received reports, both from Midway and from the Commander-in-Chief, Pacific Fleet, of the enemy force sighted to the westward of Midway. It was clear, however, that this was not the Japanese Striking Force, which was expected to approach from the north-westward, so Rear-Admiral Fletcher turned eastward once more and whilst the *Enterprise* and *Hornet* held their aircraft in readiness as an attack force, the *Yorktown*'s aircraft conducted a search of a sector between 240 degrees and 060 degrees. Rain squalls and low visibility rendered the search difficult, and it was without result.

Throughout 3 June the American task forces remained undiscovered. During the approach, the Japanese striking force had maintained antisubmarine air patrols, but the thick weather which concealed the carriers from the American reconnaissance aircraft also prevented the enemy from sending out air searches, whilst the denial of French Frigate Shoal as a fuelling base limited the aircraft from the Marshall Islands to searching south of Midway. It is an interesting fact that during the whole of 3 June, too, Task Forces 16 and 17 were in the area patrolled by Japanese submarines, without being sighted (see Fig. 1).

Rear-Admiral Fletcher moved south-southwest during the night 3/4 June, to a position about 200 miles north of Midway, on the flank of the enemy striking force whose attack on the island was expected to take place shortly. At 0420/4 the flagship launched a security search of the sector to the north and put a fighter patrol in the air. The *Enterprise* of Task Force 16 took over the direction of fighters.

The carrier force intercepted the report at 0545 of Japanese aircraft heading for Midway and a few minutes later the report of sighting two enemy carriers. Orders were at once sent to Rear-Admiral Spruance, five or ten miles to the south-west, to move westward and launch attacks when he came within range of the Japanese striking force. Since only two enemy carriers had been reported and the *Yorktown* had aircraft in the air, her attack group was temporarily held in reserve.

Task Force 16 increased to 25 knots and headed for the enemy. By 0700 Rear-Admiral Spruance estimated that the Japanese striking force, bearing 239 degrees, was about 155 miles distant. This was only 20 miles less than the combat radius of his torpedo aircraft. Nevertheless, as the reports of the enemy air attack on Midway came in, he decided to launch at once, in the hope, which in the event was fulfilled, of catching Nagumo's carriers with their aircraft on deck being refuelled for a second strike. He turned into the light south-east wind to launch his strike groups. Every aircraft not needed for combat patrol and A/S patrol was put into the air. Launching commenced at 0706 and required about an hour, deferred departure being used, the order of launching being (1) fighters for patrol, (2) dive-bombers, (3) torpedo aircraft, (4) fighters to escort torpedo aircraft. The *Hornet* launched 35 scout bombers armed with 500 lb. bombs, 15 torpedo aircraft with torpedoes, and ten fighters; the *Enterprise* 32 scout bombers (15 with 1 x 1,000-lb. bombs and 17 with 1 x 500 and 2 x 100-lb. bombs), 14 torpedo aircraft, and 10 fighters.[36]

By 0840 there had been no report of further enemy carriers other than the two already sighted, and it was decided to launch the *Yorktown*'s attack group, lest she should be caught with her aircraft on deck. The entire torpedo squadron (12 aircraft each carrying one torpedo), half the bomber squadron (17 scout bombers each with one 1,000-lb. bomb), and six fighters were launched. The 17 scout bombers that remained were held in reserve in case two more enemy carriers were sighted. The slower torpedo aircraft headed for the target at once. The scout bombers were ordered to circle for 12 minutes before proceeding to overtake the torpedo squadron. To economise fuel, the fighters were not launched until 0905. The three squadrons effected rendezvous at 0945 as they proceeded towards the target, which they found at the same time as the *Enterprise* group.

It was intended to co-ordinate the attacks of the torpedo aircraft and the dive-bombers, but owing to the inherent difficulties exact co-ordination was not achieved.

Enemy Alters Course

Meanwhile, the Japanese scouts had sighted the American task forces and Admiral Nagumo had altered course towards them at high speed (see page 135). One of the two seaplanes, either the *Tone*'s or *Hiryu*'s, which made the sighting, was sighted by the Americans, who thus knew they had been reported and must consequently expect attack unless their own attack could be made before the enemy carriers could refuel and despatch once more the aircraft which had returned from the strike on Midway.[37]

The change of course to the north-eastward by Admiral Nagumo had taken place about 0917. It was reported to the American carriers but the latter did not break wireless silence to inform their attack groups, with the consequence that some of the latter, on arriving at the estimated position of the Japanese carriers found the area void of enemy ships.

The 35 scout bombers from the *Hornet* on finding an empty sea turned southward to search along the enemy's reported course. With them were the ten fighters. No contact was made, and shortage of fuel forced all the fighters down in the sea before reaching Midway on the return journey, though eight of the pilots were rescued. All but two of the dive-bombers eventually returned to the *Hornet*, 11 of them via Midway where they refuelled. Two landed in the lagoon.

Hornet's Torpedo Squadron Attacks

The *Hornet*'s torpedo squadron, led by Lieut.-Commander J. C. Waldron, had proceeded at a lower altitude than the remainder of the attack group, from which it became separated although there were only scattered clouds. The squadron turned north to search, and found four Japanese carriers dispersed in a wide roughly circular formation, accompanied as they estimated by two or three battleships, four cruisers and six destroyers. Warning of their approach was given by the *Tone*'s reconnaissance aircraft. The *Akagi*, *Kaga* and *Soryu* were close together, with the *Hiryu* standing off some distance to the north. The Japanese carriers had just completed landing-on their Midway attack groups[38] and the Americans believed, incorrectly, that the *Soryu* and one other ship resembling a battleship were smoking from the attacks of the Midway aircraft an hour earlier.

The group attacked at once (0920) unsupported; heavy fighter opposition was encountered, the *Chikuma* opening fire with her main armament at the same time. Almost immediately the group ran into heavy A.A. fire from the supporting ships, which soon ceased as it was seen that the Japanese fighters were shooting them down. Not one of the 15 aircraft survived the attacks, and only one pilot, Ensign G. H. Gay, came through. After attacking a carrier believed to be the *Kaga* he crashed in the sea near the *Akagi*, whence he watched the subsequent attacks of the *Yorktown*'s and *Enterprise*'s aircraft, hidden under a floating seat cushion and refraining from inflating his life raft until dark. Five of their aircraft were thought by the Americans to have been shot down before releasing their torpedoes, the other ten were believed to have been launched and to have made one hit each on the *Kaga* and another carrier. The Japanese reported that the attacking squadron apparently consisted of 17 aircraft, and that four torpedoes were seen, of which two very nearly hit the *Soryu*, one missed forward and one to starboard. No hits were made either on this carrier or the *Kaga*.[39]

Enterprise and *Yorktown* Torpedo Groups Attack

The torpedo and dive-bombing groups of the *Enterprise* and *Yorktown* attacked almost simultaneously, an hour after the *Hornet*'s. First in point of time to deliver their attack were the torpedo groups of the two carriers.

The *Enterprise*'s torpedo squadron, under Lieut.-Commander E. E. Lindway, escorted by 10 fighters, proceeded to the target independently of the dive-bombers. On the way it became separated from its fighter escort, which inadvertently joined the *Hornet*'s torpedo squadron, and launched its attack without support. The altitude of the aircraft was too low to enable them to see more than three of the four Japanese carriers when they sighted the enemy about 1000 and first came under fire. It was not until 1020 that the aircraft were able to gain a position for attack on the beam of the carriers, for the violent manoeuvring of the enemy who altered course to starboard through 24 points of the compass from 270 degrees (the course which the attackers reported they were steering when sighted) to 180 degrees, kept them on the quarter of the carriers and forced them to make a wide circle. During this time the torpedo group were under both A.A. gunfire and attack by enemy fighters, and the Americans estimated that six of their number were shot down before launching their torpedoes at the westernmost carrier, apparently the *Hiryu*. Only four aircraft survived the attack.

The *Yorktown*'s torpedo squadron under Lieut.-Commander L. E. Massey made its attack simultaneously with that of the *Enterprise*, despite the difference of an hour in launching time. The squadron had been overtaken *en route* as planned, by the *Yorktown*'s dive-bombers and had proceeded at about 1,500 feet, with two of the six fighters 1,000 feet above them and four at 5,000-6,000 feet. They too, like the *Enterprise*'s torpedo squadron, sighted the enemy ships about 1000. At about 14 miles from the target Zero fighters attacked them and they dropped to 150 feet to avoid antiaircraft fire. The superior numbers of the Japanese fighters soon resulted in the heavily outnumbered American fighters becoming separated from the torpedo aircraft, which turned in to attack one of the enemy carriers from a point about a mile to the east. Seven of the twelve aircraft were shot down before reaching release point, and three of the remaining five almost immediately after launching.

It was estimated by the Americans that two hits were obtained on one carrier and one or two on a second. The Japanese reported that the attacks of both torpedo squadrons were directed against the *Hiryu*: in the first attack, at 1013 by the Japanese carrier's reckoning, by 16 aircraft, seven torpedo tracks were seen: in the second attack, at 1030, by five aircraft, five torpedoes were reported. None of the torpedoes hit, their slow speed enabling them to be avoided.

In repulsing the attacks of the torpedo aircraft the escorting cruisers *Tone* and *Chikuma* employed their main armament in addition to their A.A. guns, opening fire with the former at ranges up to 45 km. (nearly 50,000 yards).

Only two of the 12 aircraft in the *Yorktown*'s torpedo squadron survived the attack. Two of the fighters were lost, one crash-landed on board the *Hornet*, and the remainder returned to the *Yorktown*.

Enterprise Dive-Bombers Attack, 1022

The torpedo squadrons had been cut to pieces; out of 41 aircraft only six survived the attacks. Nevertheless, although exact co-ordination of the torpedo attacks with those of the dive-bombers now coming in had not been achieved and not a single torpedo hit had been made on the enemy, the unsupported attacks of the torpedo aircraft had the effect of attracting the Japanese fighters, so that few were in position to oppose the dive-bombers when their attacks commenced, two minutes later.[40]

The *Enterprise* dive-bombers took departure at 0730 and climbed to 20,000 feet. Some of the pilots experienced trouble with their oxygen masks; and observing this, the commander of the group Lieut.- Commander C. W. McClusky, Jr., removed his own mask in order to have the same reaction as other pilots.

Like the *Hornet*'s dive-bombers an hour earlier, the *Enterprise*'s failed to find the enemy carriers in the estimated position, because of their alteration of course. The commander turned northward, however, and about 1005, after searching for about ¾ hour, the Japanese fleet was sighted.[41] All four carriers were in view, disposed in a diamond shape, the *Hiryu* considerably to northward of the remainder. With them were seen four heavy ships, battleships or cruisers, and eight to ten destroyers. The entire fleet was steering a northerly course.

No damage to any of the carriers was visible at the time of sighting or during the dive, thus substantiating the Japanese report that no hits were made by any of the American high level bombing, glide bombing or torpedo attacks by either land-based or carrier-based aircraft.

The weather was clear and visibility excellent. There were scattered cumulus clouds between 1,500 and 2,500 feet, and the ceiling was unlimited. A surface wind of five to eight knots was blowing from the south-east.

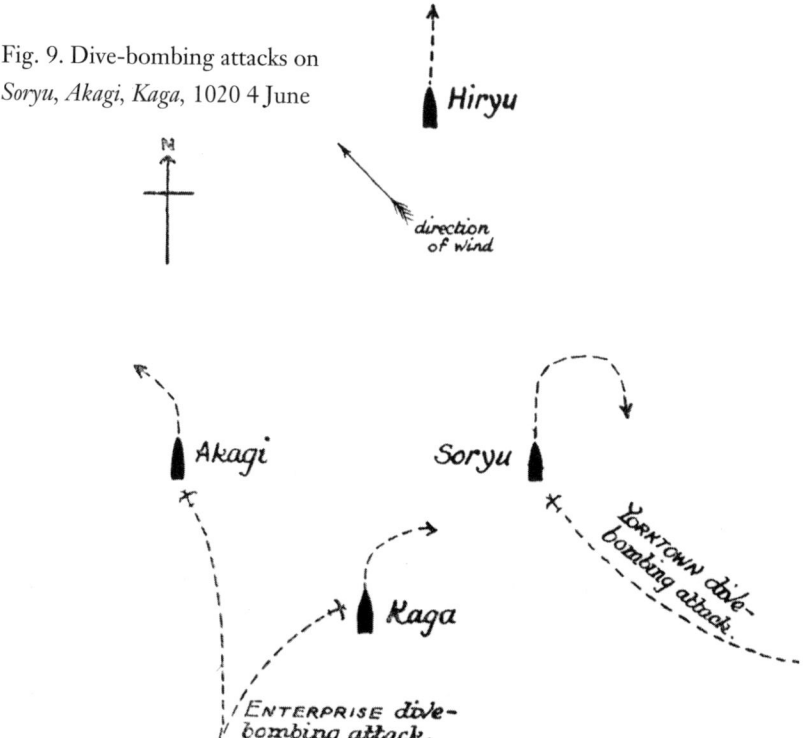

Fig. 9. Dive-bombing attacks on *Soryu, Akagi, Kaga*, 1020 4 June

Approaching from the south, the attack was made by sections on the two westernmost carriers. Targets were ordered by voice radio and there was some confusion. The group commander and Scouting Squadron 6, armed with 500 lb. and 100 lb. bombs, attacked the left-hand (*i.e.* most westerly) carrier, as did the second division of Bombing Squadron 6 armed with 1,000 lb. bombs, whilst the five aircraft of the first division of Bombing Squadron 6 attacked the right-hand carrier and the third division attacked both carriers. Each squadron leader was convinced that the carriers his men attacked were of the *Kaga* or *Akagi* type, both of which were converted, the *Kaga* from a battleship and the *Akagi* from a battlecruiser.

Anti-aircraft fire was light, and no fighter opposition was experienced until all bombs had been dropped, though the American torpedo aircraft were seen to be under heavy attack as they came in. As the dive-bombers pulled out, however, many of them were attacked by Zero fighters and came under the A.A. fire of the screening vessels which up to now had largely been concentrated on the torpedo aircraft.

Eighteen of the *Enterprise* dive-bombers failed to return to the carrier; it is thought that most of these were not shot down but were forced to come down in the sea when they ran out of fuel.

Yorktown Dive-Bombers Attack (Fig. 9)

The *Yorktown*'s 17 scout bombers, each carrying one 1,000 lb. bomb, sighted the enemy about 1000. The bombers were still in touch with the torpedo squadron, with which it had proceeded to the scene; but they lost contact when the latter attacked.

The bombers opened their dive at 1025 from about 14,500 feet, on a carrier estimated by the pilots to be of the *Akagi* class which was turning to the southward into the wind to launch her aircraft. This was probably, however, the *Soryu*. This ship, though officially displacing only 10,050 tons, little more than a third of the tonnage of the *Akagi* and *Kaga*, was actually a 17,500 ton ship and not noticeably smaller than the *Akagi* and *Kaga*, having been designed as a carrier from the first, and not as an armoured ship. The first bomb exploded amongst the aircraft assembled on the flight deck, turning the after part of the deck into a mass of flames. Four aircraft of the squadron, seeing the carrier so badly damaged, transferred their attack to a nearby cruiser and a battleship, neither of which was, however, reported hit by the Japanese.

No fighter opposition was experienced until after the dive, and the aircraft withdrew at high speed low over the water, avoiding heavy A.A. fire. The entire squadron returned safely to the *Yorktown*.

Sinking of the *Soryu*

In the attacks just described, the *Soryu* reported the number of dive-bombers that attacked her as 13. Three hits were made, and fires spread with great rapidity and caused induced explosions in the bomb storage magazine, A.A. and M.G. ammunition magazines, and gasoline tanks. Both engines stopped and the ship was abandoned at 1045. The captain, Ryusaku Yanagimoto, remained at his post and lost his life. About 1600, when the fires had died down somewhat, the air officer, who was acting commander, organised fire fighters with the intention of re-boarding the ship. Before this could be done, however, at 1913 the *Soryu* sank in 30° 42.5' N., 178° 37.5' W., torpedoed by the U.S. submarine *Nautilus*.[42]

The U.S. submarines had been notified that morning of the Japanese striking force north-west of Midway, and nine of them were ordered to close the enemy. The *Grouper* sighted the Japanese force, but was prevented by air attacks from attacking. The *Nautilus*, Lieut.-Comdr. W. H. Brockman, Jr., after shadowing a force of enemy battleships and cruisers, made an unsuccessful attack and was heavily depth charged. At 1029 she sighted on the horizon columns of smoke from the Japanese carriers under attack. On closing, the *Nautilus* encountered the *Soryu*, on an even keel, with hull apparently undamaged, smoking but with flames apparently under control, and accompanied by two ships believed to be cruisers, but actually no doubt the destroyers *Hamakaze* and *Isonami*, to which the crew had been transferred. At 1359 the *Nautilus* fired three torpedoes at the *Soryu* and the destroyers at once retaliated with a depth charge attack. When this was over, at 1610, the *Nautilus* rose to periscope depth and found the carrier completely aflame and abandoned. At 1840 heavy underwater explosions occurred accompanied by a cloud of black smoke. At 1941 the *Nautilus* surfaced. No ship, smoke, or flame was in sight.[43]

Kaga Sinks, *Akagi* Scuttled

The *Kaga* was still engaged in evasive action against the attacking American torpedo squadrons when nine dive-bombers were suddenly sighted amongst the clouds at 1022. Her manoeuvres enabled her to avoid the first three bombs, but four of the next six hit her. The third hit (bomb No. 8) almost completely destroyed the bridge and killed everyone thereon, including the captain. Although it was recognised that there was little hope of getting the fires under control, the crew continued their efforts until 1640, when the situation was recognised as hopeless and orders were given to abandon ship, and the destroyers *Hagikaze* and *Maikaze* took off the crew. By 1925 the fires had spread to both forward and after fuel tanks, causing two great explosions which sank the ship in 30° 20.3' N., 179° 17.2' W.

Only three bombs hit the *Akagi*, none of which would under ordinary circumstances have been fatal; but caught as she was with her aircraft on deck, they sufficed to destroy her. The fire quickly engulfed the entire hangar area, and aided by induced explosions spread with great intensity to the immediate vicinity of the bridge; and at 1046 the flag was shifted to the light cruiser *Nagara*. Orders were given to flood the magazines, but the pump system failed, and although every effort was made to get the fires under control it became increasingly evident that there was little hope of success. At 1925 orders were given to abandon ship, and the crew began to transfer to the destroyers *Arashi* and *Nowake*. At 0500 on 5 June, by order of the C.-in-C. Combined Fleet the ship was sunk by torpedo in 30° 30' N., 178° 40' W.

There can be little doubt that the destruction, by no more than four and three bombs respectively, of two ships as strong as the *Kaga* and *Akagi*, was due to their being caught before they could fly off their aircraft which were on deck fuelled and armed for attack on the U.S. force.[44]

Bombing Attack on *Yorktown*

The fourth Japanese carrier, the *Hiryu*, had not been troubled by the attacks of the *Yorktown* and *Enterprise* dive-bombers: as soon as the torpedo attack was over, about 1058,[45] she was therefore free to despatch her aircraft to attack the carrier *Yorktown* which one of the reconnaissance aircraft from the cruiser *Tone* had discovered two hours earlier. At 1058 the ship flew off 18 bombers armed with 500-lb. bombs, escorted by five or six fighters, and despatched them to attack the *Yorktown*.

About an hour later, at 1150, the *Yorktown* launched 12 fighters to relieve the combat air patrol which was up at the time, together with 10 scout bombers, each armed with one 1,000-lb. bomb, to search a sector between 280 degrees and 030 degrees to 200 miles, for the reports which Rear-Admiral Fletcher had of the number and positions of the enemy carriers were incomplete. Almost simultaneously, at 1152, the ship's radar picked up a large number of aircraft approaching from the westward, 32 miles distant, which were later calculated to number 18 dive-bombers and 18 fighters.[46]

At the moment, the six aircraft of the combat air patrol that had just been relieved and the surviving fighters of the group returned from attack on the Japanese carriers were on deck being refuelled and the scout bombers were still in the landing circle. The latter were ordered to fly clear, fuelling of the fighters was suspended, and the fuel system was drained and CO_2 introduced.

The 12 fighters were ordered out in two waves to intercept the Japanese attack group, which they met at about 9,000 feet, 15 or 20 miles out. Only seven or eight of the enemy bombers succeeded in breaking out of the mêlée and diving on the *Yorktown*, but three of their bombs made hits; one bomb from an aircraft which had been cut to fragments by automatic gunfire fell and exploded on the flight deck abaft the island; one made a hit in an uptake and forced the *Yorktown* to stop, largely because boiler gases were drawn into the stokeholds rendering them uninhabitable; and a third landed in the forward lift well starting fires adjacent to the forward aviation fuel tanks without igniting them. The screening vessels circled the *Yorktown* at

2,000 yards, zigzagging at high speed and putting up heavy A.A. fire. Of the 18 enemy bombers 13 were destroyed, at least 11 of them by the fighters. Three of the Japanese fighters were shot down. By 1215 the attack was over.

The *Hiryu*'s attack group considered they had made six hits, three on the starboard side abreast the island, one on the starboard side a little further aft, and two aft, all being made with general purpose bombs, except one hit aft by a land bomb.

Damage to the *Yorktown* was not serious. The hole, 10 feet in diameter, in the flight deck caused by the first bomb, was covered in less than half-an-hour. By 1412 repairs to the uptakes were completed, and the ship with two boilers disabled was able to steam at 19 knots, all fires had been extinguished and refuelling of fighters on deck was again possible. At 1320 the cruisers *Vincennes* and *Pensacola* and destroyers *Benham* and *Balch*, from Task Force 16, joined to reinforce her escort. The position of the ship at 1402 was 33° 51' N., 176° 00' W., course 090 degrees.

Torpedo Attack on *Yorktown*

When the report of sighting an enemy carrier came in to the *Hiryu* from the *Tone*'s seaplane, a type 13 experimental ship-based bomber was despatched from the *Soryu* (0830), to maintain contact with the carrier; owing, however, to a wireless breakdown the Japanese did not learn until the return of this aircraft that in addition to the *Yorktown*, there was a task force (T.F. 16) that included a carrier of the *Enterprise* class and another of the *Hornet* class. Task Force 16 had also been sighted by the *Hiryu*'s bombers, but the signal reporting the force, though timed 1140, was not received by the *Hiryu* until nearly an hour later.

At 1331 the *Hiryu* flew off against the *Yorktown* a second attack group, composed of four fighters and nine torpedo aircraft, supplemented by two fighters from the *Kaga* and one torpedo aircraft from the *Akagi*.[47] They were picked up by the radar guardship *Pensacola* at 1427 at 33 miles distance, on bearing 340 degrees, and the combat air patrol which was overhead at the time, six *Yorktown* fighters which had been rearmed and refuelled on board the *Enterprise*, was vectored out to intercept. The first four aircraft, flying at 10,000 to 12,000 feet, overran the Japanese who were coming in at 5,000 feet, and had to turn back to find them. The other two which took off a few seconds later, met the enemy 10 to 14 miles out.

Once again the *Yorktown* suspended fuelling her aircraft and introduced CO_2 into her fuel lines. Eight of the 10 fighters on deck had sufficient fuel in their tanks to fight, but there was only time to launch four of them before the guns opened up. The American force was in circular formation, with the carrier in the centre of the reinforced screen of four cruisers and seven destroyers, steering a course of 90 degrees, at 20 knots, the enemy approach being from the port quarter. The Americans apparently again over-estimated the size of the attack group, which they considered to number 12 to 16 torpedo bombers and about the same number of fighters, though the Japanese reported the actual figures to be 10 and six respectively.

Fire was opened at 1441 at a range of 12,000 yards by the cruisers *Pensacola* and *Portland* on the side of the screen towards the enemy aircraft, nine of which got through the fighter opposition and had already begun their glide to torpedo release point. They were in two groups; five aircraft headed to pass astern of the *Pensacola* towards the *Yorktown*, and two or three to pass ahead of her through the heavy curtain of fire thrown up by the screening ships. Although the Japanese report that all nine fired their torpedoes only four torpedoes were seen and only five aircraft survived the attack. The *Yorktown* avoided two torpedoes which crossed her bow, but the last two, released at about 800 yards, struck her on the port side amidships at about 30 seconds' interval at 1445.

> 'By 1447 firing ceased. The *Yorktown*, listing heavily to port, was losing speed and turning in a small circle to port. She stopped and white smoke poured from her funnels. The screening vessels began to circle.'
>
> 'Inside the *Yorktown* all lights had gone out. The diesel generators were cut in, but the circuit breakers would not hold and the ship remained in darkness. The list gradually increased to 26 degrees. Without power nothing could be done to correct it. The Commanding Officer and the Damage Control Officer thought it probable that the ship would capsize in a few minutes, and at 1455 orders were given to abandon ship. Inside, men clambered over steeply sloping decks in total darkness to remove the wounded. After an inspection in which no living personnel were found, the Commanding Officer left the ship.'
>
> 'Destroyers closed in to pick up survivors.'[48]

Only half the Japanese attack group, viz., five torpedo bombers and three fighters (two of the *Hiryu*'s and one of the *Kaga*'s) survived to return to the *Hiryu*, where preparations were at once made for a third attack on the U.S. carriers at dusk by the six fighters, five bombers and four torpedo aircraft which were all that remained. It was now known that the American force included three carriers, but it was thought that the bombing and torpedo attacks respectively had been made on two different carriers both of which had been damaged, the first by five or six bomb hits, the second by two torpedoes, for when the Japanese torpedo bombers attacked at 1441 the *Yorktown* showed no sign whatever of the damage she had sustained in the recent bombing.

Before the third attack group could fly off, however, the *Hiryu* herself came under the attack which destroyed her.

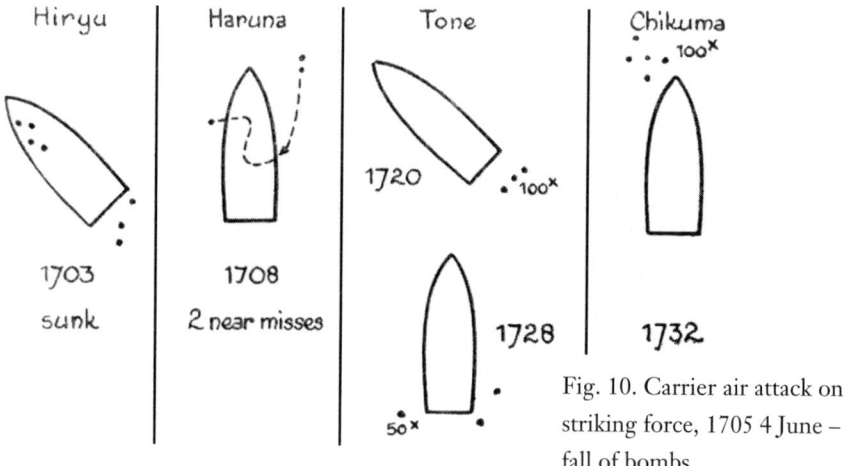

Fig. 10. Carrier air attack on striking force, 1705 4 June – fall of bombs.

Attack on the *Hiryu*

The *Hiryu* had been sighted about 1430, a few minutes before the torpedo attack on the *Yorktown*, by one of the ten scout bombers sent out on reconnaissance by the flagship at 1150. Her position was given as 31° 15' N., 179° 05' W., and she was stated to be accompanied by two battleships, three heavy cruisers (actually two and one light cruiser) and four destroyers, steering a northerly course at 20 knots.[49]

At 1530 the *Enterprise* began launching an attack group of 10 of her own scout bombers and 14 from the *Yorktown*, 11 of them armed with one x 1,000 lb. and 13 with one x 500 lb. bombs. The *Hornet* at 1603 began launching a squadron of 16 scout bombers. Both groups appear to have proceeded independently to the attack.

The *Enterprise* bombers sighted the enemy at 1650, steering a course 280 degrees and well spread out. Three columns of smoke to the southward marked the three Japanese carriers attacked earlier in the day. The *Hiryu* had fighters overhead, and they shot down one of the American bombers before it began its dive and two as they were pulling out. The Americans dived in from the sun from 19,000 feet, and four direct hits soon rendered the *Hiryu* a mass of flames. One bomber attacked a battleship, apparently the *Haruna*, without success.

Attack by *Hornet*'s Bombers on the *Tone* and *Chikuma*

By the time the *Hornet* squadron arrived 25 minutes later the *Hiryu* was burning so fiercely that it was obviously unnecessary to damage her further, and the attack was diverted to a battleship and a cruiser as the American airmen believed, though actually it would appear to have been directed at two cruisers, the *Tone* which reported ten and the *Chikuma* five bombs, all within 50 to 100 yards of the ships, neither of which suffered any damage.

B.17s Attack Japanese Striking Force

Elimination through serious damage of four Japanese carriers had given the Americans command of the air, though they were by no means certain whether there were any further enemy carriers in the area.

Meanwhile, it had been an anxious day at Midway. Owing to the great distances over water between landing grounds it was impossible to get fighter reinforcements to the island, after practically all the fighters there had been put out of action in the course of the single Japanese raid. At 1115 there was a false air raid alarm caused by the return of 12 of the *Hornet*'s dive-bombers that had failed to find the target, coming in to Midway short of fuel; they dropped their bombs on the edge of the airfield causing considerable confusion, then landed, with the exception of one which fell in the lagoon. The seven B.17s with defects that were fuelled and ready for flight took off for Hawaii, leaving only eight on the island, of which half were ready for service though later two more were repaired. In the early afternoon, before the news of the naval air attacks on the Japanese carriers arrived, the estimate at Midway was that Army aircraft had damaged one enemy carrier; the losses of the Marine air group were so heavy that it appeared their attack had been broken up before reaching the enemy; the *Yorktown* had been hit; the enemy with three undamaged carriers was still coming on and it seemed possible that before sunset Midway would be under bombardment by surface vessels. At the airfield, all confidential papers were ordered to be burned at noon.[50]

Damage to the fuelling system and other equipment at Midway rendered refuelling and servicing of aircraft so slow that the aircraft still remaining were unable to make repeated attacks on the enemy during the afternoon as would have been so desirable. At 1500, however, four serviceable B.17s which were ready were sent out under Lieut.-Colonel W. C. Sweeney Jr., U.S. Army Air Corps, to attack the Occupation Force approaching on bearing 265 degrees and thought to be then about 265 miles distant. Whilst on the way to the target, orders were received to attack a carrier on bearing 334 degrees, 185 miles distant from Midway, and the Fortresses accordingly turned to the northward.

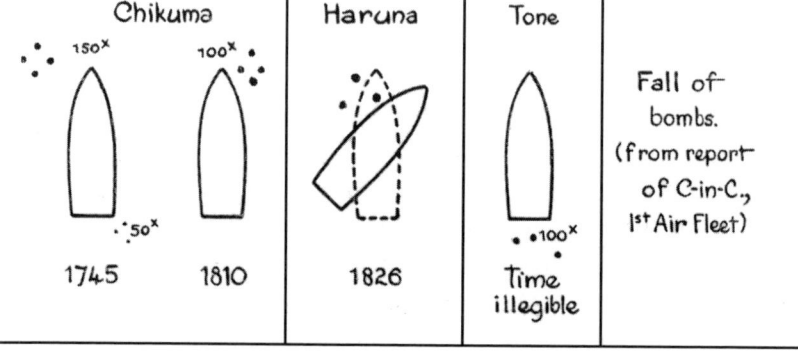

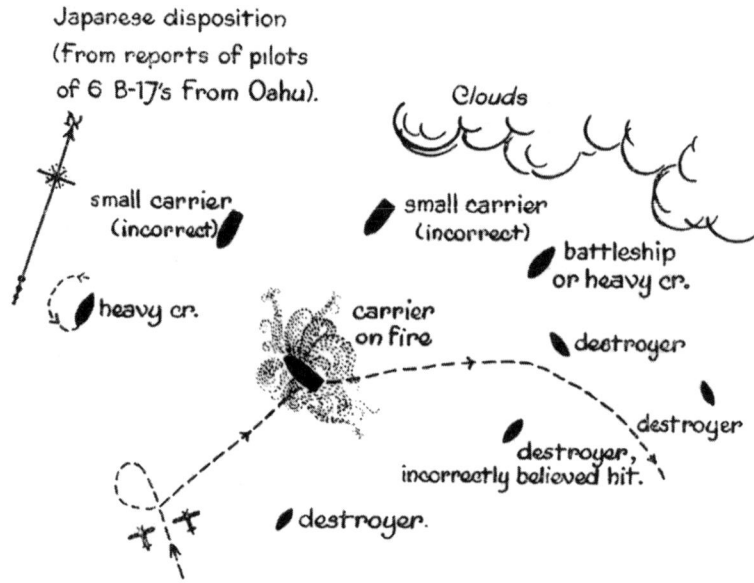

Fig. 11. Attack on striking force by Army B.17s, 1810–1830 4 June.

Contact was made about 1810, but the carrier found in the area was burning and apparently abandoned, and another ship believed to be a battleship was also thought to be on fire. Attack was consequently made on a heavy cruiser, on which 28 x 500 lb. demolition bombs were dropped from 20,000 to 25,000 feet altitude, one hit being (incorrectly) reported.

Two more B.17s were made ready and took off about an hour later under Captain C. E. Wurtele, U.S. Army Air Corps. They found the same force, estimated as two damaged carriers, two battleships or heavy cruisers, and six or eight light cruisers or destroyers. Bombs were dropped from 9,600 to 12,000 feet on various ships of the force and two hits on a battleship and two on a damaged carrier were (incorrectly) reported.

Meanwhile, during this latter attack six more Fortresses were seen to be engaged in bombing the enemy force from a lower altitude. These six aircraft, under Major G. A. Blakey, U.S. Army Air Corps, had been sent from Barking Sands Airfield, Molokai (Hawaiian Islands), each with half a bomb load and one bomb bay tank, to reinforce Midway, and were ordered at 1610 to attack the Japanese striking force, before landing. To save fuel, the squadron attacked from its cruising altitude of 3,600 feet. A large burning carrier was seen surrounded by a screen of a battleship, two heavy cruisers and destroyers; and pilots also reported (incorrectly) a second, or even two more, smaller carriers. The aircraft attacked out of the sun, on course about 60 degrees. Heavy A.A. fire was encountered, and several enemy fighters were met, four of which were reported shot down. Eight bombs were dropped on a carrier which was already aflame, and one destroyer: the latter was (incorrectly) believed hit and sunk. All six aircraft came safely to Midway after sunset.

In all, these 12 Fortresses dropped 52 x 500 lb. bombs: 18 further bombs failed to release. No hits were made and no damage was caused to any of the Japanese ships.

Midway Aircraft Attempt Night Attack

After the Fortresses at Midway had been refuelled and serviced the eleven Marine dive-bombers remaining fit to fight were got ready. About 1700, when the report of the successful dive-bombing attack on the *Hiryu* came in, Major B. W. Norris, commanding Squadron 241, was ordered to attack the enemy carrier, reported burning bearing 338 degrees distance 200 miles from Midway. In order to avoid enemy fighters it was decided to make a night attack, and about 1830 to 1900 six S.B.D.s under Captain M. A. Tyler and five S.B.D.3s under Major Norris took off.

Rain squalls were encountered, and at sunset cloud increased; and although the position of the Japanese had been reported with considerable accuracy and the striking force was still in the same general area where it had been for some time engaged in rescuing fighter aircraft crews, the bombers searched without success. All aircraft returned safely except that of Major Norris, which plunged into the sea on the return.

M.T.B.s Attempt to Attack, 1930

A final endeavour to attack the damaged carriers and other Japanese ships in the area was made by the 11 M.T.B.s which left Midway about 1930 for their 200 mile trip. However, the squally weather and low visibility which provided excellent conditions for attack also operated adversely on the chances of finding the target. The M.T.B.s searched until dawn and then returned to Midway. A Japanese reconnaissance aircraft bombed and machine gunned one of the boats in the morning without causing serious damage.

The *Hiryu* Sinks

Though the American attempts to attack during the night of 4/5 June had not produced any results, the enemy was destined to suffer yet another serious blow before daybreak.

The *Hiryu*, though heavily on fire, had remained capable of steaming for some four hours after the dive-bombing attack at 1705/4; during this time she made every effort to escape from the area and fight the fires. These could not be got under control, however; one after another the men in the engine rooms were killed at their posts; the list gradually increased to 15 degrees; further operation of the ship became impossible.

About midnight, there were hopes that the fires might yet be got under control, but another explosion re-kindled them; by 0315/5 it was evident that further fire fighting was useless, and all hands were ordered to abandon ship. The crew were taken off by the destroyers *Kazegumo* and *Makigumo*. Rear-Admiral Yamaguchi and the Commanding Officer, Captain T. Kaki, shared the fate of the ship when she was sent to the bottom at 0510 by a single torpedo from the *Makigumo* in 31° 27.5' N., 17° 23.5' W.

With her went the last of the 253 aircraft lost by the striking force on this disastrous day.

Pursuit of the Enemy

Movements of the U.S. Force, Night 4/5 June

When the six B.17s under Major Blakey landed at Midway after sunset on 4 June the situation was by no means clear. Information as to the strength and position of the Japanese forces in the bad weather area to the northward was incomplete. The Fortresses had encountered several Japanese fighters, and although these might have been, and actually were, the protective cover left in the air from the *Hiryu* when she was attacked, the possibility of a fifth Japanese carrier in the area could not be disregarded. A fifth carrier, the light carrier *Zuiho*, did in fact take part in the Midway operation, but was never sighted; she was detached with the Aleutian screening force which had not yet rejoined the main body. There was every indication that the enemy was continuing to close and no certainty that the loss of air support would deter him from the landing on Midway which it was the concern of Task Forces 17 and 16 to prevent. Battleships had been reported with the enemy force, and the latter might be superior to Task Force 16 which was now operating independently of Task Force 17 and was the only American force remaining in the area.

Rear-Admiral Fletcher with Task Force 17, after leaving the destroyer *Hughes* to stand by the abandoned *Yorktown*, moved off to the eastward, despatching the *Pensacola* and *Vincennes* to rejoin Rear-Admiral Spruance. His intention was to transfer the survivors from the destroyers to the cruiser *Portland*, which would then proceed to Pearl Harbor, whilst the *Astoria* and destroyers would return next morning to salvage the *Yorktown*. These plans were modified by a message from Admiral Nimitz that the submarine tender *Fulton* had been despatched to take over the survivors. Captain Buckmaster (*Yorktown*) with 180 key officers and men therefore returned with the destroyers *Hammann*, *Balch* and *Benham* to the *Yorktown* whilst the remainder of Task Force 17 moved on to refuel and subsequently to join the carrier *Saratoga* for operations in the Solomon Islands.

In order to avoid a night action with possibly superior forces and yet to be in a position next morning either to pursue the enemy if retreating or to break up an attempted landing on Midway, Rear-Admiral Spruance decided to move east for a time during the night 4/5 June.

At 2115/4 orders had been sent to the U.S. submarines to form on a circle radius 100 miles from Midway; they were to arrive on station and dive before dawn. The wisdom of the move was soon apparent, for it was from one of these submarines that the next intelligence of the enemy was received, when at 0205/5 the *Tambor* reported many unidentified ships about 90 miles west of Midway. The *Tambor* failed to report the course and speed of the enemy, nor did she shadow or attack.

The contact indicated to the Americans that the enemy was persisting in his plans for a landing on Midway. All submarines were directed to close the island in order to be in position to attack the enemy transports and supporting ships at a time when they would be most vulnerable.

But the expected assault never materialised. The enemy was the Japanese fast support consisting of the 7th Cruiser Squadron and two destroyers, steering for Midway, to bombard the island; and the appearance of the *Tambor* was destined to have a decisive effect on the operation.

Japanese Movements

The Japanese, who were planning a night attack with all their surface forces on the American ships, at 1728 noticed the general easterly course which Task Force 16 had steered during the afternoon of 4 June. A few minutes earlier, one of the *Chikuma* reconnaissance aircraft had sighted what was estimated to be four enemy carriers, six cruisers, and 15 destroyers, in addition to the burning and listing *Yorktown*, though fighters prevented the aircraft from shadowing. What had happened was that, unknowingly, the aircraft had sighted Task Force 16 twice, with an interval of six minutes, and failed to recognise the two forces as identical. The report was not received until 1830, and it was the first inkling Admiral Nagumo, Commander of the striking force, had of the overwhelming American carrier strength.

To an Admiral who had just lost the whole of his carrier force, the blow must have been severe, and at 1915, to his further dismay, he received from the Commander-in-Chief, Admiral Yamamoto, a signal beginning: 'The enemy fleet has practically been destroyed and is retiring eastward,' and concluding: 'The Striking Force, Occupation Force (less 7th C.S.) and

Advance Force[51] will immediately make contact with and destroy the enemy'. Such a mistaken appreciation of the situation clearly called for correction, and Admiral Nagumo pointed out unequivocally, in two separate signals, that the American force contained five carriers, four of which were still undamaged, and that all four of his own carriers were out of action. Although the Admiral Commanding his own 8th Cruiser Squadron, whose seaplanes had been doing all the useful reconnaissance, signalled that the enemy force consisted of two carriers, and there was the suspicious circumstance that the aircraft which made the original report of four undamaged carriers was unable, on demand, to supply the class and speed of more than two of them, Admiral Nagumo apparently paid no attention. At least half his destroyers were away assisting his crippled carriers and he was in no condition to undertake a night action against an enemy with which, moreover, he was not in touch. He therefore abandoned the idea of a night attack, continued his north-westerly course, and bent his energies to attempting to save his last remaining carrier, the *Hiryu*, and getting her out of the danger area.

Meanwhile, Vice-Admiral Kondo, having sent back the transport unit and air group at 1300, to be out of harm's way, was bringing the fighting units of the Occupation Force northward to co-operate with the striking force in attacking the U.S. ships, and he so informed Admiral Yamamoto. It seems probable that the Commander-in-Chief was uncertain whether Admiral Nagumo was still in company with his battleships and cruisers; he was aware that the C.-in-C. 1st Air Fleet (Commander Striking Force) had transferred to the *Nagara* and he had just learnt that he was retiring to the north-west with the *Hiryu* whose damage apparently was not very severe since she was able to steam at 28 knots. Perhaps, therefore, it was as a precautionary measure, so that he should not lose the services of these heavy ships in the prospective night engagement, that he placed the striking force, less the *Hiryu*, *Akagi* and ships escorting them, under the command of the Commander-in-Chief Second Fleet, and called for clarification of the present whereabouts and movements of Admiral Nagumo's heavy ships, the 8th Cruiser Squadron and the 2nd Division of the 3rd Battle Squadron.[52]

The immediate result of this was an order from Vice-Admiral Kondo, for the striking force, less the *Hiryu*, *Akagi* and their escorts, to reverse course immediately and co-operate with him in attacking the American task force that night; the Vice-Admiral, who was coming up at 24 knots on course 065 degrees, with cruisers and destroyers spread in search disposition, had already some hours previously explained to all concerned his tactical intentions in the anticipated night engagement. This peremptory order was addressed, not to the C.-in-C. 1st Air Fleet, but to the Commander Striking Force, for Vice-Admiral Kondo was obviously unaware that Admiral Nagumo (C.-in-C. 1st Air Fleet) was still with the striking force.[53] In any event, it elicited no response from Admiral Nagumo, who continued to assist the *Hiryu*;[54] a few minutes later, however, there came an order from the Commander-in-Chief of the Combined Fleet, that the forces with Admiral Nagumo and Vice-Admiral Kondo were both to rendezvous with the main body, and after some delay Admiral Nagumo reversed course and informed the Commander-in-Chief that he was preparing to carry out his instructions.

Mogami Damaged; Japanese Abandon the Operation

It had been arranged that the 7th Cruiser Squadron, the fast support group of the Occupation Force, should bombard Midway at 0200 on 5 June, and the four cruisers, under Rear-Admiral Kurita in the *Kumano*, had continued to steer towards the island when the second Fleet turned to a north-easterly course at 1200/4. This bombardment was now cancelled and the 7th C.S. was ordered to join the main body.[55]

At 0200/5, prior to receipt of the order cancelling the bombardment of Midway, the four cruisers with two destroyers were proceeding in line ahead in the order *Kumano* (flagship), *Suzuya*, *Mikuma*, *Mogami*, in approximately 28½° N., 179° W., when a submarine was sighted on the starboard bow of the flagship. All ships turned to port together, but the *Mogami* was late in receiving the order. The *Mikuma* had turned 60 degrees to port, but the *Mogami* had only turned four points when she collided with the port quarter of the *Mikuma*. The force of the collision damaged the *Mogami*'s bow, so that some of the plates below water were bent to port, reducing the ship's speed by a third or more. The *Mikuma* was also damaged. In consequence of this, the squadron abandoned the intended bombardment and retired.[56]

The news of this mishap, coming on top of the loss of his entire air power, decided the Commander-in-Chief that the operation must be abandoned and at 0255 a signal to that effect went out. All forces were to rendezvous and refuel during the morning of 6 June in position 33° N., 170° E., with the exception of the *Hiryu* and ships escorting her, and the landing force which was to move westward, out of air range of Midway. The three destroyers of the 15th Group accompanied the transports, whilst the *Jintsu* and the eight destroyers of the 16th and 18th Division had already approached the battle area in readiness to co-operate in the night engagement so closely that they saw one carrier burning.

I-168 Bombards Midway (Fig. 2)

At 2030/4 orders had been sent to the Japanese submarine *I-168*, whose patrol line passed close to Midway, to shell and destroy the air base on Eastern Island. *I-168* fired a few rounds at 0130/5, which caused no damage, and were answered by the batteries, which (erroneously) claimed a hit.

To the defenders of Midway it seemed probable that this bombardment constituted a diversion to cover the attack of a landing party. However, when no further developments followed, it was thought, in view of the Japanese losses, that the bombardment had been carried out by a submarine which had failed to receive the order to abandon the operation and retire.

Contact with the Enemy, 0545/5 June

It was not long before American aircraft from Midway discovered the retirement of the Japanese forces. All night long men had worked hard on the island servicing the remaining aircraft. The fuelling system had not yet been repaired, and 45,000 gallons of aviation spirit in 55-gallon drums were supplied by hand to the hand pumps from which the aircraft tanks were filled. Eighty-five 500-lb. bombs were loaded.

The morning of 5 June was overcast and visibility poor. The first reconnaissance aircraft took off before dawn, search being concentrated in the sector 250 degrees to 20 degrees, to a distance of 250 miles. Within two hours enemy sighting reports began to come in, the most important of which were as follows:—[57]

(*Mikuma* and *Mogami*)
    0630   2 battleships bearing 264 degrees, distance 125 miles, course 268 degrees, speed 15 knots.
    0632   Ships damaged, streaming oil.
(*Kumano* and *Suzuya*)
    0700   2 enemy cruisers, bearing 283 degrees, distance 174 miles, course 130 degrees, speed 20 knots.
(*Striking Force*)
    0719   5 ships, bearing 325 degrees, distance 200 miles.
    0735   5 ships, course 338 degrees, speed 25 knots, 31° 15' N., 179° 55' W.

0800   2 battleships and 1 carrier on fire, 3 heavy cruisers, bearing 324 degrees, distance 240 miles, course 310 degrees, speed 12 knots.
0815   Cruiser and destroyer screening burning carrier, battleship well ahead.
0820   1 carrier, bearing 335 degrees, distance 250 miles, course 245 degrees.

The two damaged heavy cruisers were of course the *Mikuma* and *Mogami* and in company with them were the destroyers *Arashio* and *Asashio*. The other two ships of the 7th Cruiser Squadron, the *Kumano* and *Suzuya*, had drawn ahead of the damaged vessels during the early morning hours, and altered course to the north-westward to rendezvous with the main body after the abandonment of the operation.

The main body of the enemy escaped detection since it never approached nearer to Midway than 350 miles. The Second Fleet, also, only came within the extreme range of search for a short period, before altering course at 0330/5 for the rendezvous with the main body after the cancellation of the operation.

Marine Aircraft Group Attacks *Mikuma* and *Mogami*

The Commanding Officer of the Midway Naval Air Station gave orders for attack on the two 'battleships' of the 0630 report, bearing about 270 degrees, distance 150 miles.[58] Only 12 aircraft of the Marine group remained fit for action; these took off about 0700–0730 in two groups of six, armed with 500-lb. bombs. One group of six S.B.D.2s under Captain M. A. Tyler was to make a dive-bombing attack from 10,000 feet, followed by a glide bombing attack by six S.B.2Us. under Captain R. E. Fleming from 4,000 feet.

The weather was clear with scattered clouds at 8,000 feet. After flying about 100 miles the wide oil streak left by one of the damaged ships was picked up and the attackers were able to follow it for 40 miles to the target, which Captain Tyler's group reached soon after 0800.

The S.B.Ds. dived out of the sun on the *Mogami* from about 10,000 feet. Heavy A.A. fire was encountered, but no aircraft was hit. In the glide bombing attack by S.B.2Us. that followed, however, Captain Fleming's aircraft was hit, but he held to his glide and released his bomb before bursting into flames and being destroyed. It was perhaps this aircraft which, as the Japanese report, dived into the *Mikuma*'s after turret and started fires and caused damage which reduced the ship's speed somewhat. The second section of S.B.2Us. made their glide from out of the sun, broadside to the target. The glide bombers believed they had made some direct hits, but the Japanese reported this was not so, though some near misses were made, causing slight damage. Captain Fleming's was the only aircraft to be lost.

Attack on *Mikuma* and *Mogami* by B.17s

Captain Fleming's group had barely drawn clear when the *Mikuma* and *Mogami* once more came under attack. Twelve B.17s that remained at Midway had taken off[59] armed with 500-lb. bombs and pursued a westerly course. At a distance of about 100 miles, when they had climbed to 10,000 feet, they received orders to attack two enemy battleships bearing 270 degrees, distance 130 miles from Midway.

Only eight of the Fortresses found the target, about 0830, after a period of considerable difficulty during which at one time they had turned back towards Midway. They attacked in two groups of four, one group the *Mikuma* and the other the *Mogami*, the two cruisers now being four or five miles apart. The attacks were made from 20,000 feet, the groups dropping 19 and 20 bombs respectively, whilst a further 13 hung up. The first group did not observe the results of their attack; the second group reported one hit and one near miss. The Japanese, however, reported that no hits were made. Heavy A.A. fire was experienced, but no damage was caused to any aircraft.

B.17s Attack *Tanikaze*, 1635[60] and 1840

After servicing at Midway on return from the attacks just described the Fortresses were again sent out. At 1320 seven, of Flight 92, each armed with eight 500-lb. demolition bombs, set out to the north-west under Lieut.-Colonel B. E. Allen, U.S. Air Corps, to continue the attacks on the remnant of the retreating Japanese striking force. One ship, estimated to be a heavy cruiser, was sighted on the outward journey, but no other enemy were seen. On the return, at 1636, the Fortresses attacked what they took to be the same heavy cruiser, in position reported to be 32° 20' N., 178°. Actually, the ship was the *Tanikaze*, one of the destroyers of the striking force, but it is not known why she was alone.

Four of the Fortresses attacked from 16,000 feet and dropped 32 bombs, making, as they estimated, two hits and three near misses; the other three

Fortresses dropped 24 bombs from 14,500 feet, reporting one hit and one near miss. The *Tanikaze* was not hit, however; and only five bombs were seen. Her anti-aircraft fire caused no damage to any of the bombers.

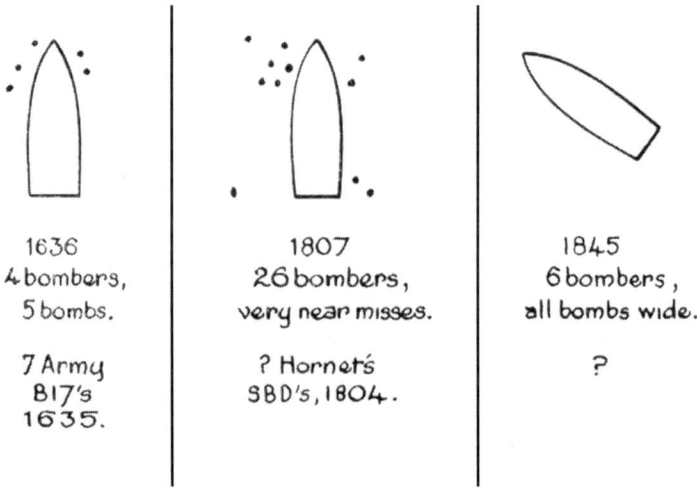

Fig. 12. Attacks on *Tanikaze*, 5 June – fall of bombs.

Five further B.17s (Flight 93) under Captain D. E. Ridings left Midway at 1545 for the last attack of the day on the carriers, by Midway aircraft, taking a more northerly course than Flight 92. By this time, clouds had gathered in the north to a heavy overcast at 12,000 feet and the group failed to find the target, but on the return journey they attacked a supposed carrier in position about 310 degrees, 420 miles from Midway, at 1840.[61] This may have been the *Tanikaze*, which reported being bombed at 1845, though all bombs fell wide. The squadron dropped 15 x 600-lb. and 8 x 300-lb. bombs from altitudes ranging from 9,000 to 12,500 feet. The results were not seen. Very heavy A.A. fire was encountered and it was probably this which caused one of the Fortresses to drop its bomb bay tank; this aircraft about 2330 reported 'out of gas and landing' and was not seen afterwards. One other aircraft was also lost through shortage of fuel though all but one of the crew were picked up. The remainder became separated in the clouds on the return and were guided into Midway by radar.

The failure of the air searches from Midway on the morning of 5 June, to sight the Japanese striking force, was due largely to the weather, though there was an additional reason, namely the change of course of the remnant of the striking force, viz. the 8th C.S. and Section 2 of the 3rd B.S., to the westward during the small hours of 5 June, after the cancellation of the Midway operation, in order to make rendezvous with the main body in about 31° N., 176° 45' E., at 1155 that morning. Consequently, the Fortresses were searching across the enemy's course, rather than along it. The *Akagi* was scuttled at 0500 and the *Hiryu* sank at 0510, so that by the time the air searches reached the area where yesterday four damaged carriers had been seen, the sea was empty of ships.

Carrier Aircraft Search for Japanese Striking Force

Meanwhile, Rear-Admiral Spruance had been doing his utmost to follow up yesterday's successes of the U.S. carriers, but the retirement of the enemy during the night had put the opposing forces too far apart for attack to be possible until the later afternoon.

When the *Tambor*'s enemy sighting report came in at 0217 Task Force 16 had just altered course (0200) to 270 degrees, after a short detour to the northward during which there was radar contact with an unknown craft about 60 miles off to the north-west, and in the belief that it betokened a landing Rear-Admiral Spruance increased speed to 25 knots and set a course to close Midway to attack the enemy. At 0600 he was on a southwesterly course about 130 miles north-east of Midway, position 29° 50' N., 175° 44' E.

The enemy reports sent in by the Midway aircraft between 0630 and 0820, indicating that an enemy retirement was in progress, were presumably intercepted by Task Force 16,[62] who estimated that there were two principal enemy groups as follows:–

(a) a transport group west of Midway followed by two damaged heavy cruisers (*Mikuma* and *Mogami*) (reported as battleships);
(b) the striking force attacked on 4 June, of two battleships (one reported damaged), three heavy cruisers, and four destroyers, followed by a burning carrier (*Hiryu*), to the north-west.

Rear-Admiral Spruance was faced with a choice of two objectives, both of which contained good targets, and he chose the one to the northwest; for although it was further away, it contained the crippled carrier and two battleships, one of which was reported already damaged. The existence of a belt of bad weather about 500 miles to the north-west of Midway was known, and the possibility that the remnants of the retreating Japanese force might find concealment therein, was accepted. At 1100 course was altered to 300 degrees to close the enemy; and except for turning into the wind when the *Enterprise* and *Hornet* launched attack groups between 1500 and 1530, this course was maintained until sunset at 1900, when course was altered to the westward, shortly after crossing the 180th meridian.

'The chase continued at 25 knots throughout the afternoon,' says the *U.S. Combat Narrative*, elaborating the few words of Task Force 16 in attempting to retrieve the situation caused by the retirement eastward during the first half of the previous night. During the forenoon of 5 June the only incident was the rescue of the crew of a patrol aircraft found on the water about 0900 by the destroyer *Monaghan*, which was then detached to join the *Yorktown*'s screen. Four M.T.B.s were sighted at 1232, returning from their unsuccessful night's search for the enemy. At 1420 Rear-Admiral Spruance received from Admiral Nimitz a sighting report of two battleships, three cruisers, five to ten destroyers, one burning carrier and one carrier smoking badly in latitude 32° N., longitude 179° 32' E. at 0800, course 310 degrees, speed 12 knots. At about 1400 a flight of B.17s passed over.[63] Rear-Admiral Spruance signalled his intention of launching an attack about 1500. The planes did not reply, but were heard reporting the position of the task force to Midway. Later Rear-Admiral Spruance received the 'disquieting information' that the B.17s had failed to find the enemy force. His last report of the enemy's position was based on a morning contact, and as the afternoon wore on prospects became less and less promising.

Attacks on Japanese Destroyers

At 1500, when the enemy force was estimated to be about 230 miles distant, launching of two strike groups began. The *Enterprise* launched 32 scout bombers, armed with 1 x 500-lb. bombs, the *Hornet*, at 1512, 26 scout bombers. The sky was heavily overcast and visibility poor.

Rear-Admiral Spruance's retirement eastward during the night 4/5 June had lost too much time. The hour was too late and the range too long, and the Japanese had escaped out of reach of the American carrier aircraft.

The *Hornet*'s group searched to 315 miles without finding the enemy. At 1804 they attacked what was believed to be a light cruiser or destroyer in approximately 33° N., 177° E. The enemy ship was apparently the destroyer

Tanikaze, which reported being attacked at 1807 and very near missed by 11 bombs from 26 bombers. The attackers saw no hits.

The *Enterprise* group searched to 265 miles, then turned to port for a leg. They, too encountered what was believed to be a light cruiser or destroyer in 33° 00' N., 177° 00' E., and between 1830 and 1900, at dusk, they attacked her with 32 bombs, none of which hit. The enemy destroyer manoeuvred at full speed and her A.A. fire was stated to be unusually heavy, and one scout bomber was shot down.[64]

The U.S. aircraft had little fuel left when they returned to their ships and landed after dark. One of the *Hornet*'s attack group had to make a water landing near the *Enterprise*, but the *Aylwin* rescued the crew.

Last Contacts and Sinking of the *Yorktown*

Mikuma and *Mogami* Sighted

Nightfall on 5 June found Task Force 16 approaching the bad weather area into which it was useless to follow the enemy. No Japanese forces had been found for 250 miles to the north-westward. There remained the possibility that the striking force might either turn westward towards Japan, or south-west to join their transports. Rear-Admiral Spruance consequently set a course 280 degrees for the night and reduced speed to 15 knots, both to economise his destroyers' fuel and to avoid overtaking any enemy battleships in the dark.

After the retirement of the enemy became apparent, the fastest U.S. submarines were sent in chase and others returning from western patrols were directed to the expected lines of retirement of the enemy.

About 0510 on 6 June, the *Enterprise* launched a search group of 18 scout bombers, each armed with one 500-lb. bomb, to search to a distance of 200 miles in the entire western semi-circle, between 180 and 360 degrees. A light wind from the south-west facilitated launching and recovery of aircraft throughout the day with minimum deviation from the southwesterly course (230 degrees) to which Task Force 16 altered at 0800.

It was not long before the first enemy sighting reports came in.

Two contacts were made almost simultaneously. The first at 0640 was of two heavy cruisers and two destroyers on course south-west, speed 15, bearing about 275 degrees, distance 400 miles from Midway. The second at 0645, bearing about 280 degrees, distance 435 miles from Midway, though variously identified appears to have been the *Mikuma* and *Mogami*, with three or four destroyers, on course west, speed 10 knots.[65] Rear-Admiral Spruance estimated that there were two enemy groups, the second about 50 miles south-east of the first, though as the hours passed and further reports came in, both from the *Enterprise* search groups, from the two scout observation aircraft which the *Minneapolis* and *New Orleans* each launched at 0720, and from the crews of returning attack groups, the positions and composition of the enemy forces became more and more confused.[66] Actually, the whole of the reports referred to the same enemy group, namely the *Mikuma* and *Mogami*, which with the destroyers *Asashio* and *Arashio* were making what speed westward the damaged condition of the two cruisers permitted.

Rear-Admiral Spruance took as his target what was believed to be the more northerly of the two enemy groups, which was, by report, the closer, and by some reports contained a battleship. It was believed to be a remnant of the striking force. The southern group was left for attack by long-range aircraft from Midway.

First Attack on *Mikuma* and *Mogami* by *Hornet* Group

At 0800 Task Force 16 altered course to south-west and the *Hornet* began launching an attack group of 26 scout bombers, 18 armed with 1,000-lb. bombs and eight with 500-lb. bombs. Eight fighters escorted the group, in case of air opposition.

The attackers found the enemy force without difficulty. To the pilots, the group of two heavy cruisers and two destroyers appeared to consist of a battleship, a heavy cruiser, and three destroyers.[67] The aircraft attacked about 0930, taking as the principal target the supposed battleship, the *Mikuma*, on which they believed they obtained three hits and two near misses, an estimate which accords with the Japanese report. Her navigation was affected, and she was left turning to starboard in uncontrolled circles. The *Mogami* was also correctly estimated to have been hit twice: the first 1,000-lb. bomb landed on top of No. 5 turret, penetrated the armour, and killed the entire turret's crew; the second hit the ship amidships, damaged torpedo tubes, and started fires below decks, which were, however, extinguished. One of the destroyers was also hit in this attack, but the ship remained navigable, though the attackers believed they sank her.

There was no air opposition, so the fighters occupied themselves by machine-gunning the enemy destroyers. Anti-aircraft fire, however, shot down one of the American dive-bombers.

Enterprise Group Attacks *Mikuma* and *Mogami*

The *Enterprise* about 1115 sent off a group of 31 scout bombers armed with 1,000-lb. bombs, escorted by 12 fighters. The target was given as two battleships, two heavy cruisers, and several destroyers in 29° 33' N., 175°

35' E., course 270 degrees, speed 15 knots.[68] The scout bombers proceeded independently and climbed to about 19,000 feet. At 1200 they sighted a force estimated to consist of one heavy cruiser, one light cruiser, and two destroyers. Part of the group searched ahead for the reported battleships. One dive-bombing squadron, however, began about 1200 an attack on the *Mikuma*, the more easterly of the two cruisers. The other squadrons came in later, and the attack on both heavy cruisers continued in this manner until after 1300, the aircraft diving out of the sun from 21,000 feet.

The *Mogami* was again hit twice, once amidships and once forward of the bridge, which started fires and slowed her down. The *Mikuma* was hit several times and was set on fire; the *Arashio* tried to go alongside to rescue the crew, but the fires were too fierce, so she lowered her boats and picked up the men from the water.

Three torpedo aircraft were sent from the *Enterprise* to take part in the attack, but they failed to make contact with the scout bombers and made no attack.[69]

All the *Enterprise*'s aircraft returned safely.

Second Attack by *Hornet*'s Group; Sinking of *Mikuma*

The *Hornet*'s attack group had returned to their ship at 1045 and refuelling and re-arming for a second attack began at once. At 1330 this group of 24 scout bombers armed with 1,000-lb. bombs took off to attack the enemy now reported bearing 264 degrees distance 110 miles from the *Hornet*. All four of the Japanese ships were still afloat when they were sighted at 1500 and the attack by 23 aircraft commenced.[70]

The *Mogami* received another hit amidships. The bomb penetrated the deck and killed men fighting the earlier fire and also damaged the doors leading to the engine room so that a number of men were trapped in the fire. About 93 men were reported killed in this attack, but the *Mogami* was still able to steam.

The *Mikuma* was hit several more times and was left a shambles. One bomb hit the *Arashio* in the stern, killing almost all the survivors of the *Mikuma* who were on deck; but the *Arashio*, like the *Mogami*, remained navigable, and both ships, as well as the *Asashio*, which apparently suffered no damage, escaped. The *Mikuma* was still afloat at 1730 when one of two photographic aircraft sent out from the *Enterprise* returned with a photograph showing her gutted and abandoned. She sank that night at some time unknown, the position of sinking being estimated by the Joint Army-Navy Assessment Committee as approximately 30° N., 173° E.

B.17s Bomb *Grayling* in Error
One other air attack took place on 6 June, by part of a flight of B.17s despatched at 1145 to attack the southern group of the Japanese transport force. The enemy were not found, but on the return by separate routes one section of six of the Fortresses, at 1640, in a position bearing about 262 degrees, 400 miles from Midway (approximately 27° 20' N., 175° 05' E.) sighted a vessel. The Fortresses were at 10,000 feet altitude, and in spite of the unlimited visibility identification of type was difficult.

The first section of three aircraft dropped four bombs each and thought they had hit the target, which disappeared in 15 seconds. No bombing run was made by the second section, since no attack signal was given.[71]

The wing aircraft, believing that a bombing run was in progress, released her bombs, which were considerably off the target; the leading aircraft returned with his bombs.

The vessel attacked was the U.S. submarine *Grayling* which crash dived when the first bombs fell near her bow, and was not damaged.

This was the only attack made by Midway aircraft on 6 June.

Escape of the Japanese (Plan 1)
The main body, the striking force (less the four sunken carriers), and the Second Fleet (less the *Mikuma* and *Mogami* and accompanying destroyers) met at 1155/5 in approximately 31° 30' N. 176° 50' E. The exact route by which the main body reached this position is not known.[72] The combined force made good its escape by a considerable detour to the westward. A rendezvous for refuelling during the forenoon of 6 June was ordered in position 33° N., 170° E. By 0900/6, however, the various forces had already made rendezvous and were in position 33° 30' N., 172° 50' E. The Aleutian screening force had joined up shortly before, and the 3rd Battle Squadron and 4th Cruiser Squadron of the 2nd Fleet here met the *Kumano* and *Suzuya*.

The combined force steered a course 270 degrees whilst fuelling, during which it fully expected to be attacked from the air. Nothing happened, however, and the main body with the remnant of the striking force turned south at 1500/6 in 33° 30' N., 169° 10' E., to a position in 28° 40' N., 169° 10' E., where it turned westerly and returned to the Inland Sea with the transports of the Occupation Force. The Second Fleet turned south some hours earlier and met the damaged *Mogami* with the two destroyers at 0900/7 in 28° N., 171° E., when the *Kumano* and *Suzuya* escorted the *Mogami* to Truk and the 4th Cruiser Squadron went to Saipan, whilst the battleships went on to Japan.

Rear-Admiral Spruance did not pursue the enemy further. The long period of high speed steaming had reduced his destroyers' fuel, and the *Maury* and *Worden* had to be detached to refuel from the *Cimarron*. With the *Benham*, *Balch* and *Monaghan* also away screening the *Yorktown*, Task Force 16 was left with only four destroyers. Enemy submarines were reported in the area, and moreover it would have been dangerous to come within range of Wake, where the Japanese were known to have concentrated an air force in readiness for transfer to Midway. Consequently, after the *Hornet* landed on her attack group at 1720, Rear-Admiral Spruance turned north-east and began to retire.

Sinking of the *Yorktown* and *Hammann*

Whilst Task Force 16 was endeavouring to follow up the successes of 4 June, some 400 miles to the eastward the stricken *Yorktown* was making but little progress. Prematurely abandoned[73] on the afternoon of 4 June, she continued to float during the night of 4/5 June whilst the *Hughes* stood by her. Her list remained about constant. On the morning of 5 June the destroyer rescued two wounded men who had been overlooked when the ship was abandoned, and also picked up a *Yorktown* fighter pilot, shot down in action, who rowed up in his rubber boat.

The minesweeper *Vireo* and fleet tugs *Seminole* and *Navajo* had been despatched to assist.[74] The *Vireo* from Pearl Harbor and Hermes Reef arrived about noon and at 1436/5 began towing at about two knots on course 090 degrees, for Pearl Harbor. The flooded carrier, with rudder jammed, proved too heavy for the *Vireo*, which by next day was barely able to keep the *Yorktown* on her course. During the afternoon of 5 June the destroyers *Monaghan* and *Gwin* arrived, the latter having been diverted whilst on passage to join Task Force 16. The *Gwin* put a salvage party aboard, but it was removed at dusk, before being able to accomplish much. The *Hammann*, *Balch* and *Benham* returned to the carrier about 0200/6.

About 0415/6, as soon as there was sufficient light, the *Hammann* went alongside and transferred to the *Yorktown* a salvage party of 29 officers and

130 men under Captain Buckmaster. In order to supply power for operating submersible pumps, and foamite and water for fire fighting, it was found necessary to secure the *Hammann* alongside, as she could not lie clear and keep position accurately, and she was secured on the starboard side forward.[75] The remaining four destroyers circled the two ships at 12 to 14 knots as an A/S screen.

By the afternoon the salvage party had made considerable progress, and the *Yorktown*'s list had been reduced some 2 degrees.

But that morning (6 June) the *Yorktown* had been sighted listing and drifting by a reconnaissance aircraft from the *Chikuma*, and submarine *I-168*, whose patrol line was near Midway, was ordered to attack her (see Fig. 2). This she lost no time in doing.

At 1335 the wakes of four torpedoes were sighted to starboard of the *Yorktown*. The *Hammann* went full speed astern on her starboard engine, but in the minute that elapsed before the torpedoes struck there was insufficient time to pull the ships clear. Apparently two torpedoes hit the *Hammann*, one of which broke her back, and two struck the *Yorktown* below the island. The hole torn in the carrier's side by the resulting explosion apparently flooded the starboard fire rooms, for the list was reduced to 17 degrees and the ship settled a little.

The *Hammann* sank within three or four minutes. Most of the crew managed to get clear, but about a minute after she disappeared a heavy underwater explosion occurred, which killed and injured a great many men. As the depth charges were known to be set to safe it was surmised that the explosion may have been caused by the *Hammann*'s torpedoes, one of which was said to have been seen running hot in its tube as the ship sank.[76]

Destroyers hunted the submarine all the afternoon. At about 1845 a submarine surfaced on the horizon and was attacked. But *I-168* escaped undamaged.

The destroyers being thus preoccupied, it was decided to defer further salvage attempts on the *Yorktown* until next day. The *Vireo* took off the salvage party and all water-tight doors remaining undamaged were closed.

At 0501/7, however, before the salvage party boarded her again, the *Yorktown* capsized to port and sank in 3,000 fathoms in about 30° 36' N., 176° 34' W.

Lessons and Effects of the Battle

Experience Gained

The Americans were not slow to recognise the lessons of the battle.[77] Some of these concerned material, such as the inferiority of the Navy fighter aircraft to the Japanese in speed, manoeuvrability and rate of climb; the fatal inadequacy of the Douglas torpedo bomber and the necessity for developing long range fighters to support the Grumman torpedo bomber which was unable to attack ships defended by fighters, whilst the aerial torpedo itself needed a larger warhead and to be designed for much higher release speed.

U.S. carrier task forces were re-organised to provide stronger close screen of cruisers and destroyers in consequence of the demonstrated value of such a screen in the torpedo attacks on the *Yorktown*; Admiral Nimitz considered that had the *Yorktown* not been slowed down by previous bombing damage she might have avoided all the torpedoes fired by the only four Japanese aircraft that succeeded in penetrating the screen.

On the operational side, both Admiral Fletcher and Admiral Spruance stressed the vital importance of timing the first attack on enemy carriers whilst the latter had their aircraft on board. In so far as the Americans were able to do this, Midway was a victory of pre-battle intelligence resulting in a tactical situation in their favour. Once battle was joined, however, there was a failure to maintain continuous contact with the enemy, one cause of which was the unsuitability of the Navy patrolbombers for carrying out their important function of shadowing due to their inability to face fighter opposition. 'The lack of information on the enemy's surface forces between 0623 and 1000 [on 4 June] was serious and jeopardized the tactical advantage we enjoyed over the enemy', wrote Admiral Nimitz.[78] The delay of the *Enterprise*'s air group attack against the enemy carriers and the failure of the *Hornet*'s scout bombers to make contact with the enemy can be attributed to this lack of information. Further, the loss of aircraft from the *Hornet* and *Enterprise* by water landings from lack of fuel can be partly attributed to the same cause.

The Japanese were guilty of the fatal omission to scout to the eastward of their striking force prior to launching their air attack on Midway, their planning having been based on the assumption that they need not fear the very thing that destroyed them, namely carrier air attack.

There were two marked failures of co-ordination in the U.S. air attacks on 4 June. The first was apparently due to lack of time not permitting adequate study and thought.[79] On the morning of 4 June, all the four groups of Midway aircraft, the Army B.26s, the Navy torpedo aircraft (T.B.F.) and the Marine dive-bombers, though flown off at about the same time, attacked separately between 0710 and 0720. Experience indicated that had they attacked together there would have been greater likelihood of damaging the enemy.

The second instance, the failure to co-ordinate the carrier dive-bombing and torpedo attacks between 0920 and 1025, as had been so successfully done at the Battle of the Coral Sea a month earlier, probably had little effect on the damage caused to the Japanese, though it resulted in the loss of 35 out of 41 torpedo aircraft.

The escape of the Japanese main body and survivors of the striking force, without being brought under air attack by Task Force 16 dive-bombers on 5 June, consequent on Rear-Admiral Spruance standing to the eastward during the first part of the previous night, can certainly be attributed to the orders of the Commander-in-Chief, U.S. Fleet, not to risk ships unduly, and to the fact that the Americans were defending a fixed point, and had been warned against a probable enemy trap.

Midway was the only defensive battle of the war in the Pacific in which American submarines were extensively employed. Lack of search radar for night shadowing was held to be a primary reason for failure; and directional (SJ) radar was installed in most of the submarines within a few months.

Effects of the Battle

The Americans repulsed the attempted invasion of Midway at a cost of the *Yorktown* and *Hammann* sunk and 307 men and 150 aircraft lost. The Japanese lost the carriers *Akagi, Kaga, Hiryu* and *Soryu* and the heavy cruiser *Mikuma*; whilst the heavy cruiser *Mogami*, the destroyer *Arashio*, and tanker *Akebono Maru* suffered major, and the destroyer *Tanikaze*, minor damage. Losses of Japanese officers and men were about 3,500 and aircraft 253.

The loss of four carriers, 250 naval aircraft and 100 pilots was crippling to the Japanese. The striking force with which they had achieved their conquests, and on which they relied to repulse American attempts to counter attack, was destroyed. Their shipbuilding capacity and air training organisation were too limited to enable them to make good their losses, with consequential effect on their future operations throughout the war.

This great American victory completely reversed the strategic situation in the Pacific. It put an end to the long period of Japanese offensive action, removed any threat to India, stopped Japanese expansion to the east, and saved Midway Island as an important U.S. outpost. It was perhaps the decisive battle of the war in the Pacific.

Appendix A

Organisation of the Japanese Forces

Admiral I. Yamamoto, Commander-in-Chief Combined Fleet
Main Body

1st Battle Squadron	*Yamamoto* (Flag of Adm. I. Yamamoto)
	Mutsu
	Nagato
2nd Battle Squadron	*Ise*† (Flag of Vice-Adm. S. Tokasu)
	Hyuga†
	Fuso
	Yamashiro†
9th Cruiser Squadron	*Kitagami*† (Flag of Rear-Adm. F. Kishi)
	Oi†
3rd Destroyer Flotilla	*Sendai* (Light cruiser) (Flagship)
	12 destroyers
Carrier Division	*Zuiho*† (Light carrier)
No.1 Supply Group	*Naruto*
	Toei Maru
	1 destroyer†
No.2 Supply Group	*Sacramento Maru*†
	Tora Maru†

Note.–Ships marked † composed the Aleutian Screening Force. Part of the 3rd Destroyer Flotilla was also employed.

Striking (or 1ˢᵗ Mobile) Force – Admiral C. Nagumo, Commander-in-Chief, 1ˢᵗ Air Fleet

Air Attack Force –
    1ˢᵗ Carrier Squadron   *Akagi* (Flag of Adm. Nagumo) Captain Aoki
                                            Kaga Captain Okada[80]
    2ⁿᵈ Carrier Squadron   *Hiryu* (Flag of Rear-Adm. T. Yamaguchi) Captain Kaha[80]
                                            Soryu Captain Yanagimoto[80]

Supporting Force –
    3ʳᵈ Battle Squadron (2ⁿᵈ Division)   *Haruna*
                                                        Kirishima
    8ᵗʰ Cruiser Squadron   *Tone*
                                     Chikuma
    10ᵗʰ and 2ⁿᵈ Destroyer Flotilla[81] (part)   *Nagara* (Light cruiser)
                                                                   16 destroyers

Supply Force –
    No. 1 Supply Group   *Kyokuto Maru*
                                   Shinkoku Maru
                                   Toho Maru
                                   Nippon Maru
                                   Kokuyo Maru
    No. 2 Supply Group   *Nichiro Maru*
                                   No. 2 Kyoei Maru
                                   Hoko Maru

Occupation Force
Screening Force or Distant Cover
(Based on 'Task Organisation for Midway Operations' –
Doc. No. 160985–B   N.I.D. 0052799/47)
(Vice-Admiral N. Kondo, Commander-in-Chief, Second Fleet)

3ʳᵈ Battle Squadron (part)   *Kongo* (Flag of Vice-Adm. Kondo)
                                           Hiyei

4th Cruiser Squadron (part)	*Atago* (Flag of Rear-Adm. G. Mikawa)
	Chokai
5th Cruiser Squadron (part)	*Myoko*
	Haguro
4th Destroyer Flotilla[82]	*Yura* (Light cruiser), (flag of Rear-Adm. S. Nishimura)
Destroyer Division 2	*Murasame*
	Samidare
	Harusame
	Yudachi
Destroyer Division 9	*Asagumo*
	Minegumo
	Natsugumo
Supply Group and Tankers	*Onoe Maru*
	Kitagami Maru
	Koryo Maru
	Kaijo Maru
	Akashi (repair ship)

Fast Support

7th Cruiser Squadron	*Kumano* (Flag of Rear-Adm. T. Kurita)
	Suzuya
	Mikuma
	Mogami
	Nichiei Maru (? tanker)
Destroyer division 8	*Asashio*
	Arashio

Close Escort and Transport Unit

2nd Destroyer Flotilla	*Jintsu* (Light cruiser) (flag of Rear-Adm. R. Tanaka)
Destroyer Division 15	*Kuroshio*
	Oyashio

Destroyer Division 16	*Yukikaze*
	Tokitsukaze
	Amatsukaze
	Hatsukaze
Destroyer Division 18	*Shiranuhi*
	Kasumi
	Kagero
	Arare
11th Carrier Squadron	*Chitose* (Seaplane carrier) (flag of Rear-Adm. R. Fujita)
	Kamikawa Maru (Seaplane carrier)
One Destroyer (of 2nd D.F.)	*Hayashio*
Minesweeping Division 16	? one minesweeper
	M.T.B. No. 5, Patrol Boat No. 3
	Patrol Boats Nos. 1, 2, 34, 35
S/M Chaser, Division 21	3(?1) Submarine Chasers[83]
Transports and Supply Ships	(?) *Kinryu Maru* (Transport)
	Argentia Maru (Transport)
	Kyozumi Maru (Transport)
	Brazil Maru (Transport)
	Nankai Maru (Transport)
	Kirishima Maru
	Kano Maru
	Toa Maru 2
	Goshu (?*Goryu* or *Gosei*) *Maru*
	Sanyo Maru
	Akebono Maru (Tanker)
	Zenyo Maru
	Azuma Maru
	Seito Maru
	(*Keiyo Maru*)
	Hokuroko Maru
	Meiyo Maru[84]

Occupation Troops

C.-in-C. 2nd Combined S.N.L.F.

1 Regiment (1,500 men) Marines (for Sand Island)[85]

1 Regiment (1,000 men) Army (for Eastern Island)[86]

11th and 12th Construction Battalions

1 Survey Force

1 Weather Group

  About 50 Marines and 11th Air Flotilla for Curé (Ocean) Island Seaplane Base, with *Patrol Boat No. 35*

16 Submarines of Sixth Fleet (Vice-Adm. T. Komatsu, C.-in-C., flag in *Natori* at Kwajalein).

24th Air Flotilla (search from Marshall Islands)

26th Air Flotilla (search from Marcus Island)

Appendix B

Organisation of the U.S. Forces

        Rear-Admiral F. J. Fletcher in command
        Task Force 16

Carrier	*Yorktown*, Capt. E. Buckmaster (Flag of Rear-Adm. Fletcher) 36 scout bombers, 12 torpedo bombers, 25 fighters
Cruisers	*Astoria*, Capt. F. W. Scanland (Flag of Rear-Adm. W. W. Smith)
	Portland, Capt. L. T. Du Bose
Destroyers	*Hammann*, Comdr. A. E. True (Broad pdt. of Capt. G. C. Hoover)
	Morris, Comdr. H. B. Jarrett
	Russell, Lt.-Cdr. G. R. Harting
	Anderson, Lt.-Cdr. J. K. B. Ginder
	Hughes, Lt.-Cdr. D. J. Ramsey

        Task Force 16

Carriers	*Enterprise*, Capt. G. D. Murray (Flag of Rear-Adm. R. A. Spruance)
	Hornet, Capt. M. A. Mitscher
	Each 35 scout bombers, 14 torpedo bombers, 27 fighters
Cruisers	*Pensacola*,[87] Capt. F. W. Lowe (Flag of Rear-Adm. T. C. Kinkaid)
	Northampton,[87] Capt. W. W. Chandler
	Vincennes,[87] Capt. F. L. Riefkhol
	Minneapolis,[88] Capt. F. J. Lowry
	New Orleans,[88] Capt. W. S. De Lany
	Atlanta (Light A/A Cruiser),[88] Capt. S. P. Jenkins

Destroyers	*Phelps*, Lt.-Cdr. E. L. Beck (Broad pdr. of Capt. A. R. Early)
	Balch, Lt.-Cdr. H. H. Tiemroth
	Benham, Lt.-Cdr. J. M. Worthington
	Worden, Lt.-Cdr. W. G. Pogue
	Aylwin, Lt.-Cdr. G. R. Phelan
	Monaghan, Lt.-Cdr. W. P. Burford
	Ellet, Lt.-Cdr. F. H. Gardner
	Maury, Lt.-Cdr. G. L. Sims
	Conyngham, Lt.-Cdr. H. C. Daniel.
Oiler Groups	Oilers *Cimarron, Platte*.
	Destroyers *Dewey, Monssen*

Submarine Force

Rear-Admiral R. H. English, Commander Submarines, U.S. Pacific Fleet

Cachalot	*Narwhal*
Cuttlefish	*Nautilus*
Dolphin	*Pike*
Drum	*Plunger*
Finback	*Pollack*
Flying Fish	*Pompano*
Gato	*Porpoise*
Grayling	*Tambor*
Greenling	*Tarpon*
Grenadier	*Trigger*
Grouper	*Trout*
Growler	*Tuna*
Gudgeon	

Midway Local Defence

M.T.B. Squadron One   11 M.T.B.s
(Lieut. C. McKellar, Jr.)

Midway Aircraft[89]
(as on 3 June 1942)
Captain C. T. Simard, Cmdg. N.A.S. Midway

Group 22, 2nd Marine Aircraft Wing, Fleet Marine Force	28 fighters (21 F2A Brewster Buffalo, 7 F4F Grumman Wildcat *(Br.* Martlett) 34 Scout [dive] bombers (18 Douglas Dauntless, 16 Vought-Sikorsky Vindicators *(Br.* Chesapeake) (only 30 pilots available)
reinforced by	6 TBF (Navy torpedo bombers – Grumman Avenger *(Br.* Tarpon) 30 Catalina patrol bombers
Seventh Army Air Force	4 B.26 (fitted for torpedoes) 17 B.17.

Appendix C

Japanese Occupation Force Messages

Extracts (paraphrased as necessary) from records of the *Kamikawa Maru*.

1 June

1. 1750 From *Chitose* to *Kamikawa Maru*. By W/T.
   S/M *I-168* reports:–
   1. Summary of Curé Is. reconnaissance. (Omitted).
   2. Sighted enemy patrol flying boats as follows:–
   1235/29 May in 228° Midway 460 miles.
   0700/30 May in 285° Midway 210 miles:
   at 0340/31 May in 170°. Curé I. 7 miles.
   They always seem to take off from Midway before sunrise.

2 June

2. 1145 From *Chitose* to *Kamikawa Maru*. By signal.
   To Occupation Force Air Group. R. *Jintsu*, *Brazil Maru*. Arrangements for approach to Curé I.
   1. This force† is to proceed to arrive at position 26° 26' N., 171° 10' E., at 1500/3.
   2. At about same time Seaplane carrier Division 11 and *Hayashio* will proceed according to plan at about 17 knots.
   3. *Patrol Boat No. 35* fuel as feasible and proceed independently to arrive at target area by 0200/5.

   †It is thought that the Transport Unit and Direct Escort are meant.

3 June

3. 0730 From *Chitose*. By signal.
   To Invasion Force Air Group. R. *Jintsu*, *Akebono Maru*.
   Separation of this unit from the Escort Force will be changed to about 1100/3.

4. 1037 From *Chitose* to *Kamikawa Maru*. By signal.
   All ships launch 4† observation aircraft.

   †The wording of the signal is 'launch one *Shotai*'. A *Shotai* is a Japanese formation of 4 aircraft.

5. 1040 From *Chitose* to all ships. By signal.
   Raise steam for maximum battle speed at 10 minutes' notice at 1300.

6. 1130 From *Chitose*. By signal.
   Sighted enemy flying boat bearing 300° at 0958: enemy disappeared course west.

7. 1235 From *Chitose* to *Kamikawa Maru*. By signal.
   When aircraft recovery completed resume original course.

8. 1250 From *Chitose* to Air Force. By signal.
   Ultra short wave will be used in inter-unit communications until otherwise ordered. Vessels operating outside visual signal range switch to medium length wave radio without further orders.

9. 1258 From *Chitose* to *Kamikawa Maru*. By signal.
   All aircraft recovered: enemy flying boats not sighted.

10. About 1622 From ? to Combined Fleet. By W/T.
    T.O.O. 1610. T.O.R. 1622. Am engaging enemy aircraft in position grid RE 1 MU 11. From *Submarine Chaser 17*.

11. About 1634 From 2ⁿᵈ Destroyer Flotilla (*Jintsu*) to Occupation Force. By W/T.
    Nine enemy land planes sighted bearing 34° Wake Is. 510 miles.

12.	About 1734	From 2nd Destroyer Flotilla to Occupation Force, 1st and 11th Air Fleets, Combined Fleet. By W/T. T.O.O. 1650. T.O.R. 1734. Attacked by 9 B.17s at 1600 with bombs. No damage. Attack repulsed by 1645.

4 June

13.	0435	From *Chitose* to *Kamikawa Maru*. By signal. Convoy is in contact with enemy aircraft.
14.	0945	From C.O. Guard Force to C.-in-C. Combined Fleet. By W/T. At 0800 today enemy force consisting of one carrier, 5 cruisers, 5 destroyers, was sighted in 10° Midway Island 240 miles, proceeding towards us.
15.	1200	From C.-in-C. 2nd Fleet to Occupation Force, C.-in-C. 1st Air Fleet, Combined Fleet, Comdr. 11th Seaplane Carrier Division. By W/T. Occupation Force proceed towards Striking Force, course 50°, speed 28 knots.
16.	1300	From C.-in-C. Occupation Force to Commander Force. By W/T. 1. Escort Unit, Transport Unit, and Air Group will retire immediately to the north-west. 2. Support Unit will join the Main Body with despatch.
17.	1350	From C.-in-C. Occupation Force to Air Regiment of 2nd Fleet. By W/T. Support Force will attack and destroy Midway base installations tonight.
18.	1355	From C.-in-C. Occupation Force to Occupation Force. By W/T. 1. *Jintsu* and two divisions of 2nd Destroyer Flotilla will join the Main Body. 2. Comdr. Seaplane Carrier Division 11 take command of remnant of Escort Force and escort Occupation Force.

	1400	From *Chitose* to *Kamikawa Maru* and *Patrol Boat No. 35*. By signal.
		Kamikawa Maru and *P.B. No. 35* maintain present course, speed 16 knots.
20.	1430	From Comdr. Seaplane Carrier Division 11 to C.-in-C. Occupation Force. By W/T.
		My position is (grid YU YU KE 44), course 285°, speed 24 knots. Expect to join Occupation Force at 1900.
21.	1445	From *Chitose* to *Kamikawa Maru*. By signal.
		Occupation Force 1300 p.c.s. 27° 10' N., 175° 11' E., 315°, 12 knots.
22.	1445	From *Chitose* to Seaplane Carrier Division 11. By W/T.
		1. Our Striking Force made contact at 0800 with an enemy force of 3 carriers, 5 cruisers, 20 destroyers. An enemy carrier was set on fire, but the *Akagi*, *Kaga* and *Soryu* were also set on fire. C.-in-C. has transferred to the *Nagara*.
		2. The *Hiryu* is continuing the attack.
		3. Main Body and Support Force of Occupation Force are proceeding at high speed to join forces to starboard. Escort Force p.c.s. (grid YU ME YU 33) 315° 12 knots. Occupation Force and Air Force have retreated one hour in a north-westerly direction.
23.	1450	From *Chitose* to Seaplane Carrier Division 11. By signal.
		The *Chitose* and *Hayashio* are preceding the Transport Unit. *Kamikawa Maru* take *P.B. No. 35* under her command and join *Chitose*.

5 June

24.	0462	From *Chitose* to Escort Force and Air Force. By signal.
		Speed at 0700, 9 knots.

25. 0820 From *Chitose*. By signal.
> Midway Operation has been abandoned. This unit will leave the area within range of enemy flying westward, maintaining A.S. and A.A. patrols.

26. 0830 From C.-in-C. 2nd Fleet to Occupation Force, Comdr. Air Forces of Combined Fleet. By W/T.
> 1, 2. 2nd D.F. in accordance with special orders, with one destroyer division and two destroyers will join Occupation and Escort Forces and take over their escort from Comdr. Seaplane Carrier Division 11.

27. 1515 From *Chitose* to Air Group. By signal.
> Ships will discontinue zigzagging and will proceed at half speed at 2000 without signal, resuming original speed and zigzagging at 0530/6 without signal.

6 June

28. 0745 From *Chitose* to Occupation Force, Air Force. By signal.
> 1. *Kamikawa Maru* is to fuel *Patrol Boat No. 35* and proceed as convenient to join first section of Third Fleet.†
>
> 2. *Patrol Boat No. 35* escort *Kamikawa Maru*, rejoining this unit with despatch after junction is made with Third Fleet by *Kamikawa Maru*.
>
> †This is thought to be a mistranslation for Section 1 of 3rd Battle Squadron *(Kongo, Hiyei* (2nd Fleet)

29.   1340   From C.-in-C. Invasion Force to 8th C.S., Occupation Force. By radio.
1. Main force of Occupation Force (including 3rd B.S., 2nd D.F., and 8th C.S.) will contact, attack, and destroy enemy aircraft carrier force; *Mikuma* will reinforce *Mogami*.
2. Supply Force will stand by at (grid FU KO N 39).
3. *Zuiho* will prepare to attack enemy aircraft carriers.
4. All reconnaissance seaplanes prepare for following action with despatch: 3-seat R/C seaplanes to search out enemy and 2-seat R/C seaplanes to attack enemy aircraft carriers and other vessels. (All aircraft will be loaded with regular bombs.)

30.   1750   From *Chitose* to all ships of Transport Unit. By signal.
At 1830 ships will proceed on planned course as follows at speeds indicated: 1st Unit *(Brazil Maru, Argentina Maru, Seicho* (sic) 16 knots) with *Oyashio* [destroyer] guide and patrol ship leave the formation and constitute the van; 2nd Unit *(Nankai [Maru], Zenyo [Maru], Coshu* (sic) *[Maru], Azuma [Maru], Hokuroko [Maru], Kirishima [Maru], Kano [Maru],* and *Toa [Maru],* 14 knots) with the *Kuroshio* destroyer, *Patrol Boat No. 2*, and *Patrol Boat No. 34* constitute left wing formation; 3rd Unit *(Akebono [Maru], Keiyo [Maru]* (13 knots) with *Akebono* (sic) and *Patrol Boat No. 1* assemble in rear. Position 1500 today was 165° 30' E., course 270°. Alter course to 250°; from position 26° 40' N., 156° 40' E., alter course again to 270°. Air Force will operate generally in the area between second and third units. Ships which lose touch should join other convoys as feasible and reassemble at Minami Tori shima (or Marcus I., approx. 24½° N., 154° E., an island claimed by Japan prior to the war).

Appendix D

Japanese Striking Force – Chronology and Signals
(Extracts, paraphrased as necessary, from Report of C.-in-C. 1st Air Fleet.)

2 June

1.	0900	2nd D.F. commences fuelling.
2.	1530	Position 37° 1.5' N., 171° 7-0' E., course 130°.

3 June

3.	0250	Fog clears.
4.	0607	Supply Unit and *Akigumo* detached, course 130°, speed 12 knots.
5.	1417	From Comdr. Striking Force to Striking Force. No. 25. Raise steam for 26 knots at 0400/4 and for maximum battle speed at 20 minutes notice from 0400/4.
6.	1500	Speed 24 knots.

4 June

7.	0330	Course 130°.
8.	0354	Speed 20 knots.
9.	0430	Midway attack units take off.
10.	0442	Course 135°.
11.	0450	Speed 24 knots.
12.	0520	From Comdr. Striking Force to Striking Force. Visual signal. Unless unforeseen changes in the situation occur, the second attack wave will be carried out today.
13.	0555	From *Tone* search aircraft to Striking Force. Enemy aircraft sighted bearing 90°.

14.	0600	Fighters take off from all ships. Enemy aircraft sighted bearing 090°, distance 23 miles.
15.	0609	Speed 28 knots.
16.	0645	From *Hiryu* Attack Unit to Comdr. Striking Force. Attack completed. Unit is returning to ships.
17.	0649	From *Chikuma* Aircraft of No. 4 search line. Am returning on account of bad weather. Position 350 miles from point of origin (bearing 11° from Midway) (0635).
18.	0700	From Air Officer, *Hiryu* to Striking Force. By W/T. Second attack wave needed.
19.	0705	*Akagi* sighted 9 enemy aircraft bearing 150°, range 27,000 yards, elevation 0.5°. Assumed battle speed No. 5, heading into above aircraft.
20.	0705	*Tone* sighted 10 enemy heavy bombers bearing 35°, to port, elevation 15°, range 20,000 yards.
21.	0706	*Chikuma* sighted about 10 PBYs distant 19½ miles right ahead.
22.	0707	*Akagi* opened fire with starboard A.A. guns.
23.	0707	*Tone* opened fire with main armament.
24.	0711	Own fighters in combat with enemy aircraft.
25.	0712	*Akagi* noted enemy aircraft launched torpedoes.
26.	0714	Enemy aircraft carry out horizontal bombing attack on carrier. No hits.
27.	0715	From C.-in-C. 1st Air Fleet. Aircraft in second attack wave stand by to carry out attack today. Re-equip with bombs.
28.	0716	*Chikuma* turned main armament on escaping enemy aircraft.
29.	0728	From *Tone* search A/C to Comdr. Striking Force. Sighted estimated 10 enemy surface ships bearing 10° distant 240 miles from Midway. Course 150°, speed over 20 knots. (Received 0800.)
30.	0738	Own attack units return.

31.	0739	Course 100°.
32.	0745	From Comdr. Striking Force to Striking Force. Prepare to carry out attacks on enemy fleet units. Torpedoes to be retained by attack [torpedo] aircraft which have not already substituted bombs.
33.	0747	From Comdr. Striking Force to *Tone* A/C. Ascertain ship types, and maintain contact.
34.	0748	From *Soryu* to Striking Force. Six to nine enemy aircraft sighted bearing 320°.
35.	0755	*Soryu* bombed (9 or 10 bombs). No hits.
36.	0756	*Akagi* and *Hiryu* bombed.
37.	0758	From *Tone* search A/C to Comdr. Striking Force. At 0755 enemy course 80°, speed 20 knots (0758).
38.	0800	*Soryu* lays smoke screen. Stopped.
39.	0806	*Chikuma* reported enemy carrier-based aircraft bearing 25° to port heading for fleet. (These were the first carrier-based aircraft sighted by *Chikuma*.)
40.	0809	From *Tone* search A/C to Comdr. Striking Force. Enemy is composed of 5 cruisers and 5 destroyers.
41.	0810	*Akagi* and *Hiryu* hit by bombs.
42.	0820	From *Tone* search A/C to Comdr. Striking Force. The enemy is accompanied by what appears to be a carrier.
43.	0820	*Soryu* bombed. No hits.
44.	0821	*Hiryu* bombed. No hits.
45.	0823	*Nagara* lays smoke screen.
46.	0827	*Haruna* dive bombed. No hits.
47.	0830	From Comdr. Striking Force to Striking Force. Carrier-based bombers will prepare for second attack. Load 250 kg. bombs.
48.	0830	From *Tone* search A/C to Comdr. Striking Force. Have sighted 2 additional enemy cruisers in position 8° Midway 250 miles. Course 150°, speed 20 knots (0830).

49.	0855	From *Tone* search A/C to Comdr. Striking Force. 10 enemy torpedo aircraft are heading towards you (0855).
50.	0855	From Comdr. Striking Force to C.-in-C. Combined Fleet, *R* 2nd Fleet. (Rec. 0930.) No. 336. Enemy force composed of 1 carrier, 5 cruisers, 5 destroyers sighted at 0800 in 10°. Midway 240 miles. I am steering towards it.
51.	0905	From Comdr. Striking Force to all ships. By S.L. After landing your aircraft proceed northward. I intend to contact and destroy the enemy task force.
51A.	0917	Course 070°.
52.	0918	All ships displayed enemy aircraft sighting signals.
53.	0918	Completed landing-on of attack units.
54.	0918	*Chikuma* sighted 16 enemy aircraft bearing 52° to starboard, elevation 2°, distance 19 miles.
55.	0918	Speed 30 knots.
56.	0919	*Akagi* takes evasive action.
57.	0920	*Chikuma* opened fire with main armament.
58.	0922	Ceased firing.
59.	0923	*Akagi* sighted 18 enemy aircraft bearing 122° to starboard, elevation 0.5°, distance 43,580 yards.
60.	0925	*Chikuma* laid two smoke screens and opened fire with main armament.
61.	0929	*Chikuma* opened fire with A.A. guns. *Tone* opened fire with main armament at enemy aircraft. *Kaga*'s fighters take off.
62.	0929.5	From *Tone*'s search A/C. My fuel supply is running low. I am breaking off the contact and am returning home.
63.	0938	From *Chikuma* to C.S.8. Aircraft off at 0938 [to relieve *Tone* search A/C.]
64.	0938	Sighted 14 enemy torpedo aircraft bearing 140° to port, elevation 1° distance 43,500 yards.

65.	0945	Friendly fighters engaging enemy flying boats bearing 40° to starboard. (About 32 enemy flying boats already brought down.) *(Chikuma.)*
66.	0946	*Akagi* noted that the torpedo aircraft groups to port were attacking Carrier Division 2.
67.	1000	*Akagi* noted that 10 of the torpedo aircraft group were brought down by friendly fighters.
68.	1000	From C.-in-C. First Air Fleet to C.-in-C. Combined Fleet, C.-in-C. Second Fleet, C.-in-C. Sixth Fleet, D(2), *R* (others): By W/T. Carried out air attack on Midway at 0630. Many enemy shore-based aircraft attacked us subsequent to 0715, causing no damage. At 0728 enemy force of 1 carrier, 7 cruisers, 5 destroyers sighted in (grid position TO SHI RI 34), course S.W., speed 20 knots. After destroying this force I intend to resume attack on Midway. My position at 1000 is (grid HE E A 00) course 30° (speed 24 knots).
69.	1015	*Akagi* sights enemy torpedo aircraft group of 12 aircraft bearing 170° to port, range 49,000 yards.
70.	1022	*Kaga* dive bombed.
71.	1023	Several aircraft suddenly emerged from clouds and dived on *Akagi*.
72.	1024	Fires break out on board *Kaga*.
73.	1026	(Description of attack on *Akagi* by 3 dive-bombers. Fatal hit.)
74.	1028	*Soryu* hit by bombs.
75.	1033	*Akagi* sights 4 enemy torpedo aircraft bearing 80° to port, elevation 4°. Ship turns to course 0°, with full helm.
76.	1036	*Akagi* reduced to cruising speed by damage to starboard after engine.
77.	1037	*Chikuma* opens fire with starboard A.A. guns on 10 enemy aircraft bearing 70° to starboard.
78.	1042	*Akagi*'s steering damaged: engines stopped.
79.	1042	Enemy aircraft retreat.

80.	1045	From *Chikuma* search A/C to Comdr. Striking Force. (Received 1118.)

      Have sighted 5 additional cruisers and 5 destroyers in position bearing 10°, distance 130 miles from point of origin. Course of enemy 275°, speed 24 knots (1045).

81. 1047   From Comdr. Striking Force to C.-in-C. Combined Fleet.

      Have sighted enemy force of 1 carrier, 5 cruisers, 5 destroyers in position 10°, Midway 240 miles. Am heading towards it.

82. 1050   From C.S.8 to C.-in-C. Combined Fleet and C.-in-C. Second Fleet.

      Fires are raging aboard the *Kaga*, *Soryu* and *Akagi* caused by enemy land-based and carrier-based attack aircraft. Intend *Hiryu* to engage enemy carriers. Meanwhile we are temporarily retiring to the north and assembling our forces. My position is (grid TO W A N 55) (1050).

83. 1050   From C.S.8 to Comdr. Carrier Division 2.

      Attack the enemy carriers.

84. 1050   From Comdr. Carrier Division 2 to C.S.8.

      All aircraft are taking off now to destroy enemy carriers.

85. 1100   From C.S.8 to *Chikuma* Nos. 5 and 4 Search A/Cs.

      Report position of enemy carriers. Lead attack unit to it.

86. 1116   From *Chikuma* No. 5 search A/C to C.-in-C.

      Weather clear in vicinity. Cloud 5, cloud base 800 to 1000. Wind direction 85°, velocity 5 metres. Visibility 30 miles.

87. 1120   From *Hiryu* to all ships.

      Second wave composed of 18 bombers and 5 fighters has taken off. Intend additional 9 attack aircraft and 3 fighters to take off in one hour. *Hiryu* intends to proceed towards the enemy on present course.

88.	1128	From Comdr. Striking Force to *Chikuma* No. 5 search A/C.
		Enemy bears 70° distant 90 miles from us (1110).
89.	1130	From Comdr. Carrier Division 2 to C.S.8.
		Am despatching one destroyer to each of the damaged carriers, and to proceed towards the Main Body.
90.	1130	From Comdr. Carrier Division 2 to C.S.8.
		Maintain contact with enemy carrier by means of float reconnaissance aircraft.
91.	1130	From Comdr. Striking Force to C.-in-C. Combined Fleet, C.-in-C. 2nd Fleet, *RD*. (2).
		Akagi, *Kaga* and *Soryu* considerably damaged by enemy bombing attack about 1030. Fires have broken out aboard them and they are unable to take part in any operations. C.-in-C. First Air Fleet has transferred to *Nagara*. After attacking the enemy intend to proceed north* with my forces. (Grid position HE IA 00.)
		* Another version timed 1150 has 'retire North'.
92.	1137	From *Soryu* R/C A/C.
		Have sighted enemy force in position 4° Midway 150 miles.
93.	1140	From *Hiryu* bombers. (Received 1230.)
		Enemy air force has as nucleus 3 carriers. These are accompanied by 22 destroyers (1140).
94.	1141	From *Chikuma* No. 5 search A/C to *Hiryu* bombers.
		Enemy bears 70° distant 90 miles from our fleet.
95.	1143	From C.S.8 to Comdr. Striking Force.
		[? I] have a part of 8th C.S., 3rd B.S. and 10th D.F. prepared to proceed to attack the enemy.
96.	1145	From Comdr. Striking Force to C.S.8.
		Hold up.
97.	1145	From Comdr. Striking Force aboard *Nagara* to *Tone*.
		Assemble and wait.

| 98. | 1147 | From *Hiryu* to *Tone, Akagi, Kaga, Soryu*. By W/T.
Leave one destroyer with damaged carriers; remainder to proceed on the course of attack. |
|---|---|---|
| 99. | 1159 | From Comdr. Striking Force. By W/T.
Assemble. We are going to attack the enemy. Form in order 10th D.F., 8th C.S., 3rd C.S. Course 170°, speed 12 knots (1130). |
| 100. | 1200 | From C.S.8 to C.-in-C. Combined Fleet, C.-in-C. 2nd Fleet.
Hiryu has attacked enemy carrier. Remainder of Striking Force retiring North to reform its strength. (Grid position TO UN 55.) |
| 101. | 1200 | From C.-in-C. 2nd Fleet to C.-in-C. Combined Fleet, C.-in-C. 1st Air Fleet, Occupation Forces, C.S.8 (received 1240) No. 2.
My P.C.S. at 1200 (grid YU MI KU 00) 50°, 28 knots. Heading for Striking Force. (1200). |
| 102. | 1200 | From Command A/C of *Hiryu* to Striking Force (received 1251) No. 1.
We are attacking enemy carrier (1200). |
| 103. | 1206 | Second attack wave takes off from *Hiryu*. *Chikuma* took station astern of *Hiryu*. |
| 104. | 1215 | From Comdr. Striking Force.
Intend to destroy the enemy through daylight engagement. Assemble. |
| 105. | 1220 | From C.-in-C. Combined Fleet to all Cs.-in-C. and Comdrs. of Divisions. (Received 1300.)
Combined Fleet Secret despatch No. 294.
All forces will attack enemy in Midway area as follows:–
1. Main Body to be in position (grid FU TO MU 15) on course 120°, speed 20 knots at 1500.
2. Midway Occupation Force will assign a portion to escort the transports and retire temporarily to the North-west.
3. Second Mobile Force will R/V with First Mobile Force [Striking Force] as soon as possible. |

106. 1300   From Comdr. 4th Destroyer Division to Cs.-in-C. Combined Fleet, 2nd Fleet, Comdr. Striking Force, C.-in-C. 6th Fleet.
  Statement obtained from prisoner, an Ensign (air) from *Yorktown*.
  1. Carriers involved are *Yorktown*, *Enterprise* and *Hornet*. In addition, 6 cruisers and about 10 destroyers.
  2. *Yorktown*, accompanied by 2 cruisers and 3 destroyers acting independently of the remainder.
  3. 4. (Omitted.)

107. 1310   From Comdr. Striking Force to C.S.8, 3rd B.S. *R. Chikuma*.
  Float reconnaissance aircraft of Supporting Force are to search between 0° and 90° to distance of 150 miles.

108. 1310   From C.-in-C. Combined Fleet to all Cs.-in-C. and Comdrs. of Divisions in Combined Fleet.
  Combined Fleet Secret Despatch No. 295.
  2. The Occupation Force will assign part of its force to shell and destroy enemy air bases on Midway. The occupation of Midway and Kiska are temporarily postponed.

109. 1310   From Comdr. Carrier Division 2 to Comdr. Striking Force and C.S.8. (Received 1345.)
  Attack unit reports that enemy composed of 5 large cruisers and 1 carrier (burning fiercely) is in position bearing 80° distant 90 miles from friendly fleet at 1240. Reliability of report, excellent.

110. 1314   From *Chikuma* No. 5 Search A/C to Striking Force.
  Enemy course 20°, speed 24 knots. I am in position bearing 265° distance 30 miles from the enemy from whence I am maintaining contact (1305).

111.	1315	From *Haruna* to C.S.8. Three *Haruna*'s float R/C aircraft took off at 1300 to carry out searches. Scope of search from 140° to 340° to distance of 180 miles.
112.	1320	From *Chikuma* No. 5 search A/C to C.S.8. Four large enemy cruisers have been detached and are proceeding on course 278° speed 24 knots (1320).
113.	1331	Second attack wave took off from *Hiryu*.
114.	1340	From C.S.8 to *Chikuma* No. 5 search A/C. Report revised position of enemy concentration (1340).
115.	1340	From *Chikuma* No. 5 search A/C to C.S.8. (Received 1346.) Bearing 20°, distance 160 miles from point of origin, course 270°, speed 24 knots (1340).
116.	1345	From *Chikuma* No. 5 search A/C to C.S.8. (Received 1358.) Enemy has altered course to 90° (1345).
117.	1355	From *Haruna* A/C to *Nagara, Tone*. At 1240 enemy bore about 90° to port. Composition of enemy force 5 large cruisers and 5 carriers; the latter were burning. (T.N. The number "5" for the number of carriers had been underlined and a question mark placed alongside it.)
118.	1355	From C.S.8 to *Chikuma* No. 5 search A/C. Report strength of enemy.
119.	1400	From Comdr. Carrier Division 2 to Striking Force. By W/T. (Received 1435.) No. 132. Our bombers report there are 3 enemy carriers along a north-south line approximately 10 miles long.
120.	1445	From *Hiryu* attack A/C to Comdr. Striking Force. (Received 1438.) Have attacked enemy carrier with torpedoes. Two certain hits observed.

121.	1445	From Comdr. Striking Force to Striking Force. Visual signal.

                3rd B.S. and 8th C.S. will take station to north-west and south-east of *Hiryu* respectively. Make distance between ships long for the enemy.(?) *Nagara* take station ahead of *Hiryu*.

122.	1502	From C.S.8 to *Chikuma*. Visual signal.

                Fall out and take station bearing 180° 10 Km. (5.4 miles) from *Hiryu*.

123.	1620	(T.N. Apparently in error for 1520.)

                From C.S.8 to *Chikuma* No. 4 search A/C.
                Report composition of enemy force.

124.	1620	(T.N. Apparently in error for 1520.)

                From *Tone* No. 4 A/C to C.S.8.

                    Enemy force has 6 cruisers as nucleus and is accompanied by 6 destroyers. About 20 miles ahead of this formation there is one apparent carrier.

125.	1531	From Comdr. Carrier Division 2 to Comdr. Striking Force. By W/T. (Received 1620.)

                  After definite contact has been established with our Type 13 Experimental Ship-based Bomber I intend to despatch all aircraft remaining (5 bombers, 5 torpedo aircraft, 10 fighters) to attack and destroy remaining enemy forces in dusk engagement (1531).

126.	1531	From Comdr. Striking Force to C.S.8.

                Ascertain the main units in the large enemy force.

127.	1531	From Comdr. Carrier Division 2 to Comdr. Striking Force. By W/T. (Received 1653.)

Result of first attack wave: 5 direct hits made on *Enterprise* class with No. 25 (250 Kg.) bombs, causing large fires to break out. The above carrier and 5 large cruisers were the only ships sighted during the attack, but Type 13 experimental ship-based bombers report 2 additional carriers about 10 miles distant. Six out of 18 of our bombers and one out of 9 of our fighters returned. Second attack wave took off at 1320, and the third (6 bombers, 9 fighters) is preparing now to take off.

128.	1535	From C.S.8 to 8th C.S. Visual signal.

Tone will take station, bearing 90° and *Chikuma* bearing 180° distance 10 Km. (5.4 miles) from *Hiryu*.

129.	1540	From Comdr. Striking Force to 2nd Fleet. By W/T.

After destroying enemy task force to east I intend to proceed north; Second Fleet will rendezvous immediately. My position at 1130 (YU YU KE 44), course 285°, speed 24 knots. I intend to rendezvous with the Landing Unit at 1900 (1430).

130.	1545	From C.S.8 to aircraft of 3rd B.S. and 8th C.S.

Position (of enemy) at 1530: bearing 67° distance 225 miles from (our) 1400 position.

131.	1545.	From *Tone* No. 3 A/C to C.S.8. (Received 1617.)

Sighted what appears to be 6 enemy cruisers in position bearing 94° distance 117 miles from my take-off point. Enemy course 120°, speed 24 knots (1545).

132.	1550	From *Tone* No. 4 A/C to C.S.8. (Received 1550.)

Enemy force consists of 2 carriers accompanied by 2 destroyers (1550).

133.	1600	From Comdr. Carrier Division 2 to Comdr. Striking Force. (Received 1635.)
		Results of second attack wave: two certain torpedo hits on an *Enterprise* class carrier (not the same one as reported bombed).
134.	1605	From C.S.8 to Striking Force. Visual signal.
		Position of enemy at 1600: 30° 25' N., 177° 26' W.
135.	1615	From Comdr. Carrier Division 2 to Striking Force. No. 193.
		From reports of returning aircraft, composition of enemy force is apparently 3 carriers, 5 large cruisers, 15 destroyers. Our attacks accounted for 2 carriers damaged.
136.	1630	From Comdr. Carrier Division 2 to Comdr. Striking Force. R. C.S.8. By W/T.
		No. 140. Third attack wave will take off at 1800 to engage enemy at dusk. Please have a reconnaissance floatplane maintain contact with enemy carriers.
137.	1655	From C.S.8 to Comdr. Striking Force. Visual signal.
		From co-ordination of reports, the large enemy force is apparently composed of 2 carriers, 6 large cruisers, accompanied by about 8 destroyers. Two reconnaissance floatplanes have been sent to obtain further intelligence.
138.	1700	*Isokaze* reports *Soryu* out of action.
139.	1701	*Chikuma* sighted a group of enemy aircraft bearing 40° to port, directly over *Hiryu*, who opened fire. Enemy aircraft dive on *Hiryu*.
140.	1705	Bombing attack on *Hiryu*, several hits, fires breakout on board. (C.-in-C. Combined Fleet, C.-in-C. 2nd Fleet, Comdr. 4th Carrier Division were informed by signal), from Comdr. (Striking Force) at 1730.
141.	1707	Dive-bombing attack on *Haruna*.

142.	1715	From Comdr. Occupation Force to Comdr. Striking Force, C.-in-C. Combined Fleet, C.S.8, Occupation Force. By W/T.

Main unit of Occupation Force intends to be in position (grid TO A WO 19) at 2400. In co-ordination with Striking Force, the remaining enemy will be destroyed. If no intelligence of enemy is obtained by above time, I intend to sweep eastward in search.

143.	1720	Three dive-bombers attack *Tone*.
144.	1728	From *Chikuma* No. 2 aircraft to Comdr. Striking Force. No. 3. The enemy is retiring eastward on course 70°, speed 20 knots.
145.	1732	Four ship-based dive-bombers attack *Tone*.
146.	1732	*Chikuma* reports 9 enemy ship-based bombers heading for her, distance 3,000 metres. A.A. guns open fire.
147.	1733	One dive-bomber attacked *Chikuma*.
148.	1737	Three carrier-based dive-bombers attacked *Tone*.
149	1745	Bombs from B.17s fell 50 metres astern of *Chikuma*. No damage caused to ship.
150.	1749	One B.17 bombed *Chikuma*, no hits.
151.	1750	*Maikaze* reported *Kaga* out of action. All survivors taken on board. (Repeated by Comdr. Striking Force to C.-in-C. Combined Fleet, C.-in-C. 2nd Fleet, and Comdr. Carrier Division 4.)
152.	1750	C.-in-C. 2nd Fleet informed all commanders and units engaged in the operation, of his tactical intentions in event of a night engagement.
153.	1750	*Chikuma* ceased fire.
154.	1800	Escorting destroyer reported enemy S/M to *Akagi*.
155.	1800	Comdr. Destroyer Division 4 to *Maikaze, Hamakaze*. By W/T.

Report whether *Kaga* and *Soryu* are in danger of sinking.

156.	1801	From *Chikuma* No. 4 aircraft. The enemy carrier is adrift.
157.	1802	From *Isokaze* to Comdr. Destroyer Division 4. By W/T. There is no hope of her* navigating under her own power. All survivors have been taken aboard this ship. * Presumably *Soryu*.
158.	1815	From Comdr. Northern Force to Northern Force. R Combined Fleet, C.N.S., Commandant Ominato Guard District. By W/T. With exception of the Second Mobile Force the Aleutians Operation will be carried out as scheduled with no change in N. Day.
159.	1828	Level bombing attack by 3 aircraft on *Tone*. Bombs fell 1,000 metres astern.
160.	1830	From Comdr. Destroyer Division 4 to *Nowake*, *Akikaze*, *Hamakaze*, *Isokaze*, R C. of S. 1st Air Fleet, D.F. (10), Comdr. Destroyer Division 17. Each ship will stand by the carrier assigned to her and screen her from enemy submarines and task forces. Should the enemy task force approach, engage it in hit and run tactics and destroy it.
161.	1830	From *Chikuma*, No. 2 aircraft to C.S.8. No. 11. Am breaking off contact.
162.	1830	From *Chikuma* to C.S.8. By S.L. *Chikuma* No. 2 aircraft sighted 4 enemy carriers, 6 cruisers and 15 destroyers steering western course in position 30 miles east of the burning and listing enemy carrier at 1713. Contact was lost shortly after sighting owing to pursuit by enemy carrier-based fighters.
163.	1832	From *Chikuma* No. 2 aircraft to Comdr. Striking Force. Three enemy carriers sighted in position bearing 95° distance 105 miles from my take-off point.

164.	1837	From Comdr. Striking Force to Striking Force. Visual signal.

  Assemble in vicinity of *Nagara*.

165.	1905	From Comdr. Striking Force to Striking Force. By S.L.

  10th D.F., 8th C.S., and 3rd B.S. cruise in that order on course 315°.

166.	1915	From *Hamakaze* to Comdr. Striking Force. By W/T.

  Soryu has sunk.

167.	1915	From C.-in-C. Combined Fleet to all Cs.-in-C. and Divisional Comdrs. in Combined Fleet. *R* C.N.S. By W/T.

  Combined Fleet Des. Op. Ord. No. 158.
  1. The enemy fleet has practically been destroyed and is retiring eastward.
  2. Units of Combined Fleet in vicinity are preparing to pursue the remnants and, at same time, to occupy A.F. (Midway).
  3. The Main Body is scheduled to reach position (grid FU ME R1 32) on course 90°, speed 20 knots by 0300/5.
  4. The Striking Force, Occupation Force (less 7th C.S.) and Advance Forces* will immediately make contact with and destroy the enemy.

  * ? Submarines.

168.	1942	From C.S.8 to Comdr. Striking Force.

  Enemy composed of 6 large cruisers and 2 carriers was retiring to south-east from position bearing 20°, distance 180 miles from Midway at 1810. I estimated position of enemy at 1900 to bear 100° distance 200 miles from us.

169.	2030	From C.-in-C. Combined Fleet to S/M *I-168*, Comdr. Carrier Division 3. *R* C.S.7. By W/T.

  S/M *I-168* will shell and destroy the enemy air base on A.F. (Midway) (Eastern) Island until 0200/5 after which 7th C.S. will continue the bombardment.

170.	2030	From Comdr. Striking Force to Striking Force. By S.L.

Float R/C aircraft of 3rd B.S. and 8th C.S. will carry out searches tomorrow morning between lines bearing 90° and 180° to as great a distance as possible. C.S.8 to arrange.

170A.	2030	Striking Force Battle Report. (Omitted in original.)
171.	2030	From Comdr. Striking Force to Striking Force. By S.L.

Report class of the 4 enemy carriers.

172.	2100	From *Makigumo* to Comdr. Striking Force. By S.L.

Hiryu is capable of 28 (sic) knots speed.

173.	2130	From Comdr. Striking Force to C.-in-C. Combined Fleet. *R* C.-in-C. 2nd Fleet, C.-in-C. 1st Fleet, C.-in-C. 11th Air Fleet. Striking Force Secret Despatch No. 560.

Total strength of enemy is 5 carriers, 6 cruisers, 15 destroyers. These are steaming westward and at 1830 were in vicinity of position (grid TO SU WA 15). I am supporting *Hiryu* and retiring to northwest, speed 18 knots. My position at 2130 is (grid FU N RE 55).

174.	2200	From *Chikuma* to C.S.8. By S.L.

Yorktown and *Hornet*. Speed 24 knots. Classes and speeds of the others undetermined.

175.	2250	From Comdr. Striking Force to C.-in-C. Combined Fleet. By W/T. Re. Combined Fleet Des. Op. Ord. No. 158.

There still exist 4 enemy carriers (may include auxiliary carriers), 6 cruisers, and 16 destroyers. These are steaming westward. None of our carriers are operational. I intend to make contact with enemy with float R/C aircraft tomorrow morning.

176.	2255	From C.-in-C. Combined Fleet to Comdr. Striking Force, C.-in-C. 2nd Fleet, *R* C.-in-C. 1st Fleet, B.S.1, C.S.8. By W/T.

C.-in-C. 2nd Fleet will take command of the Striking Force less *Hiryu*, *Akagi* and ships escorting them.

| 177. | 2320 | From C.-in-C. Combined Fleet to C.-in-C. 1st Air Fleet, *R* C.-in-C. 2nd Fleet, C.S.8. By W/T.
Report movements of 8th C.S. and second section of 3rd B.S. |
|---|---|---|
| 178. | 2330 | From Comdr. Striking Force to C.-in-C. Combined Fleet, C.-in-C. 2nd Fleet. By W/T.
Two of the enemy carriers are of the *Hornet* class with speed of 24 knots. The 2 others to the north* of these are of undetermined classes and speeds.
* Signal 195, para. 3, says 'south'. |
| 179. | 2340 | From Comdr. Occupation Force to Occupation Force, Comdr. Striking Force. *R* C.-in-C. Combined Fleet, C.-in-C. 6th Fleet. By W/T.
1. Main Unit of Occupation Force intends to be in position (grid TO E WA 12) by 0300/5, when it will search for the enemy to the east and take part in a night engagement in accordance with Striking Force Secret Despatch No. 560.
2. The Striking Force, less *Hiryu*, *Akagi* and their escorts, will immediately reverse course and take part in night engagement of Occupation Force. |
| 180. | 2400 | From Comdr. Occupation Force to Occupation Force, Striking Force. *R* C.-in-C. Combined Fleet, C.-in-C. 1st Fleet. By W/T.
1. Expect to encounter the enemy sometime after 0700/5.
2. Search disposition: From right to left, 2nd D.F., 5th C.S., 4th C.S., 4th D.F.; interval 6 Km. (3.2 sea miles). 3rd B.S. will take station approximately 10 Km. (5.4 sea miles) astern of 4th C.S. Course 65°, speed 24 knots.
3. The Striking Force will participate in the night engagement from the north. |

5 June

181. 0010 From C.S.8 to 8th C.S., 3rd B.S. By S.L. Air search today as follows:–
1. Search lines and assignments:–
   No. 1   90°   No. 2   102°, *Chikuma*
   No. 3   115°, *Tone*.   No. 4   127°, *Haruna*
   No. 5   140°, *Haruna*.   No. 6   165°, *Kirishima*
   No. 7   173°, *Kirishima*.
2. Distance:–
   Nos. 1, 2, 3, 303 miles; remainder 180 miles. All to the right 30 miles.
3. Take off at 0420.
4. Point of origin will be 0420 position.

182. 0015 From C.-in-C. Combined Fleet to all Cs.-in-C. and Division Commanders in Combined Fleet. *R* C.N.S. By W/T. No. 303.
1. Occupation Force, less the Landing Force which is standing by, and plus 7th C.S., and the Mobile Force less *Akagi*, *Hiryu* and their respective escort will rendezvous with Main Body.
2. Main Body will be in position (grid FU UR R1 31) on course 90°, speed 20 knots at 0900/5.

Note.–At 0111, the *Chikuma* began to draw the attraction of Admiral Nagumo to the above signal and inquire whether it had been received. At that moment, however, the C.-in-C. First Air Fleet made a signal 'Turn 16 points, I am reversing course.'

183. 0020 From C.-in-C. Combined Fleet to C.S.8.* *R* C.-in-C. 2nd Fleet. By W/T.
Cancel the scheduled bombardment of Midway and proceed to scheduled position of Main Body at 0900/5.

*? C.S.7 intended.

184.	0030	From Comdr. Striking Force to C.-in-C. Combined Fleet, C.-in-C.. 2nd Fleet. *R* C.S.8. By W/T.

At 2400 my position was (grid FU WA R1 55) assisting *Hiryu*. I intend to be in vicinity of position (grid FU RA R1 55) by dawn today and will be prepared to attack the enemy in co-ordination with the other forces.

185.	0030	From Comdr. Striking Force to Striking Force. By S.L.

Cruising disposition will be in the order of 10th D.F. and 3rd B.S. 8th C.S. will take up position 12 Km. (6.5 sea miles) on either beam of *Nagara**

* Executive made 0107.

186.	0120	From Comdr. Occupation Force to 8th C.S., Striking Force, Occupation Force. By W/T.

1. Position of Occupation Force at 0100 was TO A RA 23 course 305°, speed 24 knots, steering to rendezvous with Main Body whilst making preparations for a night engagement.
2. 2nd D.F. will take station astern of the Main Body.
3. Striking Force will rendezvous with the Main Body as directed by Comdr. Striking Force.

187.	0255	From C.-in-C. Combined Fleet to all Cs.-in-C. and Comdrs. of Divisions in Combined Fleet, C.N.S. By W/T.

1. Occupation of Midway is cancelled.
2. Main Body will assemble the Occupation Force and Striking Force less *Hiryu* and her escorts, and will refuel during morning of 6 June in position 33° N., 170° E.
3. Screening Force, *Hiryu* and escort, and *Nisshin* will proceed to the above position.
4. Landing Force will proceed westward, out of air range of Midway.

188.	0441	Nos. 1 and 4 aircraft took off from *Chikuma* to search (No. 1 bearing 90°, distance 120 miles; No. 4 bearing 102°, distance 200 miles).

189.	0500	By order of C.-in-C. Combined Fleet, *Akagi* was sunk by torpedo from D.F. (4) in 30° 30' N., 178° 40' W.
190.	0525	*Chikuma* commenced refuelling *(Genyo Maru)*.
191.	0620	From C.S.8 to all search aircraft. Search distances are revised as follows: Type 0, 200 miles; type 95, 150 miles.
192.	0652	From *Chikuma* No. 4 aircraft to Comdr. Striking Force. Have sighted an enemy *Yorktown* class carrier listing to starboard and drifting in position bearing 1110 distance 240 miles from my take off point. One destroyer is in vicinity. *Note.*–Comdr. Striking Force at 0750 asked *Chikuma* for, and was given, a repetition.
193.	0730	From C. of S. Combined Fleet to D.F. (10) (?). By W/T. Has *Hiryu* sunk? Report developments and position.
194.	0815	From C.-in-C. Combined Fleet to Striking Force. By W/T. My position is 33° 10' N., 177° 35' E., course 310°, speed 14 knots.
195.	0908	From *Chikuma* to Comdr. Striking Force, C.S.8 by S.L. Report of *Chikuma* No. 2 aircraft, 4 June: 1. At 1713 sighted enemy *Enterprise* class carrier in position 30° 15' N., 176° 05' W., listing and burning but with undamaged flight deck. Three cruisers and 5 destroyers were in her vicinity. At about 1720 all left the scene with exception of the carrier, on course 80°. 2. At 1810 sighted 2 carriers of *Yorktown* or *Hornet* class with 2 cruisers and 4 destroyers acting as direct escorts in position 30° 23' N., 176° 05' W. Distance between the two units was about 3 miles. Course 270°, speed 12 knots.

3. At 1816 additional carriers, class undetermined, escorted by 5 cruisers and 6 destroyers were sighted in position about 4 miles south of the other group. These were in line ahead, on course 270°, speed 12 knots.

4. The No. 2 aircraft was on course 180° from about 1800 and sighted the above-mentioned groups consecutively, so that there is no likelihood of sighting the same group twice. Moreover, the carriers mentioned in paras. 1, 2 and 3, were definitely sighted from altitudes of 300 metres, under the cloud ceilings.

196. 1259 From C.-in-C. Combined Fleet to all Cs.-in-C. and Comdrs. of Divisions in Combined Fleet. By W/T.
Second Mobile Force is returned to the Northern Force.

197. 1410 From C.-in-C. Combined Fleet to Combined Fleet. By S.L.
Aircraft have taken off from enemy carriers. (Communication Intelligence.)

198. 1725 From Comdr. Striking Force to Striking Force. By S.L.
Twenty enemy heavy bombers are on course 290°.

Appendix E

Japanese Losses
Surface Craft Sunk
Akagi (carrier) – scuttled 0500/5 in 30° 30' N., 178° 40' E.
Kaga (carrier) – sank 1925/4 in 30° 20' N., 179° 17.2' W.
Hiryu (carrier) – scuttled 0510/5 in 31° 27.5' N., 179° 23.5' W.
Soryu (carrier) – sank 1910/4 in 30° 42.5' N., 178° 37.5' W.
Mikuma (heavy cruiser) – sank /6 in 30° 00' N., 173° 00' E.
253 aircraft (about 100 pilots) lost. 3,500 officers and men lost.

Surface Craft Damaged
Mogami (heavy cruiser) (major damage).
Arashio (destroyer) (major damage).
Akebono Maru (tanker) (major damage).
Tanikaze (destroyer) (minor damage).

Japanese Aircraft Destroyed in the Air (Japanese Figures)

	In Attack on Midway	Acting as Cover Units (Syn. C.A.P.)	In first attack on *Yorktown*	In second attack on *Yorktown*
Akagi	1 fighter	2 fighters.		
Kaga	1 fighter (from A.A. fire). 1 bomber.	4 fighters.		1 fighter.
Hiryu	4 torpedo aircraft (of which 2 from A.A. fire).	4 fighters.	3 fighters. 13 bombers.	2 fighters. 5 torpedo aircraft.
Soryu	1 torpedo aircraft			
Total:	18 fighters, 14 bombers, 10 torpedo aircraft. In addition, an unknown number (9 in the case of the *Hiryu*) were damaged beyond repair by shell fire and many were lost through making forced landings in the sea after the carriers were damaged.			

Appendix F

Time (Z + 12)	No. of A/C in Attack	Target	Bombs or Torpedoes Dropped	Bombs or Torpedoes Reported by Japanese (Where Known)
3 June				
1623	9 Army B.17s, land based	Transport Unit.	28 x 600 lb. B. 5 x 500 lb. B.	9 B.
4 June				
0130–0200	4 Navy patrol bombers (flying boats).	Transport Unit.	3 T.	3 T.
0710	4 Army B.26s 6 land based Navy torpedo A/C (T.B.F.s).	Carriers of Striking Force.	3 T. 4 T. (est.)	*Hiryu* 9 T (0707) by B.26s *Akagi* 3 T. (0710) *Hiryu* 4 T. (0711) *Hiryu* 9 T. (0712) by torpedo A/C *Akagi* 1 T. (0715 ca.) by torpedo A/C.
0755	16 land based Marine S.B.D.s.	As above.	15 x 500 lb. B.	*Hiryu* 9 B. (0750) 4 B. (0808) 1 B. (0812)

Note:– The *Kaga* also reported 3 bombs (no hits) dropped at her about this time. This attack cannot be identified.

0814	14 Army B.17s, land based	Carriers of Striking Force.	108 B. (600 lb. and 500 lb.)	*Soryu* 11 B. ca. (0835)
0820	11 land based Marine S.B.2U.s	Battleship of Striking Force.	11 x 500 lb. B.	*Haruna* 5 B. (0829)
0920	15 carrier based torpedo A/C (*Hornet*).	Carriers of Striking Force.	10 T. (est.)	*Soryu* 4 T. (0930)

Summary of U.S. Air Attacks, Battle of Midway, 3–6 June

Hits		U.S. Losses	Remarks
Actual	U.S. Estimate		
3 June			
0	1 heavy cruiser or battleship hit. 1 transport hit	None	Horizontal bombing, three bombs failed to release.
4 June			
1 (on tanker)		None	One aircraft unable to attack
0	1 hit on carrier by B.26s 1 hit on carrier by torpedo A/C.	2 B.26s 5 T.B.F.s	One B.26 and two Navy torpedo A/C shot down before release.
0 0 (many casualties from near misses) Very near miss	3 (probably on *Soryu*)	8 shot down 4 unrepairable 4 damaged	Glide bombing, one shot down before release.
0	2 on *Soryu* 1 on another carrier	None	Horizontal bombing, 16 B.17s left for target, four bombs hung up.
0	2	2	Glide bombing.
0	1 on *Kaga* 1 on another carrier	15	Two other torpedo A/C did not reach target. Five A/C were shot down before release.

Time (Z + 12)	No. of A/C in Attack	Target	Bombs or Torpedoes Dropped	Bombs or Torpedoes Reported by Japanese (Where Known)
1020–1025	*Enterprise* (14), *Yorktown* (12) torpedo A/C.	As Above	13 T (est.)	*Hiryu* 7 T. (1013) by 16 A/C *Hiryu* 5 T. (1030) by 5 A/C
1020–1025	*Enterprise* (32), *Yorktown* (17) dive bombers plus 10 *Enterprise* fighters	*Soryu* *Kaga* *Akagi*	*Enterprise* 15 x 1,000 lb. B. 18 x 500 lb. B. 22 x 100 lb. B *Yorktown* 17 x 1,000 lb. B.	*Soryu* 3 B. (1025) *Kaga* 9 B. (1026) *Akagi* 3 B. (1030)
1705	20 scout (dive) bombers (10 *Enterprise*'s, 14 *Yorktown*'s from *Enterprise*, 16 from *Hornet*).	*Hiryu* and ships of Striking Force	10 x 1,000 lb. B. 21 x 500 lb. B.	*Hiryu* 13 B. (1703) *Haruna* 2 B. (1708) *Tone* 3 B. (1720) *Tone* 4 B. (1728) *Chikuma* 5 B. (1732)
1810–1830	12 Army B.17s, land based (6 from Oahu).	As above	52 x 500 lb. B.	*Chikuma* 6 B. (1745) *Chikuma* 4 B. (1810) *Haruna* 3 B. (1826) *Tone* 3 B. (time illegible)
5 June				
0805	12 land based Marine patrol bombers (S.B.D. and S.B.2 U).	*Mikuma* and *Mogami*	12 x 500 lb. B.	
0830	8 Army B.17s, land based.	As above	39 x 500 lb. B.	
1635	7 Army B.17s, land based.	*Tanikaze*	40 x 500 lb. B.	4 B.

Hits		U.S. Losses	Remarks
Actual	U.S. Estimate		
0 0	2 on one carrier 1 or 2 on another carrier	10 *Enterprise*'s 10 *Yorktown*'s	Estimated six *Enterprise* and seven *Yorktown* A/C shot down before release.
3 (sunk) 4 (sunk) 3 (sunk)	*Akagi, Kaga, Soryu* several hits; one B.S. hit, severely damaged, set on fire; another B.S. hit; one light cruiser or destroyer hit, believed sunk.	18 *Enterprise* bombers. 1 *Enterprise* fighter. 2 *Yorktown* bombers.	Estimated nine of the *Enterprise* bombers and one fighter forced down by battle damage, two *Yorktown* bombers landed in water short of fuel. *Soryu* abandoned 1045 sunk by U.S. S/M. *Nautilus* 1910 in 30° 42.5' N., 178° 37.5' W. *Aakgi* scuttled 0500/5 in 30° 30' N., 178° 40' W. *Kaga* sank 1925 in 30° 20.3' N., 179° 17.2' W.
4 (sunk) 0 0 0 0	*Hiryu* many hits, 1 B.S. – 2 hits, 1 B.S. – 3 hits, 1 heavy cruiser – 2 hits.	3 *Enterprise*'s 2 *Yorktown*'s	*Hiryu* scuttled 0515/5 in 31° 27.5' N., 179° 23.5' E.
0 0 0	*Akagi* 3 hits, 2 heavy cruisers, 1 hit each, 1 destroyer sunk.	None	Horizontal bombing. 16 B. failed to release.
5 June			
0 (one A/C dived into *Mikuma* causing some damage)	1 hit, 1 near miss	1 S.B.2U.	Dive and glide bombing. Minor damage from near misses to both ships (already damaged in collision).
0		None	Horizontal bombing, 13 bombs hung up, four further B.17s failed to find target.
0	2 or 3	None	Horizontal bombing, eight bombs failed to release.

Time (Z + 12)	No. of A/C in Attack	Target	Bombs or Torpedoes Dropped	Bombs or Torpedoes Reported by Japanese (Where Known)
1804	26 *Hornet*'s scout bombers.	? *Tanikaze*	26 x 500 lb. B.	11 B.
1830–1900	32 *Enterprise*'s scout bombers.	Destroyer or light cruisers	32 x 500 lb. B.	
1840	5 Army B.17s, land based.	*Tanikaze*	15 x 600 lb. B. 5 x 300 lb. B.	Wide
6 June				
0930–1000	26 *Hornet*'s scout bombers with 8 fighters.	*Mikuma*, *Mogami* and destroyers	18 x 1,000 lb. B. 8 x 500 lb. B.	
1200–1300	*Enterprise*'s 31 scout bombers, 3 torpedo aircraft. 12 fighters.	As above	31 x 1,000 lb. B.	
1500	23 *Hornet*'s scout bombers	As above	23 x 1,000 lb. B.	
1640	6 Army B.17s, land based.	U.S. S/M *Grayling* (in error).	16 x 1,000 lb. B. 4 x 1,000 lb. B.	

Hits		U.S. Losses	Remarks
Actual	U.S. Estimate		
0 (some very near misses).	0	1 (water landing)	
0	0	1	
0		2 (short of fuel)	Horizontal bombing.
6 June			
Mogami 2 *Mikuma* 3 1 destroyer slightly damaged	Battleship 3, heavy cruiser 2, destroyer 1 (sunk).	1 scout bomber	*Mikuma* sunk, *Mogami* damaged but navigable, *Arashio* damaged but navigable
Mogami 2 *Mikuma* several		None	
Mogami 1 *Mikuma* several *Arashio* 1		None	
0	Cruiser sank in 15 seconds (*Grayling* crash dived).	None	Horizontal bombing, one A/C did not drop.

Endnotes

1. Lat. 9° 52' S., long. 169° 35' E., not to be confused with Curé or Ocean I. 56 miles west of Midway.
2. cf. *Official Japanese Report*, part I, 2 (h), 3 (e).
3. Appendix D. 108, 169.
4. Based on *Ship and Related Targets, Japanese Submarine Operations* B.105/JAP/203/4.
5. French Frigate Shoal consists of a crescent shaped reef on which there are a number of islets and sand-banks; and La Perouse pinnacle, a steep, rocky, and almost inaccessible islet 120 feet high, is situated on the western or sunken part of the reef, nearly midway between the points of the crescent. The islets or sand-banks on the reef vary in number, according as the wind and sea may have raised or washed them away under the varying conditions of the weather. Twenty men lived there during the summer 1859 and subsisted on fish, turtle, fowls and eggs. The atoll may be safely visited during the months May to September inclusive, but, except by a few Japanese schooners in search of seal skins, seal oil, sharksfins, etc., it was before World War II generally avoided. (*Sailing Directions.*) Morison, *History of U.S. Naval Operations in World War II* states that, before the war, the lee was used as an emergency anchorage and seaplane landing. In 1943 Tern Island, at the northern end, was enlarged and developed as an emergency landing strip.
6. Gudgeon, Grouper, Nautilus, Grayling, Trout, Tambor.
7. Grenadier, Gato, Dolphin.
8. Plunger, Narwhal, Trigger.
9. Growler, Finback, Pike, Tarpon.
10. He was lost on 9 June when the long-range bomber in which he was searching for the enemy was forced down at sea.
11. But *see* footnote on Midway aircraft in App. B.
12. This rests on the authority of a MS. note on the plan in *Secret Information Bulletin No. 1*. The Commander, Patrol Wing 2 on 23rd May recommended that searches by PBY-5 seaplanes (twin-engine patrol bombers, boat (Catalinas)), should be carried out over a 180 degrees Sector, radius 700 miles; search to start at dawn daily, proceed out at average speed of 100 knots, returning at 111 knots or better in order to get back by dark. Assuming 25 miles visibility which might reasonably be expected in the Midway area at that time of year for a large force or single ship proceeding at such speed as to leave a conspicuous wake, each PBY could cover an 8 degrees sector, so that about 23 aircraft would be required. (M.051772/42, p. 9.) Comment by the Head of B.A.D. Washington, was that this search, though not watertight, appeared to be the best possible provided it was not judged to be perfect.
13. The above MS. note gives the following areas of low visibility:– 30 May, N. of 325 degrees beyond 350 miles. 31 May, N. of 286 degrees beyond 300 miles. 1 June, N. of line E.–W. and 300 miles to N. 2 June, between bearings 292 degrees:– and 315 degrees beyond 400 miles. 3 June, beyond 400 miles to N.N.W.
14. It is thought that the Japanese word which is translated 'transports' includes also supply ships and oilers.
15. *Report of C.-in-C., U.S. Pacific Fleet*, M.051642/42, p. 5, where the time of sighting is given as about 0900, as it is also in the plan attached to the report, which is, however, a composite

of all reports. The time 0924 is given in a plan reproduced in *Secret Information Bulletin No. 1*, which bears internal evidence of having been prepared on board the *Enterprise*, probably to accompany that ship's or C.T.F.17's report, neither of which is forthcoming.

16. The Catalinas, whilst excellent for long range search, did not possess the performance or defensive characteristics required to stand up against strong enemy air opposition; consequently, when the latter was to be expected, they failed in their primary requirement of continuous shadowing.
17. The *U.S. Combat Narrative*, p. 9, says the B.17 was also to search the expected enemy rendezvous at 800 miles, but this is not mentioned as one of its duties in the B.17's report in M.051772/42, p. 16, of Report by H. Q. Hawaiian Dept. Comdr.
18. One carrier was reported amongst the forces sighted on 3 June, but the contact was not verified.
19. The position given by the B.17s, 265 degrees Midway 570 miles, viz., 27° 20' N., 171° 20' E., is practically on the actual track of the Occupation Force as shown on the plan prepared by the Japanese Naval Staff College (see *Interrogation No. 65*). Nevertheless, the position given in the text of this narrative is considered to be more nearly correct, for the following reasons: *(a)* The tracks of the various forces, as shown on the Japanese plan, are obviously approximations. The track of the Occupation Force shown on the plan does not pass through the position 27° 10' N., 175° 11' E. of that force at 1300, 4 June, reported by signal (App. C.21), as would have been the case, however, assuming the position of attack to have been as given in this narrative and taking into account the alteration of course by the Occupation Force to 050 degrees at 1200/4 (App. C.15) which alteration also is not shown on the Japanese plan; *(b)* the Occupation Force was ordered to steer for a position in 26° 26' N., 171° 10' E. at 1500/3 (App. C.2), which corresponds fairly closely with that given on the composite plan in Cincpac's *Report* (M.051642/42), viz., about 26° 35' N., 172° 00' E.; *(c)* the plan *(Enterprise's)* in *Secret Information Bulletin No. 1* shows the B.17s attacking at 1640 in about 26° 25' N., 172° 20' E., but a note at about 26° 30' N., 171° 25' E. says: 'Probable position at attack assuming C. 080 degrees for "main body".'
20. 'Some of the equipment of the aircraft was received too late for the crews to become familiar with their material, and it was thought that the cases of malfunctioning of bomb releases could be attributed to this cause.
21. App. C.30.
22. The Japanese report that part of their fighters were sent on ahead to gain control of the air over Midway. The Americans, however, did not encounter these fighters separately (cf. Sect. 16).
23. The Summary of Air Operations in M.051772/42 shows one Navy PB shot down and four forced down, but no details of date, time, or place are given. The Japanese claimed to have destroyed two.
24. Presumably this was the reason why the Americans did not attempt to hold off the Japanese fighters with a portion of their force whilst the remainder dealt with the bombers.
25. Missing: 13 F2A, 3 F4F. Severely damaged: 5 F2A, 2 F4F.
26. S. E. Morison, *History of U.S. Naval Operations in World War II*, Vol. IV, says that the Japanese were vague about their losses in their official reports (since they lost all by next day) and that at least a third of the attackers were destroyed by the Marine fighter squadron or by anti-aircraft fire.
27. The Japanese report states: 'Amount of cloud 1 to 2 (tenths), ceiling, 500 metres.' This is not mentioned in the U.S. report.
28. The Japanese report says that the *Tone's* and *Chikuma's* reconnaissance aircraft were delayed, but the delay cannot have been very great, since the scheduled time for taking off was 0430 and the last aircraft was in the air by 0500.
29. This was probably an over estimate, for the Japanese report that the total number of fighters which opposed the attacks of the Midway aircraft between 0710 and 0820 was 20 of the Combat Air Patrol assisted by the returning fighters of the Midway Attack Group,

which latter did not, however, arrive back over the carriers until 0810.
30. Douglas Dauntless scout bomber.
31. Vought-Sikorsky Vindicator (Br. Chesapeake) scout bomber.
32. *U.S. Combat Narrative*, p. 18.
33. Plan in M.051642/42.
34. *Report of Commander, 7th Air Force*, M.051772/42. The *Report of the C.-in-C., U.S. Pacific Fleet* (M.051642/42, pp. 9 and 16) gives three hits.
35. Task Force 16. Carrier *Yorktown* (flag of R. Adm. Fletcher), 2 cruisers, 5 destroyers. Task Force 17. Carriers *Enterprise* (Flag of R. Adm. Spruance), *Hornet*, 6 cruisers, 9 destroyers.
36. These are the figures given in the reports of Commander Bombing Squadron 6 and Commander Scouting Squadron 6 which form enclosures (A) and (B) to the *Enterprise*'s report (Record Office Case WHS 8401, p. 155).
37. App. D 29, 33, 37, 40, 42. B.N.L.O. reported (B.A.D. Washington 1915Z/28/7/42) that it appeared probable the Japanese did not know the position of the U.S. carriers until the *Yorktown* broke R/T silence on power to vector fighters on to aircraft which subsequently proved to be friendly. (U.S. aircraft were not all fitted with I.F.F.) But it is evident that the *Yorktown* was discovered by air R/C.
38. cf. note 44.
39. The table in the Report of C.-in-C. First Air Fleet, on which App. E of this narrative is based, does not mention the attack on the *Kaga*. The action chart accompanying the Report of C.-in-C. First Air Fleet shows torpedo attacks taking place on the *Akagi* about 0915, the *Hiryu* at 0940, and the *Kaga* at 0950.
40. The Americans believed the Japanese recognised the torpedo aircraft as the greater menace and concentrated their fighters on them. But the evidence is that at this date the Japanese considered dive bombing to be more dangerous than torpedo attacks. The Americans also thought that the attacks of the *Enterprise* and *Yorktown* torpedo groups, by compelling the Japanese carriers to manoeuvre, prevented them from launching bombers to attack T.F.16 and T.F.17, but this was not the case; they were not completely ready to take off, for the Midway attack groups had not yet all been serviced.
41. The reports on this attack were rendered by the commanders of the two squadrons and not by the commander of the group; and reasons which caused Lieut.-Commander McClusky to make the most important decision to turn northward are not stated.
42. The Americans gave the time of sinking as 1840.
43. This is the account given in the U.S. reports, whilst a footnote to the American translation of the Report of the C.-in-C. First Air Fleet states that the *Nautilus* administered the *coup de grâce* to the *Soryu*. The plan attached to the Japanese report shows an unsuccessful submarine attack on the *Kaga* at 1410 (very close to the time given by the *Nautilus*), but no submarine attack on the *Soryu*. The *Final Official Report* of the C.-in-C. U.S. Fleet states that *Soryu* was sunk by U.S. carrier planes and submarine and this was also the finding of the Joint Army–Navy Assessment Committee.
44. The carriers apparently had the following numbers of aircraft on deck being refuelled and rearmed at the time of the dive-bombing attack: *Akagi*, 3 fighters, 18 torpedo aircraft; *Kaga*, 3 fighters, 27 torpedo aircraft; *Soryu*, 3 fighters, 18 bombers.
45. This is the time given by C.-in-C. 1st Air Fleet's Signal. App. D.84 gives 1050.
46. The Report of C.-in-C. 1st Air Fleet states, however, that only six fighters were launched, and the *Hiryu*'s signal (App. D.87) gives the number as five.
47. Composition as given in Report by C.-in-C. 1st Air Fleet, who does not, however, give time of taking off. Signal, App. D.87, states that *Hiryu*'s second wave took off at 1120, but it is thought this was part of the first wave (cf. App. D.84). Signal, App. D.103, states that second wave was taking off at 1206 but App. D.113 gives time of taking off as 1331, which is thought to be more probable, since the distance to the *Yorktown* was about 105 miles and time of torpedo attack 1441.

48. A *U.S. Combat Narrative*, p. 31.
49. According to the Japanese plan the position of the *Hiryu* at time of sighting was some 30 miles further east.
50. Report of Duty Officer, Marine S.B. Sqn. 241 (in M.051432/42).
51. Presumably the Submarine Force.
52. The corectness of this reading of the signals depends on interpretation of the Japanese word translated 'Escorting' in signal 176. H.S./T.S.D. works perforce on translations of the original Japanese signals, and consequently it is uncertain whether the C.-in-C. referred to the destroyers supporting the *Hiryu* and *Akagi* or their supporting ships, the 3rd B.S. and 8th C.S. It is presumed that Admiral Yamamotowould not have placed Admiral Nagumo's force under the command of an officer junior to him, if he though the Admiral was still in company with his ships.
53. 'Obviously', because his next signal (Appendix D) 20 minutes later, *re* the prospective night engagement and participation of the striking force, was not only likewise addressed to the Comdr. Striking Force but was *repeated* to the C.-in-C. 1st [Air] Fleet for information.
54. This is clear from Appendix D in which Admiral Nagumo states that at midnight he was assissting the *Hiryu*.
55. This signal is addressed to C.S.8, but this is thought to be a clerical arror, since, as far as is known, it had never been proposed that the 8th C.S. should bombard Midway. Moreover, the signal was repeated only to the C.-in-C. 2nd Fleet, whereas it is to be expected that it would also have been repeated to the Comdr. Striking had it been addresssed to the 8th C.S. which was part of the striking force.
56. Presumably they received the signal cancelling the bombardment (Appendix D) about this time.
57. The *U.S. Combat Narrative*, pp. 37–8.
58. The various reports give the bearing of the enemy as 241–278 degrees, distance 130–180 miles, composition one or two 'battleships', but it is clear that the *Mikuma* and *Mogami* were indicated. Capt. Tyler's report is not available, and Capt. Fleming was killed in the attack.
59. It is not known at what time they took off. The only available report that mentions the time gives 0430 (Midway time), which seems reasonable, since much time was spent in trying to find the target.
60. There is considerable discrepancy between the various reports on this attack. The time and place given here are as stated in Lt.-Col. Allen's report in M.051772/42.
61. The report of the Air Force Commander, Hikam Field (M.051772/42) gives the position at 320 degrees, 425 miles from Midway, and the time as 1825, but the only two available pilots' reports viz. those of Capt. Ridings and Lt. Bird give the positions 310 degrees, 420 miles from Midway, and Capt. Ridings gives the time as 1840. Lt. Bird gives no time.
62. The *U.S. Combat Narrative*, p. 37, note 29. Rear-Admiral Spruance's report is not forthcoming.
63. cf. Section 47.
64. The ship attacked cannot be identified. No attacks other that those already described were reported by any of the ships of the Japanese Striking Force, and the attack was presumably therefore made on one of the ships of the Occupation Force. For instance, the *Jinstu* and Destroyer Divisions 16 and 18 may well have been in this area at the time.
65. Admiral Nimitz's Report, M.051642/42, p.19. The co-ordinates of the above positions are respectively:– approximately 28° 50' N., 174° 30' E., and 29° 35' N., 174° 10' E. The *U.S. Combat Narrative* pp. 43–44 gives the postition of the first group as 28° 55' N., 175° 10' E., and of second 29° 33' N., 174° 30' E. According to the plan accompanying the Interrogation of the Gunnery Officer on Admiral Yamamoto's staff, all the day's attacks on the *Mikuma* and *Mogami* took place in an area centred around approximate position 28° 10' N., 175° 30' E., *i.e.*, some 60 miles east of the poistion given by Admiral Nimitz.
66. cf. the *U.S. Combat Narrative*.
67. There were certain points of just possible resemblance between the two heavy cruisers and

some of the older Japanese battleships; for the *Mogami* class had a 'pagoda' bridge structure (though not very high) and a tripod mast and the ships appeared to the U.S. aircraft crews to be far larger than their listed tonnage of 8,500, as indeed they were, being 13,000-ton ships.

68. Reports of Bombing Squadron 6 and Scouting Squadron 6 in Case 8401.
69. The *U.S. Combat Narrative* p.46 footnote 43, says: 'These torpedo planes were ordered to attack only after the bombing attack. After failing to make contact with our bombing planes they found an enemy ship independently and circled an hour awaiting our bombers which did not appear. Finally lack of fuel forced them to return to the *Enterprise. This clearly indicates the presence of two enemy groups*' (H.S. Ital.).
70. It is not stated what happened to the 24th aircraft.
71. W/T silence in force.
72. At 0815/5 the C.-in-C. Combined Fleet informed the striking force that he was in position 33° 10' N., 177° 35' E., course 310 degrees, speed 14 knots. This course would not, however, have brought him to any of the positions through which the main body is shown passing on the Japanese plan.
73. '*Yorktown* might have been saved if she had not been completely abandoned during the night but salvage work carried on.' (*Secret Information Bulletin No. 1* comment by H.Q. of C.-in-C. U.S. Fleet, p. 12).
74. The two latter did not arrive before the *Yorktown* sank.
75. Owing, presumably, to the different rates of drift of two ships of such diverse build.
76. The depth charges were rechecked after the torpedo struck, by Torpedoman First Class B. M. Kimbrel, who was not amongst the survivours.
77. The report of C.-in-C. Pacific Fleet, incorporating the experience of the battle, was dated 28 June 1942.
78. Lessons and conclusions from the action by C.-in-C. Pacific Fleet, *Secret Information Bulletin No. 1*, p. 31.
79. Op. cit. p.7.
80. Lost his life in the battle
81. Composition not known. The 'War Diary of the 10th D.F.' (N.I.D. 005279/47) gives the following organisation:–

    10th D.F. Divn. 10, *Kazegumo* (S.O.), *Yugumo, Makigumo, Akigumo*.

    Divn. 17, *Tanikaze* (S.O.), *Urakraze, Hamakaze, Isokaze*.

    2nd D.F. Divn. 7, *Ushio* (S.O.), *Sazanami, Akebono*.

    The following 13 destroyers have been identified, all apparently belonging to the Striking Force:–

    10th Divn., *Kazegumo, Makigumo, Yugumo*.

    17th Divn., *Isokaze, Hamakaze, Tanikaze, Urakaze*.

    Divn. unidentified, *Hagikaze, Maikaze, Nowake, Akikaze, Arashi, Isonami*.
82. The composition of the 4th D.F. given here is as in the Japanese 'Task Organisation for Midway Operation,' and the records of the *Yura* confirm that the ship took part in the operation though her assignment is not known. *Campaigns of the Pacific War* gives 4th D.F. *Naka* (Lt. cr.) and 16 destroyers (not named). The *Naka's* record of this date, however, is marked by the translators 'Not applicable.'
83. Names or numbers not known.
84. Did not leave Wake Island until 1000 1 June.
85. Apparently the 2nd Combined S.N.L.F.
86. Apparently the 16th Army Detachment.
87. *Enterprise* Group.
88. *Hornet* Group.
89. Morison, *History of U.S. Naval Operations in World War II*, Vol. IV, gives the figures 27 fighters and 27 Scout [dive] bombers in Group 22, and explains that certain old aircraft were inoperative or being 'cannibalised'.

John Rodgaard

Captain John Rodgaard served for over 41 years with the naval service of the United States, including 12 years as a petty officer and 29 years of commissioned service as a naval intelligence officer. He completed several active duty tours as a reservist, including two years in the Mediterranean on the destroyer escort, USS *Courtney*, DE-1021. He has also served on navy and joint intelligence tours with Submarine Group 8, Carrier Group 4, the Office of Naval Intelligence, the J2 Defense Intelligence Agency, Commander Submarines Mediterranean, the US European Command and the Navy Staff. Captain Rodgaard completed four years of active service with the National Geospatial Intelligence Agency as a senior collection officer and strategist.

As a civilian, Rodgaard has been employed as a contract intelligence analyst with the National Reconnaissance Office, the Central Intelligence Agency, the United States Air Force U-2 Programme and the Defense Intelligence Agency. He is a published author and a contributor to several TV programmes in the Discovery Channel's *Unsolved History* series. He was the US Naval Institute's Author of the Year 2000 and is a frequent contributor to the Institute's *Naval History* magazine. He co-authored the only biography of Commodore Charles Stewart USN, the most successful fighting captain of the USS *Constitution*.

Rodgaard has a BA in History and Political Science, a Masters in Political Science, and is a graduate of the United States Naval War College. He is married to Judith Pearson, PhD from Kansas City, Missouri. His two children are intelligence officers.

In retirement, Rodgaard has taken over as lead author of TS *Venomous*. His public speaking engagements in the UK have included the South West Maritime History Society, the Society for Nautical Research at SS *Great Britain* in Bristol and a Society for Nautical Research Centenary Conference in Glasgow. His speaking engagement venues in the US have included the home of USS *Stewart* at Seawolf Park, Galveston, Texas and the US Navy Museum, Washington.

Philip Grove

With a BSc (Econ) in International Politics and Strategic Studies and an MSc (Econ) in Strategic Studies, Philip Grove joined the Department of Strategic Studies at Britannia Royal Naval College, Dartmouth in 1993. His career at the College progressed and he became Head of the Strategic Studies Pillar in 2004, then Subject Matter Expert in Strategic Studies in 2008 when BRNC became part of Plymouth University. His principal research interests are naval history and policy, especially naval aviation, British defence policy and procurement.

Formerly he taught at RNEC Manadon, CTC RM Lympstone, University Royal Naval Units and Royal Naval Reserve units. He has taught at Plymouth University since 1997 on various undergraduate modules ranging from Contemporary History and International Relations, to Foreign Policy and Maritime Power. His current teaching at the University is on Contemporary Maritime Power. Additionally he continues to act as a visiting lecturer to Royal Navy vessels and shore establishments as well as having delivered papers at a number of seminars and conferences.

Philip Grove is widely published and has written, or contributed to, over 10 naval books. The papers he has given include The Lessons of Air Power at the Royal Navy Museum Portsmouth in May 2012 during the Falklands 30th Anniversary Conference.

Britannia Naval Histories of World War II

Britannia Naval Histories of World War II is a series containing reproduced historical material, newly commissioned commentary, maps, plans and first-hand accounts of specific battles. Each foreword is written by naval veterans of the highest order, including HRH Prince Philip, Duke of Edinburgh.

Never previously published in this format, World War II Battle Summaries are documents once stamped 'restricted' or 'classified' and held in the library of Britannia Royal Naval College in Dartmouth, South West England. They are unique records written up by naval officers during the conflict, and soon after 1945. Events are recorded in minute detail, accompanied by maps and plans drawn up during the period by serving officers. Where Führer Conferences are featured, these contains Hitler's words as they were minuted and typed at the time. These historical texts have been redesigned in a contemporary format. The first-hand accounts are from worldwide sources and contain individuals' reactions, emotions and descriptions, making fascinating reading 70 years on.

www.uppress.co.uk /nav

Introduction by
G H Bennett, R Bennett
and E Bennett

Bismarck
The Chase and Sinking of Hitler's Goliath

Publication Date
December 2012

Paperback
ISBN 978-184102-326-7

Hardback
ISBN 978-184102-327-4

Extent
160 pages

Format
156 x 234 mm

Category
Military and Naval Ships

Foreword
Commander Nigel 'Sharkey' Ward

- Contains the wartime British and German documents, including signals to *Bismarck* that detail this famous sea battle.
- Includes original hand-drawn tracking maps and diagrams.

Launched in 1939, *Bismarck* was the most formidable surface ship in Hitler's fleet. Sunk on her first and only war cruise, on 27 May 1941, this great victory for the Royal Navy was also a human tragedy. Only 114 of her 2,200 crew survived the Royal Navy's final storm of shells and torpedoes. The complete Battle Summary is included, detailing how Hitler's Goliath was located, pursued and attacked. Both German and British first-hand accounts embellish each turn of events.

Introduction by
M J Pearce and
R Porter

Fight for the Fjords
The Battle for Norway 1940

Publication Date
April 2012

Paperback
ISBN 978-184102-306-9

Hardback
ISBN 978-184102-305-2

Extent
408 pages

Format
156 x 234 mm

Category
JWMV2 Military and Naval Ships

Foreword
Admiral Lord Alan West, a former First Sea Lord and Parliamentary Under-Secretary of State at the Home Office

- Contains the wartime British and German documents that detail this famous sea battle.
- Includes original hand-drawn tracking maps and diagrams.

The fierce naval battles fought in Norwegian waters during the spring of 1940 were recorded in documents that were once subject to restrictions under the Official Secrets Act. *Fight for the Fjords* includes the German account, written within three years of the end of World War II, and the British report, which compiled previously unavailable Royal Navy records to produce one complete account. The combination of these two summaries forms a unique record.

Introduction by
G H Bennett

Hitler's Ghost Ships
Graf Spee, Scharnhorst and Disguised German Raiders

Publication Date
April 2012

Paperback
ISBN 978-184102-308-3

Hardback
ISBN 978-184102-307-6

Extent
224 pages

Format
156 x 234 mm

Category
Military and Naval Ships

Foreword
Admiral Sir Jonathon Band, former First Sea Lord and Chief of Naval Staff

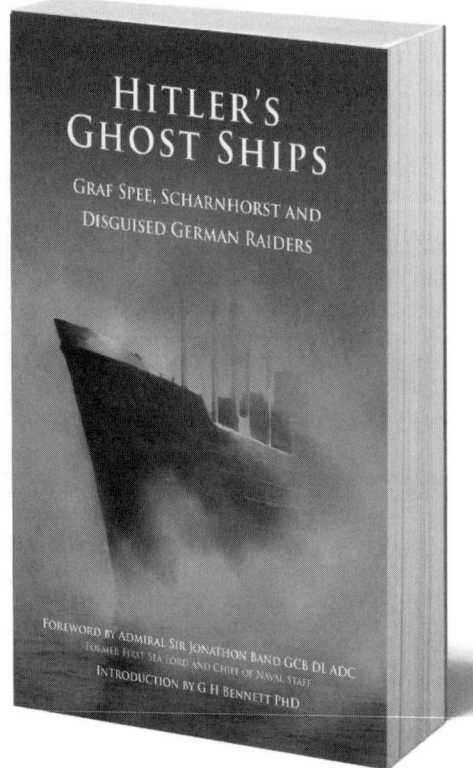

- The German Navy's tactics of disguise to oust the British fleet and isolate island Britain.
- Includes original hand-drawn tracking maps and diagrams.

Disguised Auxiliary cruisers could sidle up to merchant vessels undetected as they were flying a neutral flag, similar to 17th century pirate ships. Completion of the disguised ships was difficult and took its toll on the German dockyard workers and crews, sailing in waters dominated by the Royal Navy. The Battle Summaries chart how the Royal Navy dealt with the threat of these raiders of 70 years ago.

Introduction by
G H Bennett

Hunting Tirpitz
Naval Operations Against Bismarck's Sister Ship

Publication Date
April 2012
Paperback
ISBN 978-184102-310-6
Hardback
ISBN 978-184102-309-0
Extent
304 pages
Format
156 x 234 mm
Category
Military and Naval Ships

Foreword
Admiral Sir Mark Stanhope,
First Sea Lord and Chief of
Naval Staff

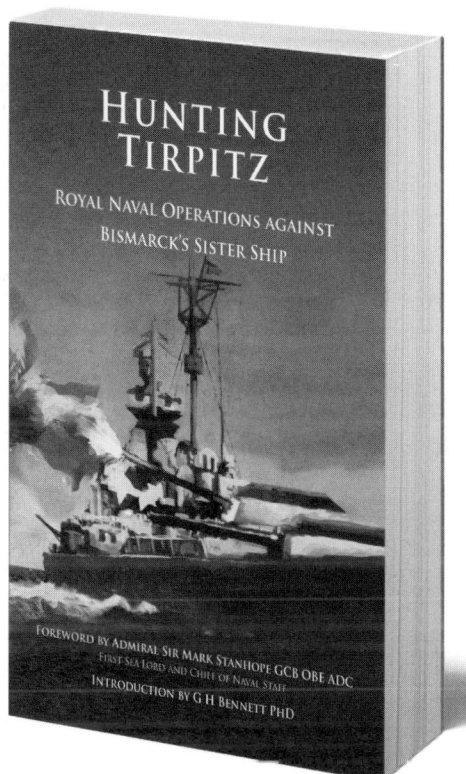

- Operation Chariot, Operation Source and Operation Tungsten are detailed and analysed.
- Includes original hand-drawn tracking maps and diagrams.
- Contains newly translated first hand accounts by German crew members of *Tirpitz*.

While it was the RAF that delivered the final *coup de grâce*, it was the Royal Navy, from 1942 to 1944, that had contained, crippled and neutralised the German battleship in a series of actions marked by innovation, boldness and bravery. From daring commando raids on the coast of France, to the use of midget submarines in the fjords of Norway and devastating aerial attacks by the Fleet Air Arm, the Royal Navy pursued *Tirpitz* to her eventual destruction.

Introduction by
J E Harrold

Dark Seas
The Battle of Cape Matapan

Publication Date
April 2012
Paperback
ISBN 978-184102-304-5
Hardback
ISBN 978-184102-303-8
Extent
160 pages
Format
156 x 234 mm
Category
Military and Naval Ships

Foreword
Written by HRH Prince Philip who served in the action

- The only publication to have a first-hand account of the battle by HRH Prince Philip.
- Includes original hand-drawn tracking maps and diagrams.

Written shortly after World War II, the summary of the Battle of Cape Matapan draws on first-hand accounts of action on both sides. Unearthed from archives, the vivid and compelling detail is reproduced and newly published as *Dark Seas*. During the battle, the enemy was hunted, trailed, avoided and engaged. Accurate intelligence combined with the inaccurate and misleading in the 'fog of war'. This is a unique insight into one of the last fleet engagements in naval history.